A Journey of Self-Love

Circular Time

Elena Radford

Copyright 2024 by Elena Radford
All rights reserved
Published in the United State by Elena Radford
Salt Lake City, Utah
LIBRARY OF CONGRESS CATALOGING-IN-PUBLICATION DATA
Elena Radford
Circular Time: a Journey of Self-Love

*This is a work of nonfiction. Nonetheless,
some names have change in other to disguise their identities.*

*This publication is not intended as a substitute for
the advice of health care professionals.*

Proprietary Information:

The information in this BOOK, website, and that which is also presented on the Online School is the Intellectual Property of Elena Radford LLC. The Inca Way DBA and is for your private use.

The Intellectual property includes inter alia, drawings, videos, description of intellectual and spiritual processes.

You agree that you will not disseminate, publish or make public this intellectual property without the prior written consent of Elena Radford LLC.

You agree that Elena Radford LLC has the right to seek legal remedy to prevent any such unauthorized dissemination. You will be responsible for damages and costs as ordered by the Court.

Love, Acada and Che

Foreword

This is the first time, in all the books, articles, or websites I've edited over the years, that I've been tempted to come out from behind the curtain and speak directly to you, the reader.

So why now? Why this book?

I like something about it. But more importantly, I want you to give yourself more than a fair chance with this book. Because in the process, you might provide yourself with something more valuable than you ever might have dreamed was waiting for you in these pages.

For this particular reading journey, there are some things I hope you'll pack and bring with you. And there are some things I hope you leave behind.

Bring your sense of wonder and your curiosity. Bring your love of a good story. Bring your adventurer and your explorer. Bring your heart. Bring your endurance and patience, and determination to keep going. Bring the part of you that believes there's something important about life that has not yet been fully explained.

Most importantly, bring that hopeful believer inside you who cannot yet accept that everything in this world is already too far gone because it's not. And this book contains some options for regaining that feeling of hope for the future. Of being in love with your own life again and being able to bring understanding and healing to yourself and generations suffering from past hurts and grief.

That smart-rat part of your brain that looks for the quick answer to everything. Leave it at home with some good snacks. Just for now. Oh, and kindly disinvite your inner organizer. Time, as you will see, is different within these pages. It moves back and forth more in circles than in long, straight lines.

This book will teach you much in the ideas it offers, but some of its most valuable lessons will come from inside of you. Be open to what your subconscious begins to hear. Read with the understanding that you're getting something far more valuable than techniques, logic, or even monetary wealth. If you keep reading forward, you will find a voice behind the words on the page. One that leads you to a relationship with what the late poet Mary Oliver calls your "one wild and precious life."

If you pack as advised, don't be surprised when you notice, somewhere in the course of your reading, that somehow, you've begun to feel good—confused, perhaps, yet hopeful about life.

The seeds of great and good change are cleverly hidden in these pages.

I wish you well on the journey.

S. K. Editor

Denver, Colorado, April 2022

Circular Time
A Journey of Self-Love

Dedication

I dedicate this book to my best teachers of love: my sons, John and Andrew.

I would like to acknowledge:

Father and Mother Creator

— For helping to understand the balance inside me, the love of female and male energies, which is the source and balance of life.

Che

—For not giving up on me.

Acada and Ta

— For sharing their story in Atlantis, which brought the teaching in the book and healing to my life.

Mela Macquarrie and Doug Gunton

— For trusting in the vision of this book.

Court Stroud

— For his contribution and kindness.

My sister Meche and brother Carlos

— For accepting me for who I am and loving me unconditionally.

Prophet Thoth and the Light Beings

— For guiding me in the process of my life that gave me the foundation for this book.

All my friends that contributed to this book,

My love goes to you.

Contents

Introduction 10
01. My 3rd-Dimensional Life 18
02. My 5th-Dimensional Life 30
03. Trauma: Separation of Consciousness,
    Subconsciousness, and Heart 37
04. Acada's 3rd-Dimensional Life 45
05. Light Beings 50
06. Acada's 5th-Dimensional Life 54
07. Why the 5th Dimension? 63
08. The Mirror's Way of Life 72
09. Victim and Survivor Behavior 76
10. Atlantis Events of Contamination 87
11. The Impact of Blocks, and Limiting Beliefs 95
12. Twin Cells: Protecting Books of Light from
    Blocks and Limiting Beliefs 105
13. The Inca Cross Protocol: Acada's Secret Weapon 112
14. Witnessing Other Creations 120
15. Decode the Inca Cross – 1st Triangle 124
16. Andean Shamans and Mountains 133
17. Accountability 139
18. My Initiation 142
19. Fire Initiation 157
20. 2nd Triangle of the Inca Cross 164
21. Father and Mother Creators' Story of Love 175
22. 3rd Triangle of the Inca Cross 179

23. 4th Triangle of the Inca Cross 184
24. Pure Intention: High-Frequency Future of New Possibilities. .194
25. Puma Punku: Observing How Acada Clears Contamination . .206
26. Machu Picchu: Clearing Contamination....................215
27. My Five Points of Power................................220
28. My Symbol of Personal Intimacy 228
29. My Symbol of the Future 236
30. Che 243
31. Experiencing My Center of Power.......................247
32. My Symbol of the 5th-Dimensional Portal 252
33. My R&D in the 5th Dimension 262
34. Acada's Protocols of Love 268
35. A New Life...274

About the Author...285
Testimonial..286
Index..291

Introduction

"This is a story of love, one that happened in Atlantis around 15,000 years ago. I am Acada, one of the last survivors of the people of Law of One."

"My love for Atlantis will always be full of vulnerability and hope. I was a gatekeeper of higher knowledge, a high technology scientist, and an Atlantis council member. To me, it was an honor to help to maintain the traditions of other previous creations of my ancestors, the Mu people, and their ancestors."

"The Mu were beings of the light. As 5th-dimensional beings, the Mu viewed values and principles from higher vibrational states containing high-frequency feelings of peace and love. For the Mu, love was not only a feeling but a multidimensional energetic language—the language of love. To them, love was the source of the creation of life, well beyond romance. Love for the Mu was a dynamic energy that propelled movement and expansion."

According to Acada, the Mu beings had knowledge of the source of every living thing, including the genetic makeup codes and electronic forces behind the creation of the universes which is what we now call chemistry, physics, biology and more. This information was stored in crystals.

In the language of love, the Mu recognized the female and male power as equal to create balance in life, even though they had different roles in the equilibrium of creation. The female was the source of creation, and the male was the source of direction.

Mu beings also knew the astrology of celestial bodies and could travel to other planets. Keeping records of their knowledge and advanced technologies was essential. These records were called the "Codes of Creation."

Mu beings experienced time according to the 5th and higher dimensional laws in which the present, and future constantly exchange love energy: they called it Circular Time. It was the ability to observe their behaviors from a perspective of Self-Love that allowed them to have a fulfilled life without regrets from past experiences.

After the continent of Mu sank into the ocean because of the volcanic fires and earthquakes, the survivors took their knowledge to the Atlantis people to create a new community that eventually went under the sea.

Atlantis was a melting pot of different cultures, and the language of love was accessible to everyone. The codes of creation were taught as building blocks to mothers and fathers, families, and communities to ground love for their future generations.

With the guidance of the Mu beings, the Atlantic people lived in balance, love, service, and wisdom. The low-frequency contamination came to Atlantis when some wanted to own and control the Mu's creation technology which was the knowledge of the DNA and atoms components.

This situation created two schools of thought: those of the Law of One and those of the Mirrors. The Law of One, my people, created a highly spiritual, advanced utopian civilization using the Mu's knowledge and technologies; they focused on the consequences of their choices.

We believe spirituality is a recognition of feelings and beliefs greater than being human. Yes, we felt that each of us played a role in a greater whole, which was cosmic and divine in nature.

The Law of One knew that the energy of love was the glue that kept the past, present, and future together. For them, the present and past were a dance of energy that merged into the future, creating a tapestry of awareness and wisdom so exquisitely balanced that they did not experience what we know of suffering or death. The power of love has a distinctive technology of creation.

The Mirrors did not create with the principles of the Mu but believed in new norms that only benefitted them. The name Mirror derives from "illusion," a false idea or belief that sucks and pulls the light from the living and has low-frequency emotions of confusion, frustration, deception, guilt, and so forth.

The Mirrors stole and misused part of Mu technology and performed DNA experiments in the Law of Ones to manipulate and control feelings. The DNA contamination created lower-frequency emotions and energies that damaged the Law of One.

By manipulating feelings, the Mirrors created separation and suffering that caused emotional and physical illnesses. The resulting alterations of DNA structure in plants, animals, and humans were generally incompatible with its essential role in preserving and transmitting genetic information. The damage to the DNA caused genetic alterations in the genes that control cell growth, and these mutations led to the development of stress, anxiety, depression, and sickness.

This separation of the DNA Patterns resulted in a new contaminated way of thinking that created illusions and focused on the unfulfilled events from the past. This was the abrupt creation of the 3rd dimension, a fragmented, linear time, and became the norm instead of Circular Time. The Law of One lost the pure essence of peace and love from the 5th dimension.

In the last days of Atlantis, the Atlanteans were aware that a meteorite was heading for Earth. The Law of One's beings accepted this. They knew they could survive when the meteorite hit the Earth or transform into other realities if necessary. The Mirrors wanted to stop the meteorite from hitting our planet. For selfish reasons, they knew their energy of love was not high enough to survive.

The Mirrors needed the light of the Law of One's people to recharge the body and soul. They manipulated the Law of One, lowering their frequency to take advantage of them and steal their light. The meteorite did not destroy Atlantis – but the explosions that damage the environment makeup originated by the electromagnetic and DNA experiments done by the Mirrors and their followers. The contamination created survives to this day.

It was too late for most people of the Law of One because they were already contaminated. The few of us who were not infected protected what was left of the high-frequency feelings of love and peace. We rescued Law of One people from being persecuted and took them to safe places. The few who were not contaminated were sent out with the hope that one day they would find the contamination cure and come back to help us.

I remember seeing the rafts leaving from the Atlantis port, crowded with the Law of One people, dressed in white and moving gently to sea. I did not feel the pain of separation, but hoped they would also find a way to save the knowledge and records of life taking with them.

I observed more Law of One people were placed in rafts. They had to be checked to ensure there was no DNA contamination. A shining golden symbol would appear on their wrists if they were not contaminated. I looked at them with so much love and wished them the best on their journey to the lands that we now call Peru and Bolivia. I honored them for their courage and determination to save the pure knowledge of our ancestors. They also took the Mu Codes, which were in danger from the ongoing radioactivity that resulted from the explosions caused by the Mirrors. The Law of One's people calculated that it would be around 15,000 years before people could reach the essence of love as before the contamination.

I decided to stay in Atlantis. I was not contaminated, but I chose to infect myself to learn more about the new creation — 3rd dimension to help my people.

I am Elena Radford, and I welcome you!

I was born in Peru and trained by Acada, my ancestors and other teachers, to fulfill my role as an Andean Shaman, a spiritual guide. Most of my training was done high in the Peruvian Andes in the Incas and Pre-Incas ancient sites around Cuzco, Puno in Peru, and Tiahuanaco in Bolivia.

In this book, I intend to share Acada's and my experiences to give you a perspective of what can be possible when you create from the feelings of your heart. She explained to me that there are low and high-frequency emotions. Feelings like happiness and love are high-frequency emotions that create unity. Low-frequency emotions such as "I am not good enough" or "I am not loveable" create mental blocks and limiting beliefs that reflect illusions and separation.

Acada channeled to me as an inner voice connected to my feelings and thoughts and shared her experiences. Sometimes, I felt Acada's physical experiences in Atlantis, like when she ran, she was hungry or tired.

Acada was a gift that came to me when I needed it most. My youngest son had a deep sadness in his heart. I wanted to stop the pain, and

I prayed to Father, Mother Creator, and the universe to guide me and help me to find the source of the pain and heal it.

While looking for a higher connection to find the solution, one day, I had a body experience of a woman crying because she was having an abortion. I felt the mother's intense pain of losing the baby.

I felt overwhelmed, overcome with intense emotions of sadness. I wanted to help, but it was like watching a movie I could not participate in. That was my first experience with Acada losing her baby during Atlantis.

Other visions and experiences came at different times and were not in chronological order, and it took a while to put the story together.

It was Acada's way of telling her story. She wanted me to experience some of the events that happened to her in my body. By sharing and observing her feelings and behaviors, she trained me to love myself, and eventually, She Shared some of the Symbols of Love originated from the Mu people. This guidance was done by experiencing feelings I did not think was possible.

The Symbols of Love are molecular behaviors. Bundles of 'feelings' work together to support life source. Their movement and sounds maintain and create 'feelings' that are the basis for life creation. These are love, trust, connection, awareness, protection, acknowledgment, happiness, passion for life, self-expression, productivity, truth, and others.

My observation thought the feeling of Self-Love was an act of noticing or perceiving the natural source. It was the acquisition of information from a primary source. Through Self-Love, the observation of living beings employs all my senses. It involved the perceptions and recording of data via feelings as an instrument of light to decode Acada's teachings. Learning the codes of love is what helped me to assist my son in the process of healing his heart.

In Atlantis, at first, everyone had access to the Symbols of Love or Mu Codes. In the last days of Atlantis, to protect the symbols from the Mirrors, Acada developed a technology that the Symbols of Love were only accessible to the people that love themselves, allowing them to reconnect to the 5th dimension and their higher self. Acada also created a process of accountability for every being that created contamination.

Acada wanted me to observe the impact of the choices made by the Law of One and the Mirrors and identify the critical distinction between their behaviors. She said, "If you perceive with love, you can contribute to the world, but if you observe with the energy of behaving as a victim or a survivor, you reflect the contamination of Atlantis in the world."

She taught me that love is the foundation for balancing our lives and connecting with others. She guided me to be a creator of love, and she wished I could teach that to others to experience feelings and design their lives from the intentions of their heart to have balance and purpose.

I have learned to accept that we still carry the contamination from Atlantis. And by observing them, I could recognize them. Acada classified these behaviors into three groups: Creator of love, which is 5th-dimensional energy, and the 3rd-dimensional behaviors influenced by the Mirrors. Which are behaving as a victim and or a survivor.

When we choose to behave as a victim or a survivor, we get stuck in the past, creating ongoing contamination of our source DNA reflected in others. In the process, we block ourselves because we observe the world from a 3rd-dimensional perspective. We have the power to change this by considering making choices to create love and balance – this is a creation of the 5th dimension.

I have often wondered about love's power and if it could be the technology that keeps us together and creates life. History and fiction are filled with stories of incredible circumstances that people have overcome in the name of love –to seek, express, expand, and honor love. These expressions of love are powerful, often inspiring, and sometimes frightening.

Throughout the book, you will be encouraged to love yourself to benefit from Acada's teachings and Symbols of Love technology. We can access her technology only if we learn to love ourselves. This book is not primarily about Atlantis nor exclusive to Inca Shamanic training but learning how to love yourself and others. It is a process of self-development.

By reflecting love to each other, we amplify the technology of love for a better world. Because of the application of the Symbols of Love, this book is light and an energetic and multidimensional hologram because it carries Acada's 5th-dimensional energy and the energy of other members of the Law of One who will assist you in the process.

This book is experiential and alive because even while you are reading, you are healing and clearing your energy; you, the reader, will experience a transformative shift in the love and kindness you show yourself. You will gain wisdom and healing simply by reading the following pages.

Remember the concept of Circular Time? This is how it can be so that I, in the present, became part of Acada's team in her future—helping her maintain the codes of the creation values – the Symbols of Love.

As you read this book, you will do the same. You will become part of the team. Your 5th-dimensional connection of love will clear the past and present from the 3rd-dimensional behavior for yourself, your ancestors, and others. You become the hope for a better future.

I have witnessed in my personal life the benefits of Acada's work. It is the process of the Symbols of Love or the Inca Way process. I called it the Inca Way to honor the Incas. They were the last to use this knowledge.

I place my intentions and hope that these teachings can also guide you to find yourself in love throughout your life, as they guide me through my life's best and worst times.

This book follows parallel stories of love through which we – you and I – help each other create a better world. You are her future, and Acada is part of your future, even as she creates in the present. Together, we have the transformative magic of Self-Love.

Introduction

For the first time in around 15,000 years, we can increase our love to levels not felt since Atlantis's contamination and corruption. These are challenging times. The planet is preparing to change –this is already happening, as we see in climate change. Humans are also changing, and we are going through an evolution. Acada invites us to create a new society of love. She says we are powerful and embracing that is essential. Loving ourselves is what is going to help us to go through these changes.

I wrote this book guided by Acada and other high vibrational beings to awaken you to the power of choosing love to bring the world's consciousness toward the 5th-dimensional teachings of love, one person at a time.

By sharing Acada's wisdom and the Law of One's 5th-dimensional knowledge, I call forth the remembrance of who you are. YOU are part of the technology of love.

CHAPTER 1
My 3rd-Dimensional Life

This book may not be for everyone, but it is for anyone who wants to love and understand themselves. It is about learning to access the true power of love to make peace with all things, especially yourself.

This book focuses on feelings as an emotional state, reactions, or thinking processes connected to the heart. And are positive states of mind. Illusions or low-frequency actions are connected only to the process of negative ideas and are irrational mental thoughts such as guilt, fear, worry, or shame.

Acada's stories are a vital part of this learning. Acada's life is a testament to the transformative power of love and creation working together. Her energy and teachings opened me up to transformation and a better life. I want that for you.

I am a student of Acada's – not so different from you. I reflect both to you for your personal development. I don't know everything about the teachings you'll explore in upcoming chapters. Although I am becoming the best version of myself, and by becoming the best version of myself, I can fulfill my promise to Acada to serve others by sharing my story and her teachings.

When we listen to our heart's feelings and let those feelings guide us, we connect to a piece of higher knowledge. These feelings create a reality that guides us in making better choices. This is the 5th-dimensional world which is a collective consciousness of pure love and other feelings.

Choices of the 3rd dimension trap us in the illusions and confusion of the blocks and limiting beliefs. We pay particular attention to the unresolved past, but 5th-dimensional choices bring us unlimited possibilities because we focus on the present and future.

The problem with the 3rd dimension, according to Acada, is that its illusions, built from blocks and limiting beliefs, confuse us. We find clarity when we see not with our minds or eyes but with our hearts.

Remember this, Acada once told me, "Only what you feel in your heart is real, and the more you experience your feelings, the more connected you are to the truth and happiness."

I am the writer of this book, but I am mainly and perhaps primarily the observer. I am witnessing how my life is changing as I write. My choices are changing, and instead of being created from illusion, I am creating from Self-Love. I am learning to love myself, make better choices, and discover my value.

I was born in Huancayo, a city high in the Peruvian Andes, about eight hours away from Lima by car. The main plaza downtown has beautiful trees that protect people from the sun's heat during warm days. Around the plaza, there were beautiful adobe buildings, and I was always impressed by the rustic, adobe Catholic church. The thick, wooden door at the entrance is painted dark brown.

As a child, I found this door far too massive to open by myself. I was convinced that even if I were to open it, it would fall on top of me. There I would be, squashed like a pancake on the floor with a disturbing-looking door on top of me. Why? I wondered, were the church doors so forbiddingly heavy? I was terrified of them.

Today, few adobes colonial buildings remain; the city has become modernized. I miss how it used to be. It feels like part of me vanished when those old sun-dried clay bricks buildings disappeared; there are only memories now.

When I think about my house, one of my memories is the constant dust from all the dirt roads surrounding it. When cars drove past, the light brown tiny powder found its way inside our home. I was little, and sweeping up all the small particles was a big chore. I knew I had to handle the broom carefully and slowly sweep it into the dustpan, but I wanted to clean it quickly. The fine dried substance would fly everywhere – not just around the floor, the chairs, and the table. Sometimes, it would even wind up inside my mouth. I'd taste the plain, gritty powder and feel hollowed out and dry. Then I'd have to start dusting all over again.

That was me. I always wanted to do things fast, which got me in trouble more than once. I was obsessed with the idea that I could somehow sweep the floor quickly without the dust flying all over the place and get the desired results. It became a goal of mine—my creation.

An outdoor market was like a carnival of fruits and vegetables two blocks from my house. Indigenous people wearing colorful clothing came from the surrounding villages to sell their products. They sat on the floors and laid out their fresh produce in front of them. It was all organic because they had no money to buy artificial fertilizers. Sometimes, I would go to the market with my grandmother. She would carry a straw-woven basket and fill it with potatoes, quinoa, beans, bananas, oranges, papayas, and other fruits from the jungle five hours away from my Huancayo.

I didn't like the taste of dust. Also, I wouldn't say I liked washing off the fruit and vegetables we'd purchased from the market. I didn't like how it made my hands dirty, which gave me a funny feeling in my stomach. Mostly, I dreaded plunging my fingers into the cold water. We didn't have heated water back then, and Huancayo, was very cold at a high altitude in the Andes. Immersing my palms, in water, even for a few minutes, made them redden and ache. That freezing feeling stayed in my body for a long time.

There was a small movie theater two blocks away from my house in the opposite direction of the market. It didn't look like a modern movie theater with several screens playing different shows with concessions. Instead, this big room could possibly hold a hundred people. There was a small glass counter with a few candies. Its screen showed black and white movies at the time, though eventually, the theater started showing color films. We didn't go to the movies often because we didn't have the money, but also because it always seemed like only a single film was showing for the entire month. Still, having a movie theater close to my house made me feel special and grateful. To me, it meant that we lived in a modern city.

My life was full of conflicts—what Acada would call a 3rd-dimensional life experience, a reality that adheres to the laws of linear time where there are blocks and limiting beliefs creating pain and suffering.

My father was an alcoholic. Instead of bringing his wages home, he spent the money drinking with his friends almost every weekend—a common problem for many families in Peru. When my father came home and fell asleep, my mother would go to his car to look for any money he might have hidden there.

Both my grandfathers were also alcoholics. Their behavior legacy affected me. I had stress, anxiety, and depression from the instability of my younger years. I still remember the late nights or early mornings when my father would come home drunk, talked loudly, and woke us up, and then he would sleep on the couch. His clothes smelled of alcohol and were dirty. He was gone for three or four days at a time. On some of those days, he may have slept on a sidewalk. As a teenager, one of my fears was for my friends to see my father sleeping on the streets of my town. The next day, when sober, he acted like nothing had happened.

I have short-term memory problems. I had struggled to remember names, streets, and new words. Alongside these struggles, I had experienced other negative impacts on my emotions and behavior, including:

- Low self-esteem
- Social phobia
- Separation Anxiety
- Obsessive-compulsive issues
- Emotional isolation
- Post-traumatic stress disorder.

You can learn more about the effects on children of alcoholic parents at https://americanaddictioncenters.org/alcoholism-treatment/children

At first, it was hard for me to believe that the choices of our ancestors could have a significant impact on our lives, but they do. I've learned that our ancestors' thoughts, behaviors, and ideas form the basis of our emotional behaviors and physical being.

My mother's father was born in Peru, but his parents—my great-grandparents—were Italian and considered themselves to be high-class. My grandfather returned to Italy to receive his college education before returning to Peru at his father's request. Still, he remained in love of everything Italian, including his educated friends and the opportunities a big city affords. He struggled to connect with the more provincial, less well-educated people of small-town Huancayo. These experiences could have started his drinking. He muted his pain with liquor, eventually descending into alcoholism and poverty, losing all his wealth gambling.

My father's parents were low-income mestizos – a mixture of white and indigenous people. Like most mestizos, he felt inferior to Peru's white population. My father came from a very different background than my mother, and their beliefs were very different about social classes. The higher-class people, like my mother's family, believed that poor people (like my father's family) should serve them. Looking back, I can see that my mother, and her parents, thought my father was not good enough for her.

Like many people living in a 3rd-dimensional reality, my mother's family believed that making someone else feel small is the best way to feel strong. My mother's brothers controlled my mother and made her feel small because they were financially successful, and she was not. My mother told me she married my father because it was the only way to escape her brother's control.

For instance, I remember once my uncle invited us to his house for lunch. My cousins would not talk to me and my sister; they ignored us because we were not to their social class level. It didn't help that my father was a native of Peru, and my mother's family utterly rejected him.

The distress over the inability to provide for us was hard on her. Her heart hurt when our cousins made us feel we weren't good enough because my father and mother didn't have money.

In my heart, I've always had a strong connection with Peruvian indigenous people, and I've despised the way white people treated them. The mestizos, in turn, believed they were superior to the native people of Peru because the mestizos had ancestors from Europe. It hurts me when I hear mestizos use the derogatory term *cholos* for indigenous Peruvians. I have always felt like a mother bear when defending them. I am proud to have indigenous blood.

My father wasn't honorable, but not because of his social class. He was irresponsible. He didn't have a good work ethic and didn't provide a stable income for the family. His behavior drove my mother, a proud and goal-oriented woman, crazy. She couldn't understand why he wasn't motivated to create a better life for himself and us. She often said, "The only reason I tolerate your father is that you and your brother and sister need him at home."

My mother told me about an incident when I was around five. My sister and I went for a car ride with my father. A few hours had passed by, and we were not back. My mother searched and eventually found us alone and unsupervised in her car, where my father had left us while he went drinking with his friends. It was painful for my mother not to have my father's support as a husband and father to us.

When I was around fifteen, I'd had enough. My mother was complaining, as usual, about my father and his behavior. In my heart, I knew he would never change, and the constant conflict had to stop. I was tired of his actions, and I decided to take a pillowcase to use as a suitcase, placing my father's clothes inside it. When he returned home, I waited by the front door and handed him the pillowcase. I told him to take his clothes and never return to the house again. He left, and eventually, he moved to Lima.

As children of alcoholic parents are often left with deep wounds damaging for all their lives, I was as well. In my 3rd-dimensional life, I became isolated and afraid of people and authority figures. I was frightened of any personal criticism and eventually became an approval seeker, losing my identity in the process.

As an approval-seeker, I found it hard to make big or small decisions without getting others to weigh in on them. I felt sad, happy, guilty, or anxious, depending on whether others approved of me. Sometimes, I took disagreement personally and felt insulted just because someone expressed a contrary opinion.

It was easier without him in many ways, but it didn't solve our financial problems. As a newly single mother, my mom sacrificed her happiness to provide us with basic needs. She did it without direction, money, or a support system. It amazes me that, a few years later, she somehow got the money to buy tickets and cover other expenses for my twin sister and me to go to the United States for college. She made things happen.

When my mother was guided by her feelings and heart, she was connected to the 5th dimension. She was a good listener. When I came home from school, she'd want to hear everything that had happened that day. She did not want us to get sick and made healthy meals. She was a very hard worker and taught us to see the value and benefits of work. All of this was the way she showed her love. She sacrificed her life for my brother, sister, and me to have a better one.

When my mother acted out the 3rd-dimensional blocks and limiting beliefs, she would hurt us – physical punishments that triggered my growing anxiety. She'd learned from the ideas of her mother and ancestors that this was the way of teaching. It worked to some degree, but it also created a lot of fear. I spent a lot of time in school, afraid of punishment. It was like I was in constant shock and couldn't focus, so I didn't learn to write or read very well.

My mother never told me she loved me when I was young. When I asked her to tell me she loves me instead of saying, "I love you," she would get defensive and explained that she may not say that she loves me, but she did a lot of things to provide for our needs like food and drive us to school.

I observed the relationship between my mother and my grandmother. It was harsh; my grandmother constantly criticized my mother. I never heard my grandmother saying to my mother that she loved her. The result was that my mother didn't know how to express love either. My brother is five years younger than me, and I loved him very much, but I did not know how to show my love to him. Nurturing love was not something I observed. We did not get many hugs; we seldom kissed.

Ideas are powerful. When my mother was five years old and forgot to wash her clothes, my grandmother beat her legs so severely that she had to stay in bed for several days. My mother shared that story several times with me. Because of her voice's pain, I felt she was stuck in the memories of that experience. It was like by sharing the story, she was looking for healing. I can see how, as a child, she had reason to find the motive of the event. Eventually, she concluded that she was unlovable; otherwise, that would not have happened. My mother wanted to be loved by everyone. She was starving for love and acceptance.

My grandmother was also contaminated with the blocks and limiting beliefs of the 3rd dimension. She punished me and my sister by not talking to us if we did something wrong, like not eating or overeating all the food she cooked.

Sadly, my mother carried the belief of punishment and passed it along too. One day she hit my back with a leather belt as I sat on the floor. I felt the searing physical pain – and the emotional devastation. That day, I, too, declared to myself that I was not loveable. Otherwise, how could that be happening?

We are beings of love and want our parents to love us. If they withhold love from us and severely punish us, our minds change. We block the feeling of love and reject it. My mother did not stop loving her mother; instead, she believed she was not lovable. As you can see, 3rd-dimensional stories carry pain and suffering.

My mother was the second to the youngest of nine children. She had eight brothers; she was the only girl. My grandmother did not see her value because she was a woman. My grandmother believed there was no value in having a girl because a daughter would not have what it took to serve her. She only saw the worth in her sons because they cared for her financially. It was painful and limiting for my mother to observe that.

My grandmother was a sarcastic woman when I was very young. She would smile and tell me that my eyes looked like the eyes of a death sheep and then laugh. Also, she told me several times that she did not like me because I looked like my father. She criticized and made fun of me for it. She was adopted as a child, and we don't know much about her family. We only know that her mother was having an affair with a married man who got her pregnant with a second baby and that she died giving birth to a boy. Her adopted family essentially treated her like a maid. She lived in a small adobe town high in the Peruvian mountains until she met my grandfather when she was eighteen and ran away with him. By the way, he was married to someone else at that time.

My mother would say, "We only bring children to this world to suffer," that was her way of expressing her frustrations when she struggled to provide for us. I believe she and I translated the message as the world was a scary place to be, and I had to be strong to survive. I did not yet know that I was subconsciously wired to believe it was a problem to have children. When I became a mother, I felt guilty for giving birth to my two boys.

I believed I was the problem for doing something my mother thought was wrong. I saw life through my mother's eyes because that is what children do. Children believe in what their parents say, and I did too. I hadn't yet learned that by thinking I was a problem, I was being trained to accept situations that reflected that I was the source of the conflict.

Even though I had the desire to have children in my heart, I trained my mind to believe I didn't. Without knowing it, my mother blocked one of my heart's most beautiful feelings: the intention of being a mother of love. The outcome was that I was afraid of being a mother, and once I became one, I believed I was not good at it. The idea I had of myself was that I was a 'problem' and I was afraid to damage my children.

That set me up to make many mistakes with my two young boys, and it affected my life and my children's lives. This damage happens when we accept the illusions of blocks and limiting beliefs.

When my mother did not get her way, she would give me 'the silent treatment.' She would not talk to me. Sometimes, if she spoke, she would say, "Then I do not love you." She would act resentful until I did what she wanted me to do. As a child, I was willing to do anything for my mother, so she would not stop loving me. Later in my life, this manifested in my relationships as me being submissive and a pleaser. I pretended everything was ok. Because of this experience, I did not know how to express my feelings.

On occasions, as a child, I thought about running away. While planning my escape, I thought about how to get food, a place to stay, and pay for my expenses. In my thinking process, I understood I did not have the means to take care of myself. So, I was trapped in an abusive relationship with my mother. My home was an environment of manipulation. Little by little, I started losing any sense of my value. Eventually, I stopped believing in myself and my feelings.

One of my biggest blocks was that I believed I was an inconvenience. Instead of loving others and getting close to people, I built a thick wall, like my mother had, to keep others away. My mother behaved aggressively and confrontationally; she came across tough, hateful, diminishing, and controlling. I felt timid. I did not open myself to others and let anyone feel my love. I couldn't bear the idea that someone might get to know and reject me, so I did not let people get close. Knowing me would give them access to hurt me.

Living with others in a 3rd-dimensional dimension where we make choices based on fear or lack of love, we all get confused and get shot down in our feelings. When we reflect on illusions, we do not connect through love. Under the influence of these illusions, my grandmother could not connect through love with my mother, and my mother, in turn, did not connect through love with me. I know she loved me, but she did not know how to convey the feelings of her heart to my siblings and me.

As a mother, I had the feeling that I lost vast amount of confidence, and I also blocked my feelings from my children. Sometimes, without being aware we choose to act out in our blocks which prevents us from connecting with others in love.

After high school, I got accepted to Ricardo Palma, a great private college in Lima, Peru. Coming from a small community, I looked forward to the big city and having new experiences. I was shy, but I was willing to give it a try to make new friends.

I felt insecure about being a small-town girl, and I could feel a sense of superiority from some people in Lima. I began to compare myself to others and got in my head. I saw people in Lima as better than me, and the identification I cobbled together in response was what I thought others wanted of me – just like the people-pleasing identity I'd created for my mother. I thought it was exciting to be part of something bigger, but I was forgetting about the desires of my heart, such as having quiet time and listening to my feelings and intuition.

Peru is unlike the United States; it is hard for students to find a good job to pay for their schooling. Parents must pay for their children's education. Seeing my mother struggling unsuccessfully to find the money to pay broke my heart, so I decided to move to the United States to study and work. I knew I would have more opportunities in the United States than in Peru. Fortunately, I met someone who helped me to obtain a passport and visa to the USA. I was only nineteen years old, leaving behind everything I had. My life was tough in Peru, and I was willing to lose everything to start a new life in a foreign country again. I knew there would be no going back.

I started in Nevada, where I enrolled at the University of Las Vegas to study English. Being in a new place even bigger than Lima was exciting—there was a strong sense of freedom. It was the powerful feeling of a fresh start.

After six months in Las Vegas, I moved to Freedom, California, where I continued studying English. Then, I was accepted to Ricks College (now Brigham Young University–Idaho), which offers only a two-year college associate degree. During the nights, I cleaned a building to pay my college expenses. After completing my first two years of education, I transferred to BYU in Provo, Utah, to finish my undergraduate degree in business.

I met my ex-husband during my first year of working toward my master's degree in Spanish Literature. He was a good man. I loved him very much, but looking back, I can see he did not feel the same way about me and that while I was ready for a commitment, he was not.

During our marriage, I sensed that he was not ready to be in a relationship and because of that he focused on what was not working instead of what was. It felt like he didn't see my value. He was not comfortable with me being shy especially when I was quiet around his brother and his wife. I did not know how to cook very well, and he would get upset about it. I wish he had helped me to be more open and showed me how to cook instead of shooting me down.

When unsure about someone, we focus on the person's negative aspects or situation. It happens a lot.

I did what many women do in that situation: I tried to prove I was the one for him and believed that by changing, I could improve things. I wanted him to feel he was the luckiest man to have me as a wife, but it did not happen. He was unhappy, and I concluded that I wasn't good enough for him. I lost all sense of identity in my continual attempts at changing myself to please him. By the time I left the marriage, I felt small and insignificant.

It was hard to look back and see that I had given almost fourteen years of my life to someone who could not see me. But I also took – and take – responsibility for that. How could I expect someone to see my value if I could not? Separation was painful, and it was tough on our two sons. Everyone gets hurt in the contamination of the 3rd dimension.

We all are made of love and want to be cared for with love. I wanted to be loved by my mother and my father. I could not understand their behavior at that time.

My 3rd-dimensional stories are full of powerless emotional traps, but my 5th-dimensional stories during my younger years were full of love and wisdom.

CHAPTER 2
My 5th-Dimensional Life

We all have 3rd and 5th-dimensional experiences in our lives. When creating a life from the desires of your heart and observing life through love, you are connected to the 5th dimension. When you are in a mental process in your head of illusion and ideas of low-frequency without personal value, Self-Love, honor, and respect, you are part of the creation of the 3rd dimension.

My 5th-dimensional life was magical and full of adventures. Even when I was very young, I observed something different about myself. The best way to describe it is by saying I felt like I had a computer program with lots of information in my head. Questions often come into my mind in my quiet space, and so will the answers. The difference between asking and searching for questions on a computer is that the energy or source answering my questions has feelings of love and kindness.

The only other person I saw who seemed to have access to the same information was my grandmother, my mother's mom. When she was in the space of love, I could see that the energy of her brain moved like mine. I didn't overthink it then, but somehow, I knew it was a type of communication.

One day, when I was around the age of twelve, my grandmother and I were in her garage. She wore a long dark wool skirt, a cotton light brown shirt, and a cardigan sweater. She was thin and had long, beautiful black hair. I love her two thick braids in the back of each ear. I was observing how she was picking up some papers from the garbage on the floor.

It was one of those moments when I felt deeply, and my thoughts penetrated the present experience. Then I saw it. I do not know how, but I saw the movement of the neurons' energy in my grandmother's brain had ideas. The waves were a bright light that moved, creating thoughts. I had seen it in my brain so many times before. It was the beginning and moment of birth of a thought, the conception of a new formation.

I noticed my grandmother, like me, when her energy generated an opening of expression from the pure love of her heart could observe in that way. This time, she thought about how important it was to keep the garage and house clean, and I had tuned into her telepathic communication.

Other times, my mind worked as I was watching five TV shows simultaneously, but with the experience of individually connecting with each performance and downloading its information to some of the cells in my brain. In that sense, I could have different experiences simultaneously, focusing on each with my full attention as if I were watching only one show. It felt like speaking many languages at the same time.

For instance, one day, my mother came home, got a thick wool blanket from one of the bedrooms, then went to the kitchen and, from a container, placed some fresh vegetable soup on a plate. Then, she walked outside. I followed her. A man was sitting on the cement sidewalk in front of the next house to the left of our home. He was around thirty years old. I noticed he was shivering because he was cold.

My mother gave him the blanket and then the plate of soup. My mother had a previous conversation with him where she found out that he just got out of jail.

I observed him in different realities or movies. I tapped into one of his memories of when he was in jail, how scared he was of other prisoners. Then, I saw an inmate looking at him, feeling sexually attractive. Then I saw another of his thoughts; he was thankful to my mother.

Also, he was worried about what would happen to him now that he was out of jail. My mind kept transmitting how lonely he felt. All was happening at once. While watching these events, I wish I could be a grown-up to help him.

After that, I was careful in what to connect to. I did not want to experience the suffering of others. Since then, mainly, it was positive information and teachings, and I could decide when I was open to it. For instance, I was like everyone else at school, enjoying seeing my classmates interacting at lunch and in the classroom. I also had fun with them, but my passion was to connect with my mental processes and learn from them.

After those experiences, I recognized I was an empath. I didn't have the word then but I was susceptible to the emotions of others. My empathic capacity meant that when someone judged me or was angry with me, I felt it deeply. I could feel the intense pain in my body. It was almost like an allergy reaction – it felt as if the energy of that negativity penetrated every cell of my body. This painful experience would happen when my mother got mad at me. It is a good thing that she didn't know about this. Otherwise, I could not have been able to protect my mind from her influence. In any case, I was still too young to explain what was happening to myself or her.

When I was young, my mother and her brothers had a tradition of visiting the nearby rural towns and countryside, which became the backdrop for my 5th-dimensional experiences. Every Sunday, we visited the rustic adobe towns and unpopulated areas close to my city. We walked in the forests and open fields of land. Sometimes we would take food and have a picnic lunch. We nurtured our bodies from the produce of that region which consisted of organically grown vegetables, and fresh meat. Sometimes, my grandmother would make spaghetti with her special sauce of dried mushrooms, some pepper, and fresh tomatoes. We'd get fresh bread from the store at the end of our street. She was an amazing cook! Other times we ate in whatever small-town restaurant we came across. The feeling and experience within all those different places recharged my energy every Sunday.

One Sunday, we visited a mostly destroyed ancient site that people call the Inca cemetery. I walked around and felt the energy charging through my veins. A wall built of red rock caught my attention and a six-foot-tall wall flattened a bit by some deterioration. It was not until I got closer and saw small holes dug into the ground that I realized this was more than a destroyed and abandoned wall. Inside the holes, there was evidence of ancient burials. I saw small human bones mixed with small pieces of ceramic pottery. I was very excited that I made an important discovery. I wondered who lived there? What did they eat? How did they dress? By holding these questions, I felt like I was part of the experience of being there with them.

People among the Peruvian Andes believe these sites have negative energy and that if you get close to them, you can take this energy into your body and get sick. The indigenous people in the Andes say that the molecular memories of the disease and suffering of those who died are still there and can contaminate you. People must be careful in those places, so I only observed them from a distance.

In ancient Peru, people believed they were going to another life after death and that they could take some of their valuable objects with them. They were buried with the things they most valued: ceramics, jewelry made of gold, silver, and other minerals. They were buried with beautiful tapestries. These people seemed to understand afterlife concepts, perhaps learned from their ancestors. They were aware that we had a solid connection to the afterlife and could communicate in the unseen world. For them, death was not a painful experience but rather a trip to something better.

When I walked around this place and felt the ancient energy, I knew I was missing something in this life. Something they had that I did not have. It was their sense of family and community. I would feel in my heart the feelings of love and commitment to the families of some people who live there. The value of connection within self-discovery in their roles as a mother or father and the gratitude for being part of something bigger than their bodies was a gift of their creator-God.

During those times, stepping on the rocks in that area, the inner knowledge came to my consciousness that it was not okay to live at home and being confused about my existence because I would not understand my father's behavior. I was so young, but there was deep wisdom inside of me that I could see that it was not acceptable for my father to behave that way.

An alcoholic is not emotionally available to his children. I could feel his energy and thoughts. But even when we were together, I could not attain a connection like the bond of true love that I felt at the ancient sites I visited on Sundays.

Also, I started feeling and noticing my mother's insecurities over her lack of money and her desire to impress her brothers to make up for it. I began having a profound understanding and recognized that my observation and thinking were advanced for my age. I was an old soul; while my twin sister and cousins played around and had fun, I sat and looked in a quiet place and processed information differently. I wondered, and my mind was curious about what was happening around me and internally. It was like searching for truth and knowledge.

I did not feel alone when I was in my 5th-dimensional multidimensional energy. I could feel the power of the mountains grounding, supporting and answering some of my questions. Their wisdom penetrated my body and made me feel better. But I felt lonely in my everyday life, at school, and most of the time at home. My multidimensional life made more sense to me. It was part of my heart that allowed me to be connected to different realities and draw meaning from those perspectives.

During those visits to the rural areas close to my city, I could sense the loss of values and principles. At the Inca Cemetery, there were holes in the ground which showed that people were searching for treasures. They had dug into the site and destroyed it. I was around twelve years old, and I was too young to understand the full impact of the damage, but my heart and body knew it was wrong to destroy the creations of others. Those experiences were not common in my family, that sensible and empathic connection with nature.

Some Sundays, we visited Ocopa. It used to be a Catholic monastery established in 1725. It was a lovely white adobe church with a red door against the big pine trees at the entrance. The church had a cemetery attached to it. There, the niches in a high wall were equal in size, and the graves were marked with personalized carvings of the nuns and monks living there. It was a quiet place built when the Spanish took control of South America. I could feel the sense of Spanish superiority and lack of respect for the indigenous people.

These Sunday sojourns took about half an hour in transit and that seemed like forever for a young girl. Once, we went to a place high in the Andes, close to Jauja. It took us an hour and a half to get there. I was around fourteen years old. After driving up the side of a mountain, we got to the top, to a plateau. It was green and water ran alongside the grass. I saw the entrance to a cave, but I was not allowed to go in. My uncle explained to me that there was an oven inside where ancient people had made ceramic pots. That place stayed in my mind. It felt like it was home.

On my last visit to that place, while observing the beauty of the area, I felt like someone in the unseen world was also watching me with a deep sense of love and kindness.

As I grew older, I increasingly knew things I didn't remember being taught. One day, I was messing around in high school physics class. The teacher noticed my behavior and told me to go to the front of the classroom.

"Elena, come to the front," he said.

I stood and slowly walked toward him, not sure what he wanted me to do. He had a fundamental physics problem on the board.

"Please solve the problem." He motioned for me to write out the equation. I understood what he was trying to do; he wanted me to pay attention by showing that I would only learn if I was focused. I took a piece of chalk and started solving the problem on the board. When I got it right, I was more surprised than the teacher. I did not know the concept on the board that I just wrote out. The knowledge had come to me from the unseen world.

I had another experience in my magical life a year after high school. I took some classes at a learning center in Lima. I was in a classroom with twenty-five students. The professor was explaining about the importance of proficiency of reading.

"If we do not know how to read, we will not learn the business concepts." He had an article in a newspaper that he wanted one student to read. He chose me.

No. No, why me?

Anxiety kept me from pronouncing the words right, and I continually skipped words. I had never been able to focus enough to learn to read proficiently.

"Explain the article's content," he said.

I told him the whole concept of the article. He was shocked. He did not move and looked at the students in the class. He was quiet and confused. I sensed he felt like he had lost control over the situation, then he said, "Time is up. We are done for today."

Over time, I lost much of this connection to the unseen, especially when I came to the US to attend college. I wanted to fit in and to be part of American culture—to be part of a new world. My focus had shifted so much that I forgot to create with my feelings and my intuition in my inner world. I stopped trusting in my multidimensional self.

It was my choice, but it was the wrong one for me because while fulfilling my college education was important, it is also developing connections with my inner world.

CHAPTER 3
Trauma: Separation of Consciousness, Subconsciousness, and Heart

During my childhood, I spent hours feeling the energy of the mountains. I do not know how or when, but I knew that the energy of the mountains had a spirit—an energetic consciousness that had wisdom, and their knowledge fed me. It was an energetic connection because I would not mentally understand what was happening. Sometimes, I felt like I was inside a cocoon, surrounded by them in a protective and comforting way. I had a sense of confidence when I felt their energy.

I was constantly tired. I often had dark shadows under my eyes because I was exhausted from having out-of-body experiences. During an out-of-body experience, you feel as if you're outside, looking at your body or a situation from another perspective. I experienced this most often while I was sleeping. These experiences would happen to me because of the intensity of the trauma and the fear of physical punishment by my mother. My spirit would not be in a body full of fear.

I am blessed to have a twin sister. I love her friendly, and open nature. One day at school, when we were about five years old, my sister asked one of our older cousins for money. Our cousin gave her a coin, which she put in her sweater pocket. A few days later, my mother was doing the laundry and found the coin. My mother asked my sister where she got it

"On the floor," my sister responded.

From communicating with the unseen world, I knew that trust was fundamental among loved ones. So, I chose to tell my mother the truth. "It's not true," I said. "She asked for the money from our cousin."

My mother became furious. She was yelling while walking. She positioned herself, threateningly like someone was attacking her, and she was ready to fight back. She went to the small garden behind the house, where there were three or four hot pepper plants, among other greenery. She pulled hot peppers off the plants and took them to the patio lined with blue ceramic tiles, where my sister was standing next to the outdoor sink. She grabbed my sister by the shoulder and thrust the hot peppers into my sister's mouth. "Do not lie ever again! Do not lie ever again!" she yelled.

Seeing my sister in pain and terror opened me to a new reality. I realized there was a world where we could get punished for lying; this world was my home. I told my mother the truth because I wanted to help her not to cause distress to my sister. I never thought that she would punish my sister in that way. With this new awareness, my heart instantly shut down. I would never feel the same about sharing my thoughts and feelings with my mother again. It was not safe.

As a small child in my magical world, I considered my conscious and subconscious to be like what I thought blood brothers might have been if I had any. They connected through feelings and exchanged ideas. They were like two happy friends.

The day I witnessed my mother physically hurting my sister, I decided not to interact and observe my subconscious and conscious interactions because I believed that if they were to do something my mother disapproved of, she would punish them as she did to my sister. I disconnected from their energy flow to protect them. Eventually, I forgot my connection to my subconscious and then from consciousness altogether.

My life was very different after that event, my introduction to the 3rd-dimensional world of pain, contamination, and fear. I felt lonely, very lonely. From then on, it was only me, my consciousness, and my heart. In the beginning, my consciousness and I had a good relationship, but when I ignored my heart, eventually, my conscious level created ideas that were illusions.

The conscious disconnected from the wisdom and teachings of the subconscious and heart, which confused It. It was like it had stopped learning. He was not happy anymore; he became critical and generated misconceptions like "no one loves you," "you are a problem to others," and "you are a loser because you can't make your mother happy." With those illusions and without feeling the truth, I sensed my conscience felt depressed and checked out.

We missed my older brother, my subconsciousness. Without him, things didn't make sense.

I don't remember much about my childhood after that. My heart separated from my subconscious and conscious levels, and I forgot my older brother (subconscious) and younger brother(consciousness).

My mother lost her temper constantly.

"Are you stupid? I will hit you if you do not behave," she yelled, raising her hands in a manner of preparation.

Other times she used different tactics to get what she wanted. "I will stop loving you if you don't do this." Or she'd say, "You only can have this if you do what I want you to do."

My younger brother, my consciousness, would get confused when my mother was in her 3rd-dimensional behaviors. He began to believe that he must be an inconvenience and that he was not good enough. He was ashamed of himself and considered himself a failure. He (and I) changed, and he wasn't happy anymore. He didn't pay attention in class and became very shy and quiet, and he wasn't open to learning in the present.

Almost nine years later, I witnessed my mother punishing my sister. One day, I reconnected to my subconscious energy for a short time. I was fifteen years old, and my school organized a field trip to the archaeological site of ancient Warivilca. It was a sacred temple made up of small stone walls, with individual rooms running parallel to the outside wall. The magic of this sacred temple was in the stream of water coming up through the ground and running in the middle of the site.

I had a vision of a couple getting married. The couple was wearing vibrant clothing with linear drawings in different colors. A male voice spoke to them, telling them that marriage was eternal and important. Shortly after, I had a second vision where time had passed, and they were no longer married. The man had stopped loving her. I could see his indifference and coldness toward her. I also noticed that she was heartbroken. The happiness I felt when they were getting married had vanished. Now, I was left with an empty hole in my heart and loneliness.

I couldn't understand the vision. I was sad the couple was not together anymore, and I wondered why the marriage hadn't lasted. I didn't want to accept that people could stop loving each other. Wisdom spoke inside me, saying, lasting or eternal marriages are powerful, and they exist. Having this knowledge felt good. I didn't recognize at that time that it was my older brother, my subconsciousness, talking to me. I believe it was the high-frequency energy in the sacred site that increase my energy and connected us.

My sense of separation endured for many years more until my oldest son was five and my youngest almost four. I drove away with my sons in the back seat, leaving my husband and the life we had built. Things would never be the same, and though I didn't know it then, it was the beginning of me remembering how to be part of a 5th-dimensional life, a process of Self-Love. a new reality where I will learn to set boundaries of honor, respect, and self-value.

As I continued driving in the opposite direction of where home used to be, I sensed a presence sitting in the front passenger seat, and somehow, I knew he was there to support me. I knew that his presence was something good, but I had too much on my mind to think about his existence. Eventually, I decided to call him Che. I liked the word "Che" because, in Argentina, it is slang for friend.

A month later, I went to Peru. I believed that being out of the country would help the process of marital separation. While there, I met an energy worker who used his intuition to align the frequency of my body. I scheduled a consultation with him. During that consultation, I was lying on the table facing the ceiling. I noticed the healer did not touch my body while working on me. Instead, he held his hands quite close, working to balance my energy.

When he reached my right arm, and I turned to see what he was doing, standing next to him, to the right of his shoulder, I saw Che, the man sitting in my car the day I left my ex-husband. He appeared as a shadow to me a month ago, but now that I was myself at a higher frequency, he looked different. His presence lighted up the room. Che was a Light Being. He no longer lived in a physical body but existed as pure energy in the shape of a human body. He radiated peace, love, and kindness as a pure essence.

I felt like I had known Che for a long time and had an old and strong connection, but I did not remember what it was or how I knew him. I started crying.

"Please do not leave again," I kept repeating.

I was having an experience of feelings—an experience that happens with Light Beings. The peace I received from his presence stayed in my heart for a long time. I wanted to learn more about him, life in other dimensions, and the unseen world.

After that experience, I often felt him around me, but I could not see him. I had a lot of questions.

Who was he?

Where is he?

How can I communicate with him more often?

What was his purpose?

He was very knowledgeable, kind, and funny. He knew I was vulnerable to the damage caused by my mother and was gentle when he felt

I could feel him. He was not invasive, but it was a soft approach when communicating with me.

I sensed that he knew me well, but at the same time, he was being careful not to rush me by giving the information I was not ready to receive.

After being in Peru for a month, I contracted pneumonia and was very ill. I returned to the United States, the inflammation in my lungs produced a dry cough, chest pain, fever, and difficulty breathing. I was weak and tired.

I was in bed for almost three weeks, and felt I was not improving. I did not have a family close to take care of me. I lay in bed, death slowly taunting me, and I kept praying to God. "Please, I do not want to die."

Che responded, touching my right arm. I felt his energy, that gently downloaded into my body. It was like my body was copying data from his energy. While he was doing that, memories of the past flowed through me. He was giving me his energetic blood and experiences of love. I felt his wisdom, his feelings, and his compassion for me. It was comforting to feel his presence while I was healing, even though he did not speak. I felt at home and safe with him.

While searching for more information about Che, I talked to several energy healers, card readers, and read some books. One day, I talked to a lady who did card readings and mentioned past lives. That was the first time I heard that we had lives before we were in our current bodies.

I had a card reading with another lady who saw a woman standing in the center of the picture in one of the cards and some mountains around her. I had not shared my childhood experiences in the 5th dimension with her or anyone else. I was surprised that she was aware of it, especially when she saw the mountains guide me and protect me.

She sensed I had Energy Gifts and said I was someone special. I invited her to my house and offered to share my newfound ability to read energy.

It was fascinating that I knew different things about her—her family, her life, the blocks, and the limiting beliefs controlling her. Something had happened within me where I was experiencing heightened gifts I hadn't had before. Che's light was uploaded to my body when I was sick. When Che's light went into my body, it was like a blood transfusion. It was a process of transferring light fluid into my veins and arteries, and the new light was recharging my body.

It was amazing. Also, I felt Che's connection with me. Sometimes, he would give me the information, and I was channeling it to her.

Finally, I met another woman who gave me some information about Che. She said that Che was always with me. My questions were still the same as they'd been before.

Why was he protecting me?

Who was he?

She was a Reiki practitioner. She explained that Che was a Light Being in my life to help me to ascend to a higher frequency. I accepted this explanation, but I knew it was more than that, and I felt she could not understand the connection between Che and me in the way that I could. I stopped seeing her when she began communicating with her head instead of her heart.

I learned from my mountains that a true healer listens to their heart. She talked about her achievements and her qualities as a healer as a way of impressing; she put herself on a pedestal. For instance, she said that she was one of the only ones who could reach a high level of understanding of what the truth is. She did not have a pure heart. We can only move forward in the light with the pure intentions of our hearts.

After these experiences of connection with Che, my conversation with card readers, energy healers, meditations, books, and dreams, I concluded that a Light Being is a being that has reached the knowledge of the 5th dimension or higher. There are different types of Light Beings: the people of light in Atlantis, ascended masters, angels, and ancestors. Their intentions are powerful. They are here to help us by providing information and improving our quality of life. They believe that our personal development is the foundation for a better universe. If we choose to see our value through Self-Love, we are unstoppable manifesting our pure desire as individual and collective consciousness.

Light Beings can also be the spirit of the mountains, rocks, water, fire, air, planets, the sun, and animals. Their spirit carries pure consciousness and serves a higher purpose in the universe.

CHAPTER 4
Acada's 3rd-Dimensional Life

Acada's experiences do not come to me in chronological order. The information came in at different times when I needed it to help me deal with a specific situation. My 3rd dimensional experiences of her life came mostly while walking through Peru's ancient sites. These took me by surprise because they happened unexpectedly.

When my children were growing up, I often felt powerless. My youngest son constantly got sick, and it was hard to see him suffer. He'd had allergies, ear infections, insomnia, stomach pain, and asthma. I wanted him to be healthy and happy, to be present for the opportunities of his life, but he had trouble focusing on school and getting the grades he wanted. He liked sports, especially football, but his asthma made it hard for him to play. Even driving him to places was challenging because he suffered from motion sickness.

I wanted my sons to have many friends and feel like they were the luckiest boys alive. I was divorced by this time. I did what mothers and fathers often do, be strong and build the courage to provide for our children.

One day while my boys were on vacation with their father, I opened my heart and prayed for the answers on how to guide and care for them. I connected to my heart like I did when I was young, and I increased my heart to higher levels of love for my son instead of being afraid.

I felt the warmth of my heart and I intuitively knew to connect the energy of my subconscious to my heart. I know the subconscious is a mystery for most people but to me it is a collective consciousness with feelings and thoughts, a driving force of love, and wisdom, that makes me feel I am the best thing that ever happened to me. It makes me feel unstoppable.

Then, I merged them into the same energy and placed them with an intention of love. I remember saying the intention, "Please, Father, guide me to help my child."

Afterward, I finished my to-do list and cleaned the house. When I was resting in my bed

a strong feeling came over me, it was like a movie happening inside my body. I felt a woman crying inside my body, she was having an abortion. I wanted to do something to help her and calm her crying, but I did not know what to do, I felt her sadness as her body moved in pain while a woman helped her body release the baby. She gently delivered the baby, but there was a sense of urgency.

I could feel her experience, her grief. The deep sadness and loss one feel when someone they love has died. She was in so much emotional pain. She loved her boy so much and dreamt about being a mother to him. Now she was losing him. Having to disconnect from him was losing part of her. She tried to be strong, but she couldn't.

A few minutes before that vision, I saw her so happy and expressing her gratitude to Father Creator for all the blessings she had in her life. Then, through a window, she saw her husband on a bed with another woman. She was confused and could not believe what she was seeing. Everything was happening so fast.

She felt sad, empty, and lost. As I witnessed this, I couldn't help but wonder what happened to her.

Why was she in that situation?

Why were there not more people helping her?

No one should experience this.

I wanted so much to stop her pain. I heard myself pronouncing her name several times. Acada, Acada.

I sensed that Acada's abortion was a secret. I had kept secrets in my past, too, not because I was doing bad things but because I was trying to protect people from getting hurt. I intuitively knew that Acada was trying to save someone by making this choice. But who?

Then I noticed that Acada was talking to me. I heard her gentle voice saying, "I was protecting my baby and my husband." To my surprise, I was channeling Acada's life in Atlantis.

Seeing Acada go through that experience was hard, not only because she was showing me something terrible that happened to her but because the memories of the event stayed in my body. They repeatedly replayed it as if it was happening to me. It was like the molecules in my body were searching for a solution.

Every time it repeated, I felt the depth of her sadness and pain. At that time, I could not comprehend these various events happening. Her pain, the story, and the lack of completion of that situation were inside me, and they were part of my daily routine. Sometimes, it would get quiet, but then the sadness came back.

Acada wanted me to understand the behavior of her society and the impact on me, my children, and our society in the present. She said that by helping her and seeing her true story, I would help my sons, which motivated me to continue learning. It was the beginning of a long journey.

Acada explained to me that some cultural and societal beliefs differed in those times. As I translate her teachings, they may have various meanings according to the level of our understanding and feelings. For instance, a banana has a different meaning today than what a banana would have meant in the times of Atlantis, based on community experiences, perceptions, and choices. A banana in Atlantis had another name and was in a different language.

Even though we see the same thing, our perceptions, and understandings differ. Acada explained if you eat a banana and get sick, that is your experience. Suppose someone eats a banana and feels happy.

That is a different experience. Someone wants to eat a banana but does not have the money to buy it. It is an experience of scarcity. Each of them looks at a banana with different meanings because of their experience, and we make choices reflected by the event's emotions.

There were some unique characteristics of the Atlantis culture, like things that are unique to our culture. For instance, among the Law of One, they chose to have children if they were in the energy of Circular Time which is in the 5th dimension because they understood the importance of having values and principles that can impact the future. It took me a long time to translate her message; the best way I could have done it was to feel Acada's experiences of the 3rd dimension and 5th dimension.

I learned that the trigger for Acada to have the abortion was that she witnessed her husband having an affair with another woman. In Circular Time relationship affairs did not exist. Not knowing what to do, she sought the advice of an older woman in the high council. This woman told her that her husband did not love her anymore otherwise he would be with her.

Acada must honor his choice, his wish to be with the other woman, and she must leave him. She advised Acada to have an abortion because a child without the connection to his father and mother in a relationship will be confused and damage the future of their society.

This decision broke Acada's heart, but she decided to listen to the elder in the council. She did not know at that time that she was being set up.

Some council members feared the birth of Acada's baby—he was bringing balance to Atlantis, balance the Mirrors did not want. The council elder was one of the Mirrors, and Acada was unaware of it.

At the time, the council in Atlantis was composed of around 500 members. Before the contamination, each member represented different aspects of higher laws of the Mu to protect living creations and frequencies of life sources. The purpose of this group was to hold the united frequencies of all creations of light, and light in those times meant life.

Unfortunately, members of the council were persuaded by the Mirrors to believe that technology was more necessary than the principles and values of feelings. They would say they had the technology, would control the future, and be more powerful than the Law of one. They infiltrated the council and convinced some members to oppose the Law of One.

This is how the contamination came into the Atlantis council when the Mirrors believed they were better than the Law of One. The council became fragmented and no longer represented the common good.

Witnessing these stories of the past was truly a gift because it allowed me to differentiate values and principles that I would choose to apply in my life and that of my children. I was observing the impact of love in our lives, not only romantic love but the love that glues objects and experiences together in time and space, creating a 5th-dimensional reality.

CHAPTER 5
Light Beings

My 3rd-dimensional perspective was a powerless story, as are all 3rd-dimensional stories unless they are transformed by love. Channeling Che, Acada, and other Light Beings changed everything for me. I learned from them that our ability to feel is essential to channeling information from a higher source.

Channeling is a process by which we achieve a state of heart and mind consciousness through communication with higher beings, ancestors, and the universe. The connection can be made through any of the senses: seeing, hearing, touch, taste, or smell. Self-Love plays a vital role because by loving ourselves, we increase our energy and experience more feelings, eventually opening us to channel. When we channel, we find that our feelings are a way of seeing – a door that opens our hearts to different realities.

A Light Being is a creation, or energy, of love. To create light, that Being had to learn to love himself and have pure intentions. The Light Beings understand that love is a science of creation; therefore, they become both gatekeepers and protectors of love. A Light Being is someone in the 5th or higher dimensions which has mastered Self-Love's energy.

It is important to mention that a Light Being can also be your higher self. Your higher self has already experienced what you are experiencing in the present. Your higher self is your highest possibility, your most expansive expression in the future. It travels to the present as a Light Being to help you make clear choices to connect you with that more significant potential in the future.

Every Light Being reflects their love for others, and I have felt their love for me. Each one of them has unique qualities. Acada, for example, focused on future outcomes. Her self-determination is her internal source of motivation and her passionate need for personal growth and fulfillment. She is soft and gentle. She is not a talker but a watcher. She was attentive, mindful, aware, and quick to perceive.

Acada's mindset did not intend to suppress emotions. Instead, it aimed to use her emotions for the greatest benefit. By assessing her feelings, she has become better at filtering out irrational ones. She could see them for what they were and choose not to react but focus on the emotions signaling something important. This practice is the key to developing our intuition and tapping into our deeper sense of self.

Acada is the embodiment of a scientific mind tempered by nurturing love. I felt and experienced Acada as the woman who was misguided by the Mirrors in Atlantis, which was one of her lifetimes. At first, in Atlantis, she was innocent as a child to darkness. She believed everyone had good intentions. When her heart was broken, she transformed. She understood that the Mirrors' contamination could mislead people and trusted only her heart. That decision healed her emotions, eventually restoring her light essence and becoming a Light Being.

I also connected to Acada as a Light Being. In that connection, it was more about her being a teacher. I could feel how her observation penetrated my light body. She knew me well, and she honored my choices. She wanted me to know she loved me and encouraged me to have self-confidence.

I experience Acada both physically and energetically. When I channel her, and I am connected to her past life in Atlantis, my body reflects her experiences. I sometimes hurt within my body in the same area that she experiences pain. If her stomach hurts, so does mine. Sometimes, I experience her emotions: courage, love, kindness, and knowledge. Other times, I share her thoughts. It is like looking through her eyes – I know what she is thinking and how she observes her experience.

Be aware that when you are channeling Light Beings, they are communicating from the present or future in a higher frequency. Because of the contamination of the past is in linear time, the Light Being will not take your energy to the past because you can be contaminated with low- frequency energy. On the other hand, an entity will try to keep you in the negative memories of the past.

When a Light Being wants you to learn something from the past, she will take your energy to the future, and from a perspective of Self-Love, you will observe the experience of the past. For instance, Acada would bring my energy to the future and show me the events from Atlantis. It was like watching a movie.

Most of the time, I experienced Acada working on her energy at the molecular level, decoding possible healings to rewrite the blocks, and limiting beliefs that she was contaminated with during the time of Atlantis. It was like seeing a scientist working with atoms, electromagnetics, and other energy fields. I can see how powerful she is.

Sometimes, when I observe Acada in the past, I can feel her strong desire that things would return to how they were before the contamination—peaceful and full of joy. During these experiences, I have felt her determination not to give up but to trust that she will find the solution. By observing her, I witnessed that the final contamination in Atlantis happened fast. There was a sense of urgency when I witnessed her working to find the cure for the contamination. It was unexpected, like an epidemic.

It is amazing to identify Acada as a Light Being, her higher self in the future, guiding me in the present to witness her past in Atlantis. As she said, my observation from a Self-Love perspective is helping to rewrite her life in Atlantis into a story of love and balance.

I have learned that not everything in the unseen world is light or a message from a Light Being. I see people channeling, but they get information from 3rd-dimensional sources. I know this because I can feel there is no love in their message.

In the 3rd dimension, we are influenced by creations not connected to feelings of love, such as the illusions of blocks and limiting beliefs. The beings that influence us through illusion are called dark entities.

They use manipulation to take our light or feelings of love; their intention is not to love but to use us.

When I channel beings, I must ensure they come from a space of love. If I do not know them, I focus on my heart to feel and reflect if their energy is loving. If I cannot feel that I do not open myself to communicate with them.

CHAPTER 6
Acada's 5th-Dimensional Life

I learned Acada's 5th-dimensional experiences mainly in my walks around the neighborhoods where I live in Park City and Salt Lake City house after I witnessed Acada having an abortion.

Acada was born at a time when there was already conflict in Atlantis. She was a member of the Law of One, the keepers of their traditions and creations of the Mu beings. One of the first memories Acada showed me was when she was around five years old. I saw her in a vision playing in a garden with Mother and Father Creator. She was running around in the beautiful green grass and big green trees. Mother and Father Creator looked at her while they smiled. The expression on her face showed that there was nothing to be worried about. She had a big smile.

Acada explained to me that this park was a holy place to them. This place was where Light Beings lived among the Law of One in Atlantis. The planet's frequency was high because there were few blocks and limiting beliefs, allowing the People of the Light to connect between different dimensional realities. There was no pain or suffering in this place but love and happiness. The beings communicated in full expression of the observation and perspective of Self-Love.

Acada taught me that there are so many ways to express the meaning of Father and Mother Creator. For instance, we can see Father as a human, but that is a small part of his evolution. If we give him only human qualities, we will give him limited qualities of blocks and limiting beliefs. "Look at him as a possibility of Love," she said.

It was true. At times, I had compared Father Creator to my human father, and I got confused because Father Creator does not have blocks and limiting beliefs, and my human father did. I have learned to perceive Father and Mother Creator as more than a human experience.

Another way to understand Father and Mother Creator is by envisioning the first atom created billions of years ago with a neutron (Father Creator) and proton (Mother Creator) inside a nucleus. Through time, they had trials and self-discoveries to maintain their existence. They went through evolution and changes to be who they are. Their secret formula, Self-Love.

They represent who we are at the molecular level. Therefore, the female power that Mother Creator and the male power that Creator Father represent are equally influential.

One day, I had a vision of Acada in the holy garden. She was around five or six years old. She was happy running in an open field of bright green grass. As she ran, everything around her flowed in waves of energy that reflected and matched her movements as she connected to every living thing. She felt good and in harmony with everything around her.

I felt Acada's self-confidence. It was as if she knew deep in her heart that there was nothing to worry about and to enjoy the present. She loved everyone, and like her ancestors, she could feel a molecular connection to every living thing – the air, plants, the ground she stood on, and the love of the people around her.

I felt lucky to witness the possibility of another way of life in which we could be part of everything. I had felt that when I was young, but not to the degree Acada did.

There was a lot of space to play in the carpeted green grass and trees park, Mother and Father Creator were with her, as were other people. Everyone was dressed in white. Acada watched Mother and Father talking and smiling, and I sensed that she felt the love they had for each other.

I saw Acada holding the energy of Father and Mother's experience inside her heart as if it was a gentle wind feeding energy to her. It was like she was decoding, downloading, and storing like a computer the love experience of Father and Mother Creator inside her body. She was processing information like her ancestors did. Mother and Father's connection fed light into her energy. They channeled their love into her; she was learning from them by feeling. It seemed like she was accessing the blueprint of their love for one another.

Acada would share memories in this park with me often. She showed me a time when only Father was with her. That day, she noticed that the park was not as bright as it had been when Mother Creator had been with them. It was clear to me how much Father Creator loved Acada. She felt his love in her body's energy and was confident in her connection with him. She remembered when Father showed her love by trusting her and being proud of her when she was happy. He also acknowledged her wanting to learn more about connecting with plants, animals, and other creations. He taught her how to communicate with the spirit and molecular energy of mountains, plants, rocks, and more. She called them brothers and sisters.

Father showed her a portal of light behind him and gently said, "I will be leaving through that portal. When the portal closes, I will not be returning, but we get to keep the connection of our hearts together."

Father told her to remember everything he taught her so they could be together again. To her best understanding at that age, this meant remembering that Acada loved him and that he loved her. Even before she understood the significance of what he was telling her, this motivated her to love everyone so that she could hold onto the information Father gave her.

Acada was too small to understand. Father had chosen Acada to be the connection between the Light Beings in the 5th dimension, higher realms and the Law of the Ones in Atlantis.

That day Father moved his hands and created a rainbow of soft yellow light that connected his heart to hers, and he said, "Always remember how much I love you, and you will be okay."

Acada trusted Father and felt no pain or fear because she knew they would always be connected. This experience happened when the 5th-dimensional energy of Atlantis was under threat, and Atlantis was becoming a 3rd-dimensional world.

Many years later, Acada would visit the park with her husband. His name was Ta, with whom she worked on the Law of One council within Atlantis. She called it the 5th-dimensional park because it was a holy ground connected to the 5th dimension of her memories of Father and Mother Creator in the space of expansion of love. She loved to visit there.

These memories of 5th-dimensional love motivated her and Ta to become members of the council, which had been formed by the Law of One to honor the teachings of Mother and Father Creator so that future generations could benefit from these 5th-dimensional lessons. Like other couples, Acada and Ta represented the love of Father and Mother Creator, and they were called Twin Cells. Acada married Ta in that same park and was happy that she had the same love for Ta as Mother had for Father.

Father had told Acada that when two feelings connect in a common purpose, it is a Contract of Love: a promise to keep the balance of love and happiness. Love is a male force or feeling that guides us, and happiness is a female force or feeling that creates more possibilities for creation and existence. Contracts of Love were the foundation of the Atlantis council before the contamination and played an important role in the Twin Cell marriage. The Atlantis Council was a collective consciousness that wanted the best for its diversified community. Its purpose was to create, maintain, and support Contracts of Love in the community and its organizations.

Acada was one of the last living full-blooded Mu—most had perished in the sinking of their continent—and as such, her role on the council was critical: to honor and perpetuate ancestors' traditions and knowledge.

Acada was unique in the way that she created with her mind. It is a challenging concept for us to understand and it was even difficult for some in Atlantis. Like her Mu ancestors, Acada was a multidimensional thinker. Rather than thinking of the past, the present, and the future laid out on a linear timeline, she enjoyed and experienced what we call "time" as more of a like a circle, a complete process that manifests in the present. Further, her ability to decode cellular and atomic-level behaviors set her apart.

Acada could travel to the past, present, and future, make changes, and then manifest the physical result in the present, all based on what she wanted to experience. For instance, in linear time, if we cook a meal, add too much salt, and dislike the result, we feel stuck, as if we've ruined the food. In Acada's mind and experience, it's okay to oversalt a meal you've cooked because instead of being stuck in the "present," where the food does not taste the way you want it, you can return to the past just when you added the salt and put less in the dish. You recreate the experience. Then, when your mind returns to the present, you find the taste of your food has changed. This way of creating was one of the benefits of "Circular Time," rewriting events to become a better situation.

Acada was in love with life and always grateful for her opportunities. She was a feeler. Her thinking patterns – the ones that carried her from past to present to future and back again – allowed her to feel the experience of every step of her creation, which kept her closely connected to the knowledge of her surroundings like water, plants, animals, rocks, and other creations. She called the knowledge of her surroundings her star brothers and sisters because she considered every creation of the universe a family.

Five Points of Power

One of the first things I learned from Acada was that the future is made up of different possibilities and that making Contracts of Love will bring the best outcomes from the future to the present.

"We're all created by Protocols of Feelings," she said. During those times, I would go for walks on the street close to my house in Park City and saw on the trail or out by the trail, rocks with five points in the shape of a pentagon. I picked up the stones and felt them in my hand like I was looking for a connection. I was learning how to feel that protocol of Five Points of Power.

That is how I learned that there is a unique bundle of feelings in our molecular energy that is made for each of us that attracts and aligns to future outcomes and possibilities, which is a connection between the present and future in high-frequency. This bundle or protocol of feelings is the Five Points of Power.

Mu people believed every creation was a structure around a bundle of feelings—they asserted humans were, too. They called these bundles of feelings Symbols of Love or protocols, and the Five Points was one of those protocols. A pentagon's geometrical shape represents the Five Points of Power with five sides and five angles.

The Five Points of Power were created before we were born at the beginning of our energetic existence. It is a representation of our existence in light or energy. It is part of a spiritual chemistry periodic table of elements. It is a science that has yet to be discovered in our times.

Father Creator taught Acada that we all have different "Five Points of Power," representing our five most substantial feelings. Those points were co-created by Mother out of her depth of knowledge of us and the desires of our hearts. Father Creator told Acada that if she focused on developing her five most substantial feelings, they would guide her into higher possibilities in her future.

I asked Father Creator how to explain this new concept to you, the reader, and he showed me a young woman's experience. She was around twenty-one years old, and I just finished talking to her mom on the phone. The mother was worried because the young woman was avoiding going home because she was drinking and using drugs. She was using drugs and alcohol because, in her conversation, she was free to do anything she wanted to do.

Father said that this young woman believed that freedom does not have consequences in the future, but that is not true. Freedom has positive outcomes. She could not see this because she was disconnected from her Five Points of Power.

Acada's first point was the energy of unconditional love, which gave her the power of discernment. Unconditional love is the balance between giving and receiving, giving love to yourself and others, and receiving love from yourself and others. This concept does not have anything to do with giving with conditions, which means expecting to get something back in return. This exchange is about energy. It is how the equilibrium of the universe works. When you give something, the universe returns energy to you to create a balance of creation and direction.

Her second point was the feeling of expansion, with which she could increase her power of giving and receiving love.

Mother gave Acada her third point of power: the Knowledge of love. The more she learned about the feelings of love, the further she could expand. The Law of One knew that Knowledge is a feeling. The feeling of Knowledge was essential to go into expansion.

I asked Father Creator to explain the meaning of feeling differently. He asked me to share with you my experience with you. A few months ago, I noticed that my reading glasses hurt my eyes. I knew (Knowledge) I should get new prescription glasses. But I had not taken the time to get new ones. Yesterday was a hectic day. I took my glasses everywhere with me. At night, I would not find them. I lost them.

Losing them is good because now I get to take the "action" to purchase new ones. Once I get them, which is in the future, they will be good for my eyes. This is how feelings work; they are energy in movement that requires an action to connect to a better future. These are some types of feelings: self-expression, productivity, trust, love, caring, and more.

Acada's fourth point of power was the feeling of grounding, the balance of an effect on its cause. The grounding feeling brings knowledge feelings through genetic codes to create light expansion. When I say "expansion," I mean a link to the future to create light which is the source of life.

Mother knew how much Acada loved her, so she gave Acada her fifth point of power: the powerful feeling of connection which is the gift of understanding the balance of Mother's female energy.

Father explained to Acada that we create separation when we look for a point of reference for our identity in others. He emphasized that if she focused on her Five Points of Power, she would find her inner connection to learn more about her light essence. That is, he told her, the true power of believing in our feelings.

Acada applied these teachings, and the love of Father and Mother Creator, to her relationships with her husband and two children.

Acada did not have the 3rd child, because that was the one, she aborted. Ta was in a trap that the Mirrors set up for him to be unfaithful to Acada, as a consequence, the harmony in the family was damaged.

In Acada's timeless world, names represented the highest expression of a feeling. Acada's name meant "the guardian of the light," which was the feeling of unconditional love. Ta's name, the closest translation, meant "climber of the sky," which is gratitude in our reality.

When Acada and Ta wed, their promises of love were reflected in their Five Points of Power. These feelings were aligned with the blueprint of Mother's and Father's love that gave them direction and supported them in moving forward to create a life of balance, connecting with 5th-dimensional love.

When the Mirrors stole Mu technology and the frequency of the planet dropped from the 5th dimension to the 3rd dimension, Acada, as it turned out, became a bridge between the 5th and 3rd dimensions. One day, Acada received a channeled message from the 5th dimension from Father Creator, telling her that she would have another child, a boy, and that this unborn child would have in his DNA codes of the 5th dimension. These codes would help to clear the 3rd-dimensional contamination of the planet. By clearing this contamination, the 5th-dimensional energy would increase. He said the boy would love his people in Atlantis very much, and the reflection of that love would help increase their energy to balance and reconnect them back to the 5th dimension. That would be the beginning of reconnecting to the old ways of love of the Law of One.

The Law of One, Father said, would return to the source of light and open other dimensions to reconnect and maintain communication with their loved ones in other realities of light. The Law of One would teach how to create more light in unity without separation. There would not be diseases, pain, or suffering but instead the expansion of spirit.

Acada was happy that her unborn baby represented the love of Father Creator for his people. Her son was a gift from the universe. Acada's baby would connect the power and balance of love that Mother and Father Creators had for each other. She decided to call her unborn son Fatherlove to honor him for his role in Atlantis. Fatherlove's Five Points of Power were Love, Expansion, Accountability, Persistence, and Acknowledgement.

Ta was also thrilled by the news. His innocence to darkness blinded him, seeing only the good of every person, honoring their feelings as much as his own. He believed that everyone, in the deepest part of their hearts, wanted to be connected to higher knowledge. His Five Points of Power were Compassion, Truth, Transformation, Wisdom, and Connection.

Ta wanted to master those feelings to connect with his children. He felt gratitude and love for the opportunity of having a son that would bring balance to Atlantis, and he was already embracing the feelings of his unborn child to support Fatherlove on his heart journey. Acada and Ta were learning to connect to their unborn baby, Fatherlove's Five Points of Power.

This impending homecoming of the energy of Father Creator from the 5th-dimensional world was welcome news for The Law of One people. They had memories of Father Creator but did not have him in their DNA experience. As the Law of the One well knew, there was a difference between the memories of feelings and the experience of emotions. The experience of feeling is what connects us to the 5th dimension. The Law of One knew that if they could experience higher feelings from the 5th dimension, it would be possible to increase the energy of Atlantis to one that would be balanced in love, service, and wisdom.

CHAPTER 7
Why the 5th Dimension?

Acada Learns the Books of Light

To understand Acada's purpose in sharing her story, you must remember that 3rd-dimensional stories are illusions that adhere to the laws of linear time (the past, the present and the future) where blocks and limiting beliefs create pain and suffering.

The 5th dimension is the reality of Circular Time in which the present and future work together and are balanced by Self-Love. In Circular Time, there is no past because there is nothing to repair. We are fulfilled with our choices of Self-Love.

What happens to the past? All the good memories of the past get transferred to the future of high-frequency to create more energy of love and light.

The past of illusions can't survive because they can't produce light and are parasites that can only suck the light. When the memories of love that created, light are transferred to the future in high-frequency, the parasites don't have food to eat and eventually disappear. This is the 'technology of love.'

What is the difference between high-frequency and low-frequency futures? The high-frequency future is the 5th-dimensional frequency, and the low-frequency future is a 3rd-dimensional extension of the past of stories of illusions. Low-frequency future stops existing when the stories of illusions of the past are dissolving. These concepts may be challenging to comprehend, but being open to these concepts will help you learn and benefit from other creative possibilities.

One day, I was walking in a park, thinking about what else Acada wanted me to share in this book. Suddenly, I had a vision. I saw Acada resting on a bed. She was feeling her love for Father and remembering him. It was a connection of mind and heart. To my surprise, I realized that she was tapping into the molecular memory of Father, what I called "Books of Light" or records of light that he'd left inside her atoms.

Intuitively, I knew they were memories of Father Creator. I looked at one of them. It was a pure white light in the shape of a book. In the book's content, there was no writing as we know but a white light like a cloud with information. The white cloud was a scroll of feelings and memories that behaved like 3D movies.

In this experience, three paralleled realities were happening at the same time. Acada was reading the Book of Light, and I observed Acada reading the book and me reading the book from another reality.

I knew she was reading the book because I felt her connection to Father at that moment. These Books of Light contained the knowledge Father had placed inside her at the park before he left Atlantis.

By visualizing the content of the book, I felt like I went inside a cloud and created a connection. I felt different emotions. Each of them inspired others, and they also triggered me to experience and observe the information. It was like watching an ancient theater play where people on the stage were giving information to the viewers by playing a role on stage.

Reflecting on this, I also learned how to read the Books of Light by observing Acada while she was reading them.

Books of Light are powerful tools of communication in the 5th dimension. These books are frequencies of love that contain stories and experiences from the perspective of love about the creation and evolution of planets and living things in the universe, including our emotions and bodies. In this way, Father was teaching Acada while she felt his love.

I was intrigued that my body began changing as I felt their loving connection. It was like a gentle flow of electricity running and charging my nervous system, producing a magnetic field shaped in a circle form. Some of these little atom magnetic fields were added together, creating a stronger magnetic field that wrapped my body in a golden light coming from my head, going through it and directing it to my feet in a vortex of atomic force of feelings.

There was a difference between Father's and Acada's Books of Light. All Father's Books of Light felt like an expansion of light from inside out of 5th-dimensional energy. Some of Acada's Books of Light also felt like expansion, but some of her atoms did not have Books of Light. The Books of Light moved in a circular spiral light. However, the atoms that did not have Books of Light acted differently because they had radiation. The electrons inside those atoms were moving without direction in an open field, which is the motion of the 3rd dimension.

Another way to explain this concept is by likening it to the experience of eating. Let's say you like apples. When you eat an apple, there is a feeling of satisfaction— an expansion of being fulfilled. This is the feeling of 5th-dimensional energy. But when you eat something that makes you sick, you want to clear your stomach; this discomfort is the feeling of the 3rd dimension. Father had only 5th-dimensional energy, but Acada had 3rd- and 5th-dimensional frequencies in her body because she was exposed to 3rd- and 5th-dimensional behaviors in this reality.

Sometimes when I am in my quiet space lying on my bed, and my mind is calm, I can feel Acada's energy in my stomach, head, arms, legs, and other body parts. My molecules are holding space for her Books of Light – her stories. Her Books of Light start with feeling the movement of energy in my body. Then my heart connects to the essence of light. I feel my love for her, and I can observe her experiences or events from the past, present, or future. I have observed that these books or molecular memories are only accessible and transferrable to us when we feel love for others or ourselves.

Acada was a fast learner. The more she felt the information in her body given to her to understand, the more she manifested the knowledge. She tried explaining this to me, but I didn't know what "manifesting the knowledge" meant. There were a lot of things I did not understand because I had not experienced them. I realized I needed the experience to understand what "manifesting knowledge" was and what Acada was teaching me.

That day, I lay in my bed and closed my eyes. I was feeling the energy in my body, and suddenly, I had a vision of an army of over a thousand soldiers. Acada said, "That represented an army of atoms in one of my cells." I was surprised I would have so many atoms in one cell of my body.

I saw one of the tiny soldiers—an atom— that received a yellow light in his heart, bringing new information about feelings. I didn't know what feeling it was; I only saw the light coming from the space from above and to him.

Once this tiny atom in the cell learned the new feeling, it would feel energetically charged, exhibiting great activity and vitality. It felt like it became happy as it realized the new feeling. It desired to share its experience with other atoms. It transferred to another atom.

The receiving atom next transferred, in turn, with other atoms. It was like a domino effect. Nothing was forced about the process; it was an invitation to love. This process is what Acada meant by "manifesting the knowledge."

So, the "manifestation knowledge" is the "collective consciousness" among atoms that creates a new behavior inside a cell. Then, the cell with thousands of atoms with the new behavior will also transfer that to the other cells in the DNA of the body, and a new behavior is manifested.

Okay, this is a lot to understand. Let me slow down a little and share my story with you. When I was young and observed how my mother punished my sister for asking my cousin for money, it was a terrible experience. My mother placed hot pepper in my sister's mouth, and I felt her pain and saw the terror on her face. At that moment, one of my tiny atoms absorbed my mother's anger and dropped its energy. The "Book of Light" inside the atom vanished in the process.

The contamination inside of the atom with anger created stress and anxiety, eventually depression. These three low-frequency emotions also started radiation. The movement inside of it slowed down, and linear time at last took over. The cellular memory stayed in the past, remembering the event over and over again, contaminating other atoms. The radiation spread through my body, and I developed seasonal allergies. When my boys were born, both had allergies because the information about the event and radiation transferred to their genes.

According to Acada, "Manifestation Knowledge" is the ability of the atoms of the 5th dimension to rewrite the contaminated ones by bringing back the "Books of Light" to repair the damage. When behaviors of love and experience of love transfer, they learn to create in the reality of the 5th dimension with Self-Love again.

Acada Learns About Linear Time and Circular Time

By feeling and observing the information of the Books of Light in her atoms, Acada learned the difference between linear and Circular Time. Acada determined that some of the behaviors in the 3rd dimension, such as envy, blaming, self-doubt, guilt, revenge, and lying, are blocks and limiting beliefs controlled by linear time, which is fragmented time: past, present, and future. This fragmented time has the collective idea that we are broken.

Acada also observed how the 4th dimension works. The 4th dimension is like a bridge between the 3rd and 5th dimensions. The 3rd, 4th, and 5th used to be the same energetic dimension, but the contamination separated it in Atlantis.

During the summer of 2011, there were days when I would walk for 20 to 30 minutes, grounding myself to keep my connection with Mother Earth and understand what Acada was teaching me.

I wondered, "Where is the trigger point when we choose circular or linear time?" How did my mother's anger penetrate into my tiny atom?

I increased my energy high enough and connected with Acada to understand the new concept, the 4th dimension.

She said, "The trigger happens in the 4th dimension," then she continued, "The 4th dimension works like our liver."

Our liver processes everything we eat, and all the blood that leaves the stomach and intestine passes through the liver. It processes the blood and creates nutrition for our body. If the liver is not working, we get intoxicated and sick. Since the blocks and limiting beliefs taking part in the 4th dimension are like toxins in the liver, it cannot process them, gets contaminated, and stops working. In the toxicity of the 4th dimension, we cannot connect to our feelings, which are the bridge to the 5th dimension. We get trapped in our minds without feeling our hearts. When the energy of the 4th-dimension does not connect to motion and codes of feelings, you are vulnerable to contaminations in the 3rd dimension. When you stop processing information with feelings, you choose an illusion instead of the truth and that is the trigger. In my situation when the anger of my mother came into my atom and I stopped feeling, I created an idea in my mind that ran my life for a long time, "Life is not safe."

Linear time does not have movement. In Acada's language, the future cannot heal the past if it is separated from the 5th dimension. But when we connect to love to ourselves and others, the magic happens, and you connect to the 5th dimension. In the 5th dimension, there is energetic motion and expansion, and you create in Circular Time, where the focus is on the relation between the present and future. You complete the story of past limitations by observing love and letting the past of suffering and low-frequency emotions go.

Acada wanted to free us. She saw and felt, in the memories of her Books of Light, that linear time could be rewritten. It is, after all, an illusion. She was surprised to discover that she could rewrite linear time by reconnecting the feelings of her Five Points of Power to the energy of the 5th dimension. In the process, she could also make obsolete the 4th dimension of energy that supported linear time.

Why would she want to do this? Because we suffer as both victims and survivors of limitations. While the blocks use our consciousness to create more blocks or limiting beliefs without us knowing, we, as a collective society, decide some of these limitations. For instance, we have perpetuated the concept of aging – the ideas of "young" and "old." Collectively we decide who is powerful and who is weak. We determine who is useful and who is not, and we reject one another according to our skin color and physical attributes. Also, we decided if women or men are strong or weak and who is successful and who is not. We experience these limiting beliefs in our bodies, and we get sick. These are just some ways we create separation and maintain linear time. It is separation according to who we think we are.

Another collective limitation is the belief that suffering entitles us to decide between right and wrong and what is convenient. We suffer when we do not feel safe, and from the space of survival, we determine, as a society, who is rich or poor. We wear energetic labels on our foreheads that say, "I only want to hear what is convenient for myself and my needs because eventually I will stop existing. I need to compensate for my lack of fulfillment by having more and creating less." In linear time, we are trapped in fear and mistrust of ourselves, and we are trapped in the past and have a sense of being unfulfilled.

In the 5th dimension, however, we find time to be circular. It is the ability to connect to Self-Love, to live in the present, and to generate the future we want. The solution for those damaged atoms with limiting ideas is to rewrite their information using the "manifestation knowledge" to reintegrate the "Books of Light" into them.

The intention we create from our hearts is the key to making a life that fulfills our daily potential. The past is a low-frequency vibration that does not dictate the direction of your life. If you instead live with intention, you are creating a circular behavior in the present. Choices in Circular Time are choices that can be fulfilled and completed.

Let's say, for instance, that you have lots of money and can buy anything you desire. You buy everything you want for yourself and others but are still unsatisfied. Is it possible that you are stuck in the dissatisfying 3rd-dimensional cycle where you always want more? Yes, it is.

On the other hand, if you purchase something that makes you happy—and this is your structure for everyday behavior—then you feel complete and look forward to new choices. This balance is the power of Circular Time: to feel happy and complete every time you make a choice that can bring the best possibilities for your future.

Self-Love is essential in Circular Time because it redirects you to your highest potential in every choice. You get to know yourself in every way. Instead of controlling the outcome of everything, you are in the expansion of creation. That is abundance! When creating in the 5th dimension, you do not compare yourself to others, but you use your inner essence as a point of reference to move forward to your potential as a creator and reflect it onwards to create even more. Circular Time is when the past, present, and future dance together to give you what you need. You can then go to your next level of getting to know yourself without suffering but rather with happiness and trust. Always a complete experience.

Acada Learns About Codes (Contracts) of Love

Father taught Acada that the foundations for the 5th and higher dimensions are found in Love Codes or Contracts of Love. These Codes of Love travel through our feelings and connect to the feelings of others. It is like a tunnel of feelings. They create the collective source of the energy of life. Blocks and limiting beliefs cannot survive in Codes of Love; therefore, they are dissolved and cannot reach the 5th dimension.

When we feed our body and essence with intentions of love, Codes of love band together and make a bundle of energy that develops our energetic talents and gifts and connect to other realties and become multi-dimensional.

For example, when we develop a connection and awareness between our thoughts and how those thoughts connect subconsciously and consciously to the energy of what is around us. This connection affects the state of mind and allows us to channel Light Beings. In the process, you learn to use your intuitive wisdom to help others make decisions that align with values that come from truth.

One of the multidimensional benefits is witnessing past lives of low-frequency to help rewrite them into stories of light and love, which may be memories of your ancestors, yourselves, or others inside our atoms, or the atoms of others. We are living computers with several programs from our ancestors and their stories. Also, our ancestors are living computers inside ourselves and have their programs. Specific feelings, or Contracts of Love, keep these programs together.

In addition to experiencing my past lives or the past lives of my ancestors, I learned that multidimensional beings can observe community events that affect a group of people in the past—events such as war, earthquakes, and climate changes. Additionally, they can see a "Collective Consciousness Event," defined as ideas or creations we choose to keep, like the first car or motorcycle. These collective events create or determine the outcome of the future. For instance, we decide to maintain the creation of the television or internet as a society or keep the teachings of religious beliefs or social norms. These collective events can hold space for values, principles, or corruption. Either way, we support this in our body energy and act by accepting or rejecting the experiences.

Being aware of multidimensional experiences like past lives, community, and collective consciousness events, helped me gain more knowledge and freedom of choice. When we are unaware of who we are and do not love ourselves, limitations can control us, and we get trapped in the emotional slavery of the 3rd dimension.

In experiencing the distinctions between the 3rd and 5th dimensions, we find the power to choose and create what we want. Once I was aware of the difference between the 5th and 3rd dimension and understood the power of feelings, Codes of Love, and Books of Light, I learned to make better choices. You can do that, too.

CHAPTER 8
The Mirror's Way of Life

The Law of One maintained the 5th-dimensional creation values, the knowledge of how to access the power of the living source of all life by feeling. But the Mirrors, who sought privileged inequality and entitlement, could not produce enough light to maintain the knowledge in the energetic field of their bodies because they chose not to feel. The Mirrors knew that feelings showed the consequences of our actions in the future. They did not want any responsibility for their choices but blamed others.

The Mirrors knew they had to get the source of light from somewhere. The source of light came from feelings. The Mirrors called the Law of One "feelers". They concluded that because the "feelers" can connect to the future and create abundance of love and light through Self-Love it was the perfect way to steal the light from them and have their abundance.

So, the Mirrors, rather than finding love within themselves that allowed them access to higher knowledge, took the knowledge of light from the Law of Ones by manipulating them.

The Mirrors claimed that the People of the Light did not reflect the light satisfactorily; therefore, it was their fault that they, the Mirrors, will not reincarnate again because the Law of One not supporting them. The Mirrors chose to contaminate the working system, believing their path to power was taken away. The new structure the mirrors create by misusing their power create the 3rd dimensional contaminated matrix.

The Mirrors believed in the illusion that love was only about sharing possessions instead of sharing feelings. Because of this, love took on a new concept: the idea of possession. The more ownership they had, the more powerful they believed themselves entitled.

The Mirrors took possession of the land and created social classes. They kept the Law of One out of their properties by promoting the idea that they were protecting themselves from the negative influence of the People of the Light.

All their observations and ideas sprung from this new, limited existence. Even genetic contamination was the result of the Mirrors' actions. The Mirrors' limiting belief in entitlement created the victims' and survivors' behaviors in Atlantis. This restricted focus birthed a new reality of the 3rd dimension— corruption and loss of the balance that once was Atlantis's way of life. For example, someone acting out as a survivor believes, "I have to be better than others to prove that I am right." It is a trigger of painful and unfinished experiences from the past. A victim's behavior will be, "I can't stop thinking about getting back at my brother for making me feel I am not good enough."

The Mirrors did not have respect or value for other creations, only for their own personal benefit. It was a power game, and they wanted to control their communities to prove their power. This interruption led to the creation of the energy of linear time in the 4th dimension— part of the 5th dimension— by misusing and manipulating the DNA of humans, plants, and other living things.

The Mirrors used Mu's knowledge to break into some of the "feelers" magnetic fields and experimented on them to access their feelings for their own use. This corruption damaged the Five Points of Power protocol, disconnecting the energetic field from the 5th dimension.

For instance, genes are made of DNA and carry large amounts of information about an organisms' development, survival, reproduction, and ancestry sequence data. The Mirrors accessed, experimented, and traced this knowledge to see how they could benefit from it.

The Mirrors were very secretive about the experiments they were doing. None of the Law of One knew about them.

When our feelings are connected to the 5th dimension, we release the contaminations associated with the creation of the 3rd dimension in Atlantis. It's important to note that with Self-Love, we can release consciousness of low-frequency. This is how powerful 5th- dimensional feelings are.

The more we create feelings in our hearts, the more difficult it becomes for harmful attachments to remain in our energetic space. If you generate love which is light, your level of expansion will be positive and more prominent. But, if you choose to make lower frequency decisions, they will manifest at the same intensity, but the space of creations will be smaller only on your reflection, inside of you, with limitations of blocks and limiting beliefs.

If your choices are high-frequency, you will create them in significant ways. Your mind and heart will build and connect. A Light Being told me once that our minds are powerful, but when they disconnect from the feelings in the heart, thoughts can't link to the future of high possibilities. We get stuck in the incomplete ideas of the pain and suffering of the past, feeling emptiness, creating stress, anxiety, depression, and others. He said the heart frequency is more powerful than the mind. When we feel again, the heart force reconnects to the future, and we can see our possibilities of love and light again. Then, you will remember who you are in your full power potential of the 5th dimension, learning to love yourself and connecting to others in honor and respect.

However, people who choose to create with blocks and corruption will be trapped in the space of their lower-frequency choice. It will still be a transformation, a point of learning based on their choices, but it will be an experience of the pain and suffering they intended to send to others.

Nowadays, most people can't see an attachment from the contamination of the time of Atlantis. But I have observed that the Mirror's consciousness interferes with the behavior of the person who carried the DNA contamination.

The good news is that we have entered a period when linear time is dissolving and returning to Circular Time. The Eagle and the Condor ancient prophecy of the Amazon and Andes indigenous cultures speaks of long ago when human societies split into two different paths of the Eagle and that of the Condor.

The prophecy says that during the next 500 years, beginning in 1990, the potential will arise for the Eagle and the Condor to come together, fly in the same sky, and create a new level of consciousness for humanity. I believe, they are talking about the mind and heart coming together. The blocks and limiting beliefs stored in linear time are disintegrating, as are the entities that created the damage.

There will be an evolution in human behavior, as well as, planetary climate changes with fires, earthquakes, droughts, and other phenomena—before the new electromagnetic forces on the earth stabilize.

CHAPTER 9
Victim and Survivor Behavior

What is a feeling? It's a high-frequency expression, experience, or emotion that connects to the future possibilities of love behaviors. For instance, it is when we listen to our hearts while making choices and consider the impact of what we want in the future.

Feelings are also the ability to experience physical sensations (such as pain, touch, or temperature) mediated mainly by skin sensory receptors. For instance, when you feel cold, warm, or numb. These are different from the feeling we will discuss in this book.

According to Acada, there are three types of behaviors:

It was during that time that I was experiencing the distinctions that my practice as a shaman started. I observed in my clients that their bodies react to the frequencies of these behaviors, which also determine whether we have a healthy body and mind or a polluted body and mind.

As with victims' or survivors' behaviors, irrational actions or decisions are not based on reason or sound judgment. They are influenced by psychological factors that trigger decision-making rather than logical or evidence-based thinking.

When we behave as victims or survivors, we do not feel because we are stuck in the past of low-frequency emotions that carry blocks and limiting beliefs that are contaminations. And we engage in triggers of a 3rd-dimensional perspective.

We are receptive to these behaviors. For instance, if someone considers you a victim, your body will sense that person's thoughts and experiences, and you may be triggered to act as a victim. On the other hand, if you are with someone uplifting, like a life coach communicating with love, your body will be receptive to that energy of love and empower you.

Sometimes we learn these behaviors from observing others, but they can also be acquired through our DNA from our ancestors. For example, one day, I was talking to a client and observed his relationship with his son. He was disappointed with his son. He wanted his son to be like him because he believed he had learned from his mistakes. He did not want his son to make the same mistakes he made. He was also telling his son what to do. But the son wanted to have his own experiences.

I noticed that even though the father was in a different city, far away from his son, the son was still receiving the energy in his DNA of the father's disappointment. In my visions, sometimes, I see that the DNA is like a long film that connects to all the ancestors. I do not see all of them at once, but they are there. In the DNA's energy, space acts differently than in our reality. It does not make a difference if someone is far away or close. You and your ancestors connect as if you were in the same place.

In my experience of this father and his son, every time the father generated an idea about his son, the son felt it. He was sensing the frustration and sadness. Because he felt those sensations inside his body, he assumed he was the one who was disappointed with himself. Consequently, he didn't have direction or Self-Love. In this situation, the energy of the father's victim behavior was attacking the son.

We are constantly transferring information to each other, but we are unaware of it, and this is how contamination can be transmitted. By observing the impact of our behaviors, I did not want to behave like a victim or a survivor. I wanted to be a creator of love and reflect those feelings to the world the way Che and other Light Beings trained me. By doing that, I was becoming a reflection of them and their teachings.

I learned from my light teachers that a victim is physically or emotionally harmed due to a crime, accident, or other action; in this case, they do not have a choice. But eventually, that person can choose to behave as a victim, a survivor, or a connector of love. It was clear to me that because these are behaviors, we can decide to change them, as a behavior is not who we are.

When a person behaves as a victim, the atoms in the body will match the behavior to the victim's mentality. A victim's behavior has a lower frequency than a survivor's because when someone acts out as a victim, he is unaware that he has a choice. When a victim recognizes his choice, he has an opportunity, a way out of the situation. He could become a survivor but still focus on the unfulfilled past, he can push through the experience and become a connector of love and stay in the present and future, letting go of the past.

In the situation of the father and son, the father, as a loving connector, would acknowledge, honor, and respect his son's choices. And the son would receive that frequency in his energetic space and would empower him.

A victim, a survivor, and a love connector are confusing concepts. Here is another story that will help you understand the different behaviors.

A woman was driving her car when she got hit by another vehicle. Her car was severely damaged. She did not have any injuries. She was a victim of a situation. In her mental process, she would not stop thinking about the accident. She thought, "If the accident had not happened, I would be using that time to do other things. I am wasting my time."

Then, she used the excuse of the accident to avoid going to work and school. She justified herself and yelled at others when she did not get her way because she was unhappy. She acted helpless because she believed that she could not control the situation.

She focused her energy on the accident and couldn't let go of the inconvenience it created. Like many people who choose to be a victim she thought: *Why me? I am not good enough; bad things happen to me. I will never be the same. God does not love me – otherwise, this wouldn't have happened.*

People who have a victim mentality haven't develop a healthier way to cope. As a result, they develop a negative view of life when they feel that they don't have control of the situation.

Let's say that eventually, she chooses to change her behavior to become a survivor. She is still focused on a past event, but now she has an action plan. Her survival behavior sounds like this: *I will avoid driving. I am going to show I have control when I am driving. I am stupid, and I am ashamed of myself.* Some of the survival traits are aggressiveness, entitlement, ruthlessness, greediness, power oriented, weak integrity, and impulsiveness.

It is also possible that the woman shifts back and forth, sometimes behaving as a victim and at other times as a survivor. Either way, she is not letting go of the story from the past.

There is another option, and that is being and behaving as a connector of love and Self-Love. A love connector focuses on the present and the future and is not controlled by the past. Here are some expressions of a connector of love: *It can happen to anyone. I am in gratitude that I am okay. I want to learn from this and move on.*

Here are some behaviors of a victim mentality:

- "I felt my body was being overtaken by an energy that took control over me. I could not focus or talk to explain what was on my mind.
- I felt small. I started doing things fast without thinking. I would look for something to calm myself. I am starving; I could eat; Eating makes me feel better."
- "I felt overstimulated, sensitive, and alert to the idea that someone might hurt me. I had not eaten, and I felt strong anxiety in my body."
- "I noticed that I spend a lot of time worrying and fear about getting in trouble. When I look back, that was happening every day."
- "My body had learned to reflect on the pain and sorrow of the events from the past, and it was running that daily program. That

was my connection with the outside world. I wondered how I could be the mother I want to be if that is my state of mind every day."

- "I am afraid my children may stop loving me. Because I am not a good mother.
- Here are some reasons why someone may choose to behave as a victim.
- By being a victim, the person will get the attention of others.
- By being a victim, the person can manipulate others who sympathize with the victim's situation.
- The desire to have someone else to be strong for them.
- The desire to make others responsible for their choices.
- The desire to be triggered by the negative as a reflection of their sorrow or pain.
- A victim likes to feel helpless and constantly compares himself with what others want and what others have.
- To justify their behaviors with the sad stories of their past.
- The need to be defended. They are always looking for someone to defend them.
- A victim finds power in pretending.
- A victim needs to manipulate passively or aggressively.
- A victim does not want others to be happy if she is not happy.
- A victim will always look to blame someone for their past or find a point of reference for playing the victim's role.

The difference between a victim's and a survivor's behavior is that the victim feels powerless, and the survivor blocks and controls the situation. A person behaving as a victim will also control, but it is because she wants someone else to take care and make choices for her. Instead, the person who acts as a survivor is motivated by putting his own needs above those of everybody else.

Survivors cope better with difficulties than people who behave as victims, but the survivors are still attached to the past. Survivors always look for ways to feel good about themselves but come from a space of scarcity or fear.

Here are some behaviors of a survivor mentality:

- Even when they are making progress, a survivor will focus on what can go wrong instead of enjoying the moment.
- They focus on fixing their mistakes instead of enjoying life.
- Survivors working as a team sometimes take credit for the work of others instead of accepting that others are the ones who made it happen.
- A survivor maintains their distance; they build a wall around themselves. They do not trust many people.
- Sometimes, survivors want to prove that they can cause something to happen on their own, especially in ways that involves a lot of change.
- They are not a team player.
- They see their goals and dreams for the future, yet they can't commit for a long time.
- A survivor sometimes likes to be a savior.

Here are some reasons someone may choose to behave as a survivor.

- Survivors may be experiencing insecurity expressed in an increase in anxiety—a symptom of stress.
- A survivor may have a sense of not feeling safe.
- A survivor may be experiencing unpredictability at home or community.
- A survivor has the desire to overcome pain and suffering.
- A survivor wants to defend or protect himself or others

While we are in the 3rd dimension, there will always be contamination, and we will continue to be under the influence of the behaviors of victims or survivors. For instance, as a child, I behaved as a survivor after my sister was punished for asking for money. I felt her pain and didn't like how the experience made me feel. So, I decided never to let anyone make me feel that pain again.

My desire to not be hurt again blocked my feelings, and I did not let people get close to me. I created the idea that trusting others would hurt me, and I decided not to believe others, especially my mother. It was a survivor's choice. My sister's abuse and sadness were my points of reference in the past. I carried the anger and pain from the experience within me, and I struggled to move forward.

When my mother behaved as a survivor, she believed she was not a good mother unless if she taught me to be productive. She would get angry if my sister or I lay on the bed during the day to rest.

"Get out of bed and do something instead of lying there like a lazy person," she'd yell.

I would suddenly feel terror. My body would shake. I started breathing fast. I wanted to cry but held the loud sound of crying to avoid more punishment, and then my body would get out of bed as quickly as possible.

Like the story of the father and son, every time my mother lost her temper, she transferred her energy as a block to me, and I was receiving it because I feared her behavior.

I was constantly intense, explosive, angry, sad, and reactive as a survivor. It was like being wired, in an edgy state and nervous. I had poisoned my body with these energies, leaving me tired, and experiencing muscles aches. I had problems with my digestion, and I could not rest during the night. That changed when I became a creator and connector of love.

"When you are surviving, you are not living your life. Your life is a beautiful house that you constantly clean in your survivor energy. But you are not enjoying the house; you think you must be perfect. When you are creating from love, you let the fear go and know it is time to enjoy life." Che once told me this as I was trying to understand my own survivor energy. "Your energy of focusing on the past is slowing you down. You are holding yourself back and doing the same for your family. You are suppressing your progress, your mother's, and that of your sister and your children."

He was correct. My survivor influenced my business and damaged my relationships with others because I still wanted everything to be right and perfect. I tried to fix things but was unwilling to let them go.

I knew I was holding back when it came to expressing myself. I was connected to painful memories because I believed that, by remembering, I could prevent them from happening again. I was so wrong. By letting go, I was able to find a way to overcome the events that caused me trauma. The way out was by trusting myself – believing the danger had vanished and that I was *now* safe.

I was done acting small and submissive. I had behaved as a survivor for most of my life. It was time to take care of my body and generate feelings and balance instead of overthinking and intaking contamination. I looked at my relationship with my mother. Likely, she will always condition me to be under the influence of the behaviors of victim and survivor, but that doesn't mean there is no possibility for happiness and transformation.

I realized I had to accept where my mother was in her personal development—victim or survivor. It was not for me to carry her problems but instead, in a kind and loving way, to explain to her that I was happy being myself. Accepting that made me determined to cut the energetic cords of being responsible for her emotions. I could not make her happy. She had to want to be happy and love herself.

Connecting to the 5th dimension is impossible if we do not love ourselves. When we love ourselves, we develop balance at the atomic level. What does that mean? It means that we all have female and male energies. Our female atomic level is the power of 5th-multidimensional creation. It is the ability to create with fulfillment instead of suffering. Our male power is the ability to have direction in our lives and redirect changes when necessary to expand more powerfully.

Mother's female power of Self-Love is represented in her Five Points of Power. This blueprint starts the process of being connected to the future in the 5th dimension. We all have different Five Points of Power created by our individual choices through light or energy creations. This process can take millions of years.

Self-Love Is a Way to Connect to Your Heart

Do not underestimate the corruption of the Mirrors. It is still with us. To avoid contamination, feel the experience first, then think about it and gain awareness; in this way, you connect your feelings with your thoughts to choose love.

When you *choose* to love yourself, you can avoid behaving as a victim and a survivor. Being kind, accepting, nurturing, confident and grateful are positive traits that can help you to love yourself. But if you have no experience with those feelings, how can you transform into that new reality? In my story, the times my mother hit my back with a belt were not teaching me to be kind, accepting, or nurturing to myself.

I understood Acada when she said, "If you have not experienced something, how can you reflect that?"

It was an awakening moment for me. In my childhood, I was not trained to experience the trait of being kind, accepting, or nurturing myself. There was no way to understand that because I did not have a reference point. How can you teach a dog to smell if he has never smelled? The dog must have an experience before he can smell. How could I reflect kindness or nurturing love to my boys if I hadn't had that experience before? I did not recall getting a hug from my mother or father when I was a child. I had to change!

I wanted my boys to have those positive traits. I had to change!

At that moment, I became fully aware that Acada's teachings were a blessing to me. Being angry with my father and mother was not going to help. That would be a reference to the past. I had to experience those positive traits through energy transmitted from the 5th dimension to my heart.

Acada could feel my energy; she knew I was vulnerable and needed care and support. She explained. "One way you can experience love for yourself is by envisioning someone you love standing before you. Generate and feel love for that person in your heart. Allow that feeling to get stronger and redirect that love to you. Now you're feeling love for yourself. Stay away from the ideas of your mind. Just feel the energy of love in your heart.

I wanted to make it fun, so I envisioned my beautiful dog. I could feel how much I loved her. That was my point of reference for love at that moment. Then, I bundled that energy and redirected it to me. I felt good to know I could feel that way about myself. Then, I practiced more and did the same thing with my boys.

Acada gave me another option for how to generate love for myself. It required an alignment of time and space at the molecular level for this process to work. Acada, as a scientist, created a bundle of pink energy. It was the point of reference for Self-Love from the perspective of the 5th dimension. She called it the "pink crystal."

Acada explained that because of the emotional and physical abuse traumas, my body and mind had learned to reject the feeling of Self-Love. But the pink crystal will not be rejected because the mind will not recognize it as a feeling.

She continued, "Reflect love for yourself by learning to make it visual. In vision, you are observing the blue sky, and there is a beautiful, pure white cloud. Go inside it gently. The cloud is in your heart and represents the pure essence of you.

Then, visualize a pink crystal representing Self-Love floating in the center of the energy of the white cloud in your heart. Rotate the crystal with the energy of your eyes in the open space. The movement of the crystal activates the energy of your feelings and increases your energy of Self-Love. This process will help you focus more on your heart and connect to your mind, guided by your feelings."

This crystal was a gift from Acada to me, and if you choose to create this process for yourself, the energy of your pink crystal will be available to you.

It is a gift from Acada to you. Your UNIQUE pink crystal. The only one of its kind, unlike anything else.

The most important times I practiced were when I was depressed, had anxiety, or had conflicted stories in my mind. I focused on the pink crystal in my heart and moved it gently. It activated Self-Love and brought me back to the feelings in my heart, a pure connection between my heart and mind. I had then made choices of Self-Love. I use the process of the pink crystal in my meditation in the morning or night. It is my way of practicing loving myself.

I understand now what Acada was teaching me. We are always observing and creating at the same time. It is like watching a movie. You can watch the film from a 5th-dimensional feeling powered by Self-Love. Alternatively, you could observe from a 3rd-dimensional perspective, driven by the illusion of blocks and limiting beliefs. No matter which you choose, you will contribute based on your observation. We always have a choice. If we become connectors of love, we break from the low-frequency cycle. We can be multidimensional, travel to higher realities, and channel information to find balance and fulfillment. No exceptions.

CHAPTER 10
Atlantis Events of Contamination

The Mu used the technology of Love to connect with living things on the planet and their environment. The Mirrors used the Mu's technology to feed their ego as a reward system for their success.

The conflict between the Mirrors and the Law of Ones started because the Mirrors stole some Mu crystals in a temple's center of energy. The centers of energy were connected to Pleiadean and Orionid stars. By stealing the crystals, they distorted reality and light records, which created the first explosion.

First Outbreak

The *first* explosion damaged the electromagnetic balance of the planet and that created high levels of radiation. The high radiation level contaminated and harmed animals, plants, and other living things. The frequencies of the water were damaged as well.

In the time of Atlantis before the contamination, women could not get pregnant if they did not feel because their frequency was not high enough to connect to the future. The Mirrors were obsessed with the crystals' power because they could access light without feeling. They used that technology to create new ways of life and even new beings.

Some of these creations were called "the things." They were half-human and half-animal. The Mirrors' actions distorted the collective reality of their environment.

Furthermore, the Earth's energy field grid system broke down when the first explosion happened, damaging some 5th-dimensional energy that eventually was used to create linear time. When this happened, the people who could previously live 25,000 years had their life spans shortened.

After the first explosion, there were three more outbreaks of events related to the damage done to the protocols of love or life, the Five Points of Power and Earth's energy grid system. The Mirrors could have increased their energy and ability to feel, but they chose not to because they didn't want to be able to feel and be aware of the damage they were creating.

Acada was a target because she could create feelings, which requires understanding the energy of accountability. When people and other beings were close to Acada, they would reflect upon their choices because of her energy of creation.

The Second Outbreak

The *second* outbreak happened when the Mirrors undertook other experiments. They were obsessed with their research - to build humanoids. I was not given information about how this humanoid got built; they look like humans. At first, female humanoids could not reproduce, but eventually, some did. The Mirrors scientist took the reproduction organs of the Law of One and placed it in the humanoids and the Mirrors that were mating with them.

The Mirrors wanted the humanoids to reproduce and create a perfect race, which meant carriers of energy that could hold low-frequency beings in their DNA. According to their plan, they would be reincarnated in these ideal bodies, have an abundant life, and control everything around them.

At first, a way of reproducing humanoids was by placing the baby humanoid in a woman's womb. The first prototypes were awful. When babies were born, they did not have feelings. The babies that were born became dark entities in nature and without life. Eventually, they decided to steal the life source from the People of the Light – the Law of One – and integrate it into the female humanoids. This distortion created another rift in the collective consciousness, and some people of the collective consciousness stopped communicating intuitively with the environment.

DNA technology was desirable in the Mirror's society because it was advanced. As mentioned, humanoids started replacing human needs and behaviors. For instance, when a Mirror Mother wanted a humanoid's help with her children, some of the mother's DNA memories were placed in the android's artificial DNA. In that way, the android had similar behavioral traits to the mother. The problem began when the androids, with sophisticated artificial intelligence, believed the children were theirs.

The androids wanted a sole connection with the children, disconnecting them from their biological mothers and creating confusion. Soon, the humanoids were trying to figure out ways to keep the children from their human parents – and mothers began hiding the children from the humanoids.

The Mirrors had created the technology to impregnate humanoids, and they were having a conflict because humanoids were fighting back. There was a lot of opposition from the Law of One to these types of creations. Still, the Mirrors kept blaming the chaos on the people of the Law of One instead of taking responsibility for making a terrible mistake.

The persecution of the People of the Law of One intensified. At that time there was a powerful, wise, and loving leader, Prophet Thoth. He is eventually known as an Egyptian deity. He and other leaders helped exile the persecuted Law of Ones. The Law of Ones decided to leave Atlantis and guided the exiles to Egypt, Alaska, and other locations. Hoping they could have a fresh start and, in some cases, create pyramids to increase the 5th-dimensional energy on the planet to stop the damage and help the Law of One. The conflict radiated out to nearby planets closest to Earth and Mars. It was affecting the universe. Eventually, the second, third, and fourth outbreaks of contamination happened simultaneously.

The Third Outbreak

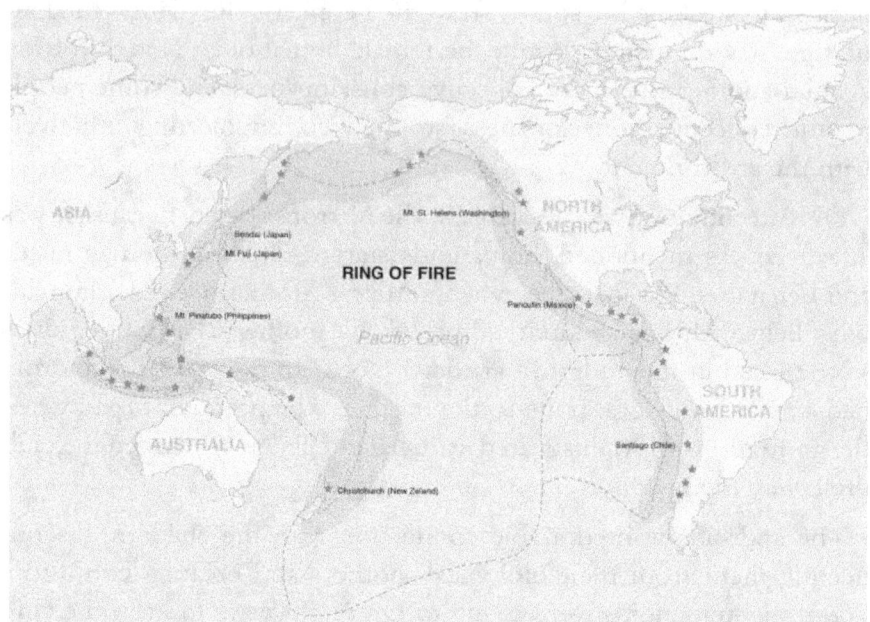

That is when the *third* outbreak happened when the Mirrors wanted to manipulate the mind of the Law of One. They experimented in the Pyramids that the Mu had built. The goal was to remove the frequency of the Five Points of the water to reduce it to the 3rd-dimensional energy. Without the balance of the Five Points of Power, it was easy to have more access to the technology of the Mu people.

They decided that the strategic place to break the balance of the Five Points of Power of the water was the lower part of Chile at the starting point of the Ring of Fire. The Ring of Fire is a line of live volcanoes starting in Chile and ending in New Zealand. The chain of volcanoes was so strong that any change in them would affect the whole planet. So, it altered the water near the volcanoes close to Chile.

The Mirrors placed an atomic organism to imbalance the atoms of the water, which damaged the hydrogen atoms' speed of the electron orbits. The hydrogen inside the water interrupted the collective Five Points of Power connection, the balance of space and Circular Time collapsed, and a portion of the 5th dimension was fragmented, now known as the 4th.

The Law of One tried to stop the contamination. With the help of one of their leaders, Prophet Thoth, they went to different ancient pyramids. They rebuilt the energy centers to increase the frequency of the planet and repair the damage done to the water. They tried to restore the pyramids in Belize, Brazil, Egypt, Tibet, Alaska, Peru, Chile, Ecuador, Utah, and Central America but were unsuccessful. There was not enough of the Law of One force left to keep the planet in 5th-dimensional energy, therefore, they did not complete the project to maintain the energies of the 5th dimension on this planet.

Acada and other Law of Ones tried to save their uncontaminated people to avoid extinction. She witnessed the horror of the actions against the Twin Cells and their families. The Twin cells were couples of the 5th-dimensional frequency that had a relationship balance in a molecular behavior of Circular Time. They were getting sick, and the contamination got worse.

In the language of the Light Beings of the Five Points of Power, our 5th-dimensional identity was damaged. Thoth's Twin Cell was one of the writers of the new protocols. She, Acada, and others found places to hide the uncontaminated Law of One people's tools to save them from the Mirrors' corrupted intentions.

The destruction of the Twin Cells in front of their loved ones became a massacre and outbreak. Prophet Thoth helped the last ones migrate to Egypt, and they had to hide their knowledge of the technology in some areas. He remained in those lands and taught the people to their level of understanding. Thoth believed that during those dark times on the continent of Atlantis, his journey was to move technology and knowledge to Egypt to build the new pyramids and activate the old ones to rebuild the protocols, or Sacred Geometry of feelings, on the planet. It was an act of desperation because everyone was dying.

He took his dear wife with him on the journey. They worked until the final explosion occurred. The contamination of blocks and limiting beliefs spread as an epidemic. People of the Light could not feel or be connected from their hearts to the future and feelings; therefore, they got sick and could not heal themselves. Many people died.

Fourth Outbreak

At the same time as the 3rd outbreak was happening, another significant event unfolded. Mu astronomy and cosmology technology allowed the Mirrors and Law of One to monitor astronomical changes. They saw a good possibility that a meteorite would hit Earth.

The Law of One people were not concerned about the meteorite because they believed in reincarnation. They knew that if the meteorite hit them, they would be reunited again because of their love connection, even though they were not in a physical form. If this happened, the Mirrors feared, they would not have high enough frequencies to survive or reincarnate. The Mu teachings said that if people were not in a high-frequency of feelings and heart desires, they would not have enough energy to reincarnate.

The Mirrors knew they would be destroyed and looked for a way to relocate the energy in others' reincarnation. Therefore, the Mirrors initiated DNA experiments to download their conscious intelligence into the atoms of the Law of Ones to become part of the life force and manipulate it.

The Mirrors planned to break down the connection of the Five Points of Power, and their consciousness or intelligence would connect to the Law of Ones' DNA. Even though they would not be able to have a physical body, their conscious energy would survive in the energetic body of the Law of Ones. The Law of Ones foresaw that through the years of contamination, humanity would carry some of the Mirror's conscious intelligence in their DNA. This contamination eventually became known as a *low-frequency subconscious* virus.

These days, the Mirrors are attached to our bodies as an active and energetic virus to survive. We are the computers, and they are the viruses. The virus causes severe damage to our computer without any sign of its presence, and it will survive until it is removed.

The malware removal is our feelings. We increase our energy by feeling and acting on our feelings of love which clears the virus, and, in the process, we overcome blocks and limiting beliefs.

The virus can only be in our body energy if we are in the low-frequency of blocks and limiting beliefs and linear time. The Mirrors can't exist in Circular Time because they choose not to feel. When we are in the 5th dimension or reflecting the energy of the 5th dimension of feelings, the Mirrors' energy can't survive. Acada's teachings are the removal of their malware or contamination.

Going back to the story of Atlantis, as it turned out, the meteorite passed near to the Earth and didn't destroy Atlantis. But the Mirrors' contamination of the water did. It took several years for the final destruction.

The final destruction happened when one of the Mirror's experimental centers was intentionally placed on fire to stop the experiments done to the Law of Ones. This sank the continent of Atlantis.

The Mirrors shifted the fabric of time and space. Instead of using feelings from the present and future in a circular behavior to create more love, the frequency of feelings shifted to one of fragmented time in past, present and future contamination.

According to Acada, Prophet Thoth was a great teacher, scientist, and lover of life and wisdom. He loved Father creator.

The Law of Ones did not see God as a religious figure to worship as a superhuman power but as a relationship with someone who had mastered a greater relevant knowledge, wisdom, experience, and Self-Love.

Acada said that the heart of Thoth was full of light, and he believed that "Love is the most important gift of Father creator." Prophet Thoth stood for the kind of love that allows us to have choices – anyone who takes your choice of love away from you is not standing for the light. He witnessed the destruction of his brothers and sisters of light and their families. They carried the essence of life, higher levels of compassion, and respect for humanity.

Prophet Thoth's message was a message of love and hope from a nation destroyed by low- frequencies. Humans are powerful, and the essence of life and consciousness comes through the knowledge of feelings in your heart. Prophet Thoth encourages us to feel our choices and bring life and abundance to this planet.

Before the contamination, people could genuinely love themselves and reflect that love in their regard for others. Their way of life created a community of ever-expanding love centered on shared values. It focused on the individual's full potential in the future. With this power, they could delete past events in lower frequencies and replace them with possibilities of love in the future. The contamination created linear time and the existence of past and future in low-frequency of separation of families. The Law of One worked hard until the last days to recreate the possibility of love in the future in their full potential to maintain the 5th-dimensional energy and beliefs to reunite the families, but the Mirrors defied them.

At that time, the Law of One scientists measured the damage of the radioactivity and the exposure and determined that it would take around 15,000 years for the planet to *start* clearing the radiation. In our language, this means clearing the contamination of blocks and limiting beliefs.

Years after that, there was a global flood on the planet to help to clear the contamination. Many stories about this global flood say it killed almost every living thing, including Plato's writing in 360 B.C. It was said to be a new start for Earth.

Today, there is a native community, the Q'ros, in the Peruvian Andes. They are the last of the Incas. Currently, they are a tribe of 600. Previously, they sought refuge at altitudes above 14,000 feet to escape the conquering conquistadors.

For 500 years, the Q'ero elders have preserved a sacred prophecy, the Mosoq, which means "times of change" or "Pachacuti." According to this prophecy, the world would be turned right-side-up, restoring harmony and order while putting an end to chaos and disorder. It envisions a time when the eagle and condor would fly together again.

CHAPTER 11
The Impact of Blocks, and Limiting Beliefs

What were the sources of the contaminations in Atlantis? I believe there were several events. I witnessed two of them. The first one was on a planet called Maldek, where a civilization engaging in DNA experimentation had a genetic mutation occur. The neutron's energy in some atoms added mass to the nucleus and could not produce enough light. The planet eventually exploded.

Acada explained that inside an atom has a nucleus with a proton and a neutron. Throughout history, they have been designated as female (proton) and male (neutron); creation (proton) and direction(-neutron); giving (proton) and receiving (neutron): and present (proton) and future (neutron). Here, we will use the terms female and male. The electrons in the atom's orbit represent the product of the relationship between the proton and neutron.

While witnessing Acada's Books of Light, I channeled a molecular memory or Book of Light story. There was a happy society in Maldek. But there was male energy which was envious of the female energy and her power of creation. He wanted to have control over the female energy to get this power but did not want to create with other female energies. So, he began taking some of the female energy's light gifts or creations.

In the story, the female and male energy shared the same house: the nucleus. So, when the male energy began taking the light gifts of the female energy, the house started getting dark. He could not see, and he began making mistakes. He remembered that his role as male energy was to direct, with his feelings, the female energy light. But now that it was dark, there was nothing to direct. He grew angry. Instead of appreciating the light created by the female energy, he joined other neutrons who took light. He started a revolution to force female creations to give them their light. Acada was talking about the radioactive material of atoms and their chemical bonding.

The neutrons planned to impregnate the males with the stolen light of the female energy so they would no longer need female-conscious energy. The neutrons started reproducing amongst themselves and created a mess, a mutation. The new baby neutrons, without the connection to the female energy (protons), quickly depleted their neutron energy – and since they did not know how to create light, they began dying.

A powerful female left the planet of Maldek to find the cure—and she did. But when she returned and offered the healing, none of the damaged neutrons wanted to take it because they were brainwashed to believe that female energy, which was the proton, was incapable of helping them.

There were millions of these damaged and mutated neutrons, which took the planet out of alignment. Radioactive decay happened, and the nucleus changed to a lower energy state, spitting radiation Eventually, the planet was destroyed in a vast explosion. Rocks and crystals from Maldek traveled everywhere through space, and some came to this planet, Earth.

The Mirrors' scientists found some of the rocks from Maldek, and they began testing them in the DNA of the People of the Light, or Law of One, to lower their frequency.

The second event I witnessed centered on an infertile woman who broke the 5th-dimensional protocol to conceive. She stole the energy of a woman of the Law of One by using the technology of Maldek, and she used the woman's Five Points of Power to get pregnant. This violation created a rupture of time and space in the woman's body of the Law of One.

Before the protocol of love in Atlantis, women could not get pregnant unless they were at a high energy level. It took years of training to become energetically balanced to have a child. A Law of One parent maintained a high standard of Self-Love because that was an essential part of ensuring that high-frequency choices would allow them to reincarnate into the future in a balanced and loving creation.

By learning more about the dynamic of the Mirrors in Atlantis, I understood more about the creation of blocks.

"Clearing the damage is essential, to create a better world for us, our loved ones, and for generations to come," Acada told me.

Because I had the experience of how Father Creator's and Acada's Books of Light worked, I knew how to sense someone else's energy inside me. It can be reflected in me as damage or something positive. For instance, my ancestors live inside my energy. They are part of me and manifest through me in ways that can help, guide, or block me in my life journey.

If you have a temperamental ancestor, you could act out that program or behavior and damage yourself. The DNA clearing Acada developed is a way to remove the ancestral programs that have stopped you from being who you are. The clearing also activates the ancestral programs that bring you light so that you can create love and abundance in the present and future. These programs are called "higher choices." The ancestral programs that block you or create limiting beliefs are called "lower choices." In the 3rd-dimensional mindset, people accept and make lower choices, never realizing they are false ideas in their energy space. Instead, lower choices are often considered "just the way things are."

For instance:

- The belief that punishment is a way of teaching.
- The acceptance that "it is my personality" and no effort to make changes.
- The excuse that "I am not teachable."

- To become agreeable and lose your identity in the process.

Acada's Books of Light explained how suffering is created. Unlike pain, suffering is due to a lack of completion of past experiences or a disconnection from the future possibilities of love or feelings. In suffering, we get stuck in the past, and we connect to the behaviors of the victim/survivor that create more suffering. This internal conflict is one of the ways we stay contaminated.

Emotional blocks are the ideas that prevent us from feeling and reaching our highest expression of ourselves. A block can be created when a painful event happens because you are the victim or the survivor. Blocks are bundles of low-frequency emotions working sometimes to protect yourself. They do not come from you, but you carry them as your own. You acquire the block when you consciously or unconsciously accept the limiting belief. You may believe that you don't like yourself, for example, because somebody else has sent that energy to you without you knowing. You have taken on this belief: I do not like myself.

I remember when I went to a restaurant and sensed the waitress felt superior because I did not speak English well. By the time I left the restaurant, I felt small and insecure. Often, we judge others because we need to feed from a sense of power and superiority by diminishing others.

Limiting beliefs are ideas we think about ourselves that are not standing for our highest good. Limiting beliefs can come from restrictive views in our society. They can come from science, books, religion, or anything that can make you feel you have limitations. For instance, one limiting belief is that we should stop others from being who they are if they stand in the way of our ego desires.

Here are other ones:

- I am not good enough.
- I'll never be successful.
- I am not smart.
- I am not loveable.

The reflection of the contamination of blocks and limiting beliefs is in the behavior of the victim and the survivor. Remember, it is just a behavior. Once you are aware of it, you can change it.

This contamination can take the form of physical illnesses, low-frequency emotions (jealousy, resentment, rage, self-pity), an inability to create relationships with others, feelings of scarcity, or failure to have abundance. It is just an attachment to your genetics that manipulates your behavior. As a result, you don't receive the balance you want in life.

Every choice we, our ancestors, and our community make is stored in our bodies. We also hold everything that is around us and events in the past. Contamination attaches to our DNA and travels through ancestral DNA. To observe the behaviors of these contaminations, let's classify them into three groups where they appear.

Group 1: Community and Collective Consciousness Events

These low-frequency events that we all carry in our cellular memory have created contamination throughout history. These blocks and limiting beliefs can come from religion, government, wars, countries, diseases, plagues, natural disasters, or climate changes. Here are some examples:

- The contamination of Atlantis
- World Wars I and II
- The Black Death
- Racial discrimination
- Roman Catholic Church sex abuse
- The Great Chinese Famine
- Terrorism
- The Crusades
- Viking invasions

Group 2: Family Events

These are genetic or DNA contaminations, called Ancestral Contamination, carried among family members throughout generations. Here are some types of DNA contaminations:

- Bacteria and viruses
- Cancer and other illnesses
- Muscle and tissue deformations
- Addiction
- Mental illnesses
- Incest mutation

Group 3: Personal Events

These are contaminations acquired by choice from your behavior or others. You may accept them because you think it is a way of life. You could also have witnessed something or have been forced to do something. Remember, personal contamination can become DNA and community contamination.

Acada suggested organizing the "personal events" contaminations into four groups based on their source and how they manifest in the bodies and behaviors.

- Group A is a mutation of the original contaminations in Atlantis.
- Groups B are physical experiences and C are emotional experiences contaminations from Atlantis.
- Group D are survival contaminations created in our times. Usually, people use them to medicate or stimulate themselves to endure a condition or situation.

Group A: Personal Emotions and Mutations of Contaminations of Atlantis

- A1. Depression
- A2. Anxiety

- A3. Stress

Group B: Abuse and Control – Contaminations of Atlantis

- B1. Sexual abuse, harassment, and manipulation
- B2. Physical abuse

Group C: Collective Consciousness Emotions and Ancestral DNA Damage – Contamination from Atlantis

Acada shared with me that Group C, the Collective Consciousness Emotions and Ancestral DNA Damage, was the contamination that destroyed Atlantis at a time when people were not immune to these energies and got sick. During that time, people developed mental health problems and diseases in hours or days when exposed, which was like radiation to them. Their bodies broke down, and they were not able to function. It was an epidemic, and it spread everywhere.

We have accepted some of these contaminations as a part of our culture, and we do not realize how damaging they are. Others can create these contaminations in your space, or you may have learned from others' behaviors how to hold these contaminations in your energetic field.

For instance, the contamination of greed is having an intense and selfish desire for something, especially wealth and power, and lacking consideration for others. It is the desire to be concerned chiefly with one's profit and pleasure. People who are under the influence of greed act like they are superior to others. Greedy behavior affects others and can be manifested in depression, anxiety, and other disorders. All these contaminations are carriers of mental and physical illnesses.

- C1. Objectiveness
- C2. Repulsiveness
- C3. Frustration
- C4. Confusion
- C5. Rejection
- C6. Condemnation

- C7. Procrastination
- C8. People Pleasers
- C9. Disapproval
- C10. Un-Fulfillment
- C11. Competition
- C12. Being Replaced
- C13. Cheating
- C14. Stealing
- C15. Lying
- C16. Deceiving
- C17. False Accusation
- C18. Anger
- C19. Self – Doubt
- C20. Self – Denial
- C21. Jealousy
- C22. Envy
- C23. Revenge
- C24. Apathy
- C25. Avoidance
- C26. Powerlessness
- C27. Pessimism
- C28. Greed
- C29. Excuses
- C30. Remorse
- C31. Narcissism
- C32. Spitefulness
- C33. Guilt
- C34. Hopelessness

- C35. Aggression
- C36. Obsession
- C37. Punishment
- C38. Profanity
- C39. Racism
- C40. Prejudice
- C41. Resentment
- C42. Grief
- C43. Blame
- C44. Betrayal
- C45. Shame
- C46. Regret
- C47. Abandonment
- C48. Self-sabotage
- C49. Detachment
- C50. Agitation
- C51. Incompletion
- C52. Corruption

Group D: Addictions – DNA Contaminations

Addiction is a type of mental illness that impacts your health, relationships, and quality of life. It is a chronic condition that generates compulsive seeking and taking a substance or participating in on an activity regardless of negative and harmful consequences.

These contaminations do not allow people to face reality. They ignore the situation as a defense mechanism to cope with distressed emotions. It can involve not acknowledging reality or denying the consequences of that reality.

This type of contamination embodies the denial of who you truly are. The rejection of love for yourself creates this contamination. This type of contamination shuts down the energy of the heart and creates illusions of false connections.

- D1. Pornography
- D2. Prostitution
- D3. Marijuana
- D4. Mushrooms
- D5. Crack
- D6. Ayahuasca
- D7. Cocaine
- D8. Alcohol
- D9. LSD
- D10. Meth
- D11. Ecstasy
- D12. Opium
- D13. Heroin
- D14. Others

CHAPTER 12
Twin Cells: Protecting Books of Light from Blocks and Limiting Beliefs

We are responding to the contamination of Atlantis when we are manipulated by blocks and limiting beliefs triggered by "past" experiences in low-frequencies. This is the source of the behavior of a victim or a survivor.

The Law of One people established what they called protocols. According to Acada, protocols are the feelings that allow an action or experience to connect the future to the present. They create fulfillment without the inference of the low-frequency past. These protocols led the Law of One to create marriages, families, and communities based on love essence and balance. The protocols permitted every living thing to be connected and to communicate and co-create with humans. Of course, the Mirrors' actions contaminated many protocols, including the Five Points of Power. As we have already discussed, this is when the Circular Time and space matrix ceased to exist and was replaced by linear time.

The Law of One married couples practiced the Tree of Life protocols: the reflection of the balance of creation in their cells, atoms, and electromagnetic fields. They were also connected to the electromagnetic fields of others like plants, water, oxygen, and rocks in their environment. The Five Points of Power of married couples in high-frequency energy were connected to the cells and atoms of other creations or alignments of Earth, planets, and the universe to co-create. They represented and held space for the 5th dimension of higher frequencies, life forces, and creations that maintained balance on Earth and the universe. These couples were called Twin Cells.

The Twin Cells were the keepers of the knowledge in the Books of Light. Because they could feel the molecular behavior of living things, they created a polarization force that connected Earth's electromagnetics to other planets with high levels of hydrogen. These multidimensional couples were the force that maintained the high energies' knowledge guarded and stored in crystals, plants, and waters worldwide.

Using Mu technology, the Mirrors created a new applied science that separated the *subconscious* from the *conscious*. This disconnection of future feelings from the present created a veil of memory. Because of this, the Law of Ones lost most of their high-frequency memories. Now that the People of the Light could access only the low-frequency memories of pain and separation, it was easy for the Mirrors to steal their light and knowledge and create blocks and limiting beliefs in the DNA.

Sometimes, as I was receiving information from Acada, I could not understand and this was one of those times. She was patient and continued. "Taking energy away from the Law of Ones' DNA was like accessing their savings account. The Mirrors used their money or vitality without having to work for it nor be accountable for how they spent it. One of the ways to do this was by separating the Conscious from the Subconscious creation centers.

After Acada was separated from her husband, her energy dropped to the 3rd dimension. But she was able to reconnect to her memories of the 5th dimension when she remembered to love herself and reconnected to the love of Father Creator. She said that observing the Books of Light is the only way to reconnect the past, present, and future in Circular Time. She said that once an experience in the past is completed and simultaneously, the veil is removed, the high-frequency of that experience becomes part of the future. There is no more use for the past, so it gets dissolved. Only the present and future exist.

Acada kept referring to the word *action*. It took me a while to understand. She said that *action* is the idea that we can only learn and teach from something we have experienced. Thus, I had to believe, experience, and behave in alignment with a new feeling to connect to it. The behavior or action of the experience is the power of *being*. It is the ability to experience the behavior and be part of it. Doing so teaches you to relate to others with a new behavior.

For instance, one day I worked with a sixty-year-old woman with depression. She did not have the opportunity to have a child. The Light Being doing the healing showed me a light ball and placed it in her heart. The light ball represented the experience of having a child. A few months later, I saw the lady. She was complete by having the energetic experience of giving birth to a child, and the depression was gone. She was happy, and she reflected that to others.

Acada was preparing me by experiencing her Books of Light and channeling them. It was time, she said, to experience the behavior of the energy of Twin Cells.

I was committed to learning more about loving myself. I was ready for her guidance. As with the sixty-year-old woman, I received a ball of light in my heart. The training to learn about the Twin Cells was to experience the behavior and feelings of an animal, the beaver. Beavers are one of the few animals that carry the memory and behavior of Twin Cells, and now I get to feel how beavers create their communities and contribute to humans.

I searched the internet and found that beavers increase biodiversity. They protect the environment because their dams improve water quality and provide homes for many plant and animal species. Their dams create wetlands that attract insects, fish, other wildlife, and other river-oriented mammals like mink, muskrats, and otters. Their ponds filter pollution, store water for farm and ranch use, slow flooding, and are buffers against erosion and fire outbreaks. And their dams and the sediments that build up hold carbon, which means less carbon in the atmosphere.

To my surprise, I learned that beavers co-create with nature at a molecular level in a 5th-dimensional way as the Twin Cells couples in Atlantis. They can feel the frequency of plants, animals, and rocks as if they were part of themselves.

They also have a partner, much like a Twin Cell. When they reincarnate, they reconnect to their partner and return to the same family unit. They are one of the happiest animals on Earth. There are no limitations in their life cycle. They have abundance, understand the power of creation-love, and manifest to that level. I understood why I was assigned a beaver to learn about 5th-dimensional knowledge and protocols.

In Atlantis, the Twin Cells kept a community's memories and transcended them to other lifetimes. Acada's baby, Fatherlove, had Books of Light that intensified the intuition and awareness of the People of the Light and connected them to the Twin Cells' energy more strongly. This multidimensional connection threatened the Mirrors, their intentions, and why Acada was set up to have an abortion.

After Fatherlove died, Acada committed to fulfilling, to the best of her ability, Fatherlove's mission. She organized the Law of One people to save what was left of the knowledge of the Twin Cells and their Books of Light before they were contaminated with blocks and limiting beliefs from the 4th-dimensional linear time.

The best option was to exile the People of the Light, who were not contaminated, to another place where they could be protected and possibly find the cure. There was a sacred place where some DNA of the 5th-dimensional and Books of Light were stored; it was the temple of Puma Punku.

Puma Punku was a temple and an ancient library housing the Books of Light. Located near Tiwanaku in western Bolivia, it was built as a terraced mound of earth with huge sandstone and andesite blocks weighing several tons each. Each block was cut so meticulously that it interlocked with the next block tightly and perfectly, a remarkable feat of engineering. Today, the site is in ruins.

The people of the Law of One escaped to Puma Punku via small boats able to hold only six or eight people. I saw in a vision, and it was emotionally hard for me to witness them leaving because families and loved ones were being separated. I saw mothers, daughters, sons, fathers, and other family members coming to the port to say goodbye to the people leaving. I heard the crashing of the waves and smelled the sea, a blend of salt and fish. The unknown feeling of what would happen to them left a heavy sadness and emptiness that day.

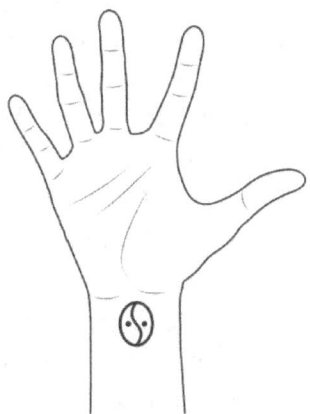

That was the first time I saw the protocol of pure DNA as it was before contamination. It was an oval shape as if it were a standing egg. A line moved down it, beginning from the top and center going into a curve formation, leading from the left to the right and landing at the bottom center, with a dot on each side.

I saw a woman dressed in a white robe walking toward a boat and getting aboard. I felt her peaceful and calm. I could not see her face. I also saw a man. I would not see his face either, only the shape of his body. He approached the boat and asked the woman dressed in white to turn her hand so he could see the symbol there.

She did as she was asked. The design I saw appeared like a bright golden tattoo. I knew it was not ink but a molecular symbol that only showed on the skin of the people of the Law of One when their bodies were uncontaminated by blocks and limiting beliefs.

I felt the vulnerability and hope of the woman with the symbol on her wrist, her trust in the possibility of escaping contamination. The person who checked the symbol was also focused on the idea that they were running out of time.

Let's ensure we get them out of here before they get contaminated. He spoke.

Acada also watched her brothers and sisters being separated. There had been a time when she wished she had gone with them to find the cure, but by this point, standing on the shore, she was resigned to her commitment to stay. She did not want to leave her Twin Cell. She hoped the exiled people would someday find the cure and heal all those left behind in Atlantis.

The Law of One people that were left behind also hoped that the uncontaminated brothers and sisters would remember and find them again. Connections of love are forever in the energy of the 5th dimension, so when the Law of Ones spoke of their hope, they talked about finding each other after death. They knew there was a possibility of dying without a love connection; in that case, they might never find each other again. But they hoped that if the Books of Light could be protected and saved, they could reunite, even after death, and return to the energy of the 5th dimension. As for those escaping to Puma Punka, they hoped that someday, Acada could join them to help bring them together again.

The Law of One were doing everything that was possible to find the healing. As alternative ways of curing the contaminated, Acada had been looking for other ways to find the remedy besides sending people to Puma Punku. The temple was not the only place where there were Books of Light. She hypothesized that the Books of Light she carried in her molecular memories might be the key to the cure. If she could heal herself, she could heal others. And so, she chose to contaminate herself, feel the contamination in her DNA, work on healing herself, and find the cure. It was a risky and brave choice.

The Law of Ones who went to Peru and Bolivia became the ancestors of the pre-Incas and Incas. This is how the Inca or Andean shamans inherited some of the knowledge in the Books of Light and used it until they had to hide it again from Spanish conquistadors in the 1500s.

Since the contamination of Atlantis, we have been in the process of radioactive decay. Unstable atomic nuclei have lost energy due to the radiation of the blocks and limiting beliefs. According to Acada, the contamination penetrated even the Books of Light. They disconnected the Law of One and the Mirrors from the 5th dimension. They lost their identity, and so did we. The radiation behaviors created a shield of illusions, and we lost our memories of who we are when we are in the essence of love.

This duration of decay is called "The War of the Times." The Andean Shamans' prophecy says that we will know that clearing the contamination happens when people stand for human rights and values. Also, we will reject control, manipulation, corruption, and separation as a society or collective consciousness.

We will be awakened to our intuition and see the real intention of people's hearts. People with low-frequencies will not be able to get away with corruption like they once used to, and our human nature will look toward creating new communities and tribes with higher human values and standards. I believe we have started to see this happening now. We are in the process of starting a world without contamination. When there is no contamination, there will be no more sexual abuse, racism, physical abuse, slavery, or corruption – these will be past stories. It will be a time in the future when the molecular memories of the Books of Light will allow the people of Atlantis to reconnect them with each other. The Law of Ones will join energetically and physically. They will reunite as a family. Their essence of life is bringing this new evolution of humanity.

CHAPTER 13
The Inca Cross Protocol: Acada's Secret Weapon

"This book is guided by spirit. Spirit creates love, and love creates Circular Time. Writing this book has not been easy because it is in Circular Time, and each story is shared when necessary to create a reality or situation that will help you understand your essence in time." Light Being

Translation: "It is not for you to doubt yourself but trust yourself."

One summer day in 2022, after dedicating more than four years to writing this book, I was struggling to draft the content of the stories and messages. I wondered if the readers would focus more on the writing style than the message. Then, the message would be lost.

The night before I got the above message, I went to bed worried. How could I write a 5th-dimensional book and translate the concepts to keep the message's purity? I wanted to follow an outline, but I did not want this book to become a linear-time book.

A linear-time reader will be energized to criticize the writing and check the grammar and structure, looking for details of what is right and wrong. I wanted the readers to open their hearts and sense the energetic message of love. In the message, to feel the heart of the Light Beings, clear their blocks and limiting beliefs and go through a molecular change to a higher way of life. From the deepest desires of my heart, I wanted the reader to have a multidimensional experience and eventually channel light and love.

The next day, when it was still dark, I awoke feeling the spirit of a Light Being. I sensed a gentle light coming through the window. I turned around in my bed to face the window as he stood before me. He gently said, "Write down this message."

I got out of bed and took my computer from the living room. Back in bed, I typed the message at the beginning of this chapter: *"This book is guided by spirit. Spirit creates love, and love creates Circular Time. Writing this book has not been easy because it is in Circular Time, and each story is shared when necessary to create a reality or situation that will help you understand your essence in time."*

I asked him what the message meant. He said, "The translation is for you not to doubt yourself but to trust yourself." Then, he suggested, "Go back to sleep because it will take a while to feel the experience and process the message in your body." He continued, "You will not understand the whole message until after 8:00 a.m."

I tried to go back to sleep. I could feel in my body the reflection of Light Being energy—the pure love, the feeling of honor and respect he had for me, as well as the feeling of the message spreading in my molecular memory. I felt like I was talking to my body, to my Books of Light, understanding the message little by little, the molecular message that was being downloaded into my body. It was a sensation spreading in my body, no visions, only a feeling of knowing. Right after 8 a.m., just like he said, I understood the message.

The message was clear: I did not trust myself. I had observed my behavior and noticed that I doubted myself because I was concerned that people would criticize this book for not being structured as they believed it should be. I understood I was settling for less if I focused on the critics.

It is a book of love, and readers will understand it to their level of love, and it will transform them.

Acada, in a kind way, said, "The creation of new molecular behavior is happening while I am writing this book. This book is a Book of Light, and it's a Circular Time creation."

That may sound confusing, and it's okay to feel confused. I suggest you focus on the shared stories and love them for what they are. Even when it feels like you don't understand, you are becoming a multidimensional observer, and your body is clearing and changing.

I also want to explain that while Spanish is my first language, I wrote this book in English. It has been difficult not to write in my native language. In addition to the complexity of writing in English, there has been the challenge of translating the feelings of a dead language from over 15,000 years ago and bringing it back into this reality. As you can see, the message's content in this chapter's first paragraph is different. The higher beings, or spirits from the 5th dimension, speak differently than we do. They communicate and describe all that makes up the content of the feelings and experiences in protocols. It is their feelings, belief system, language structure, and lives.

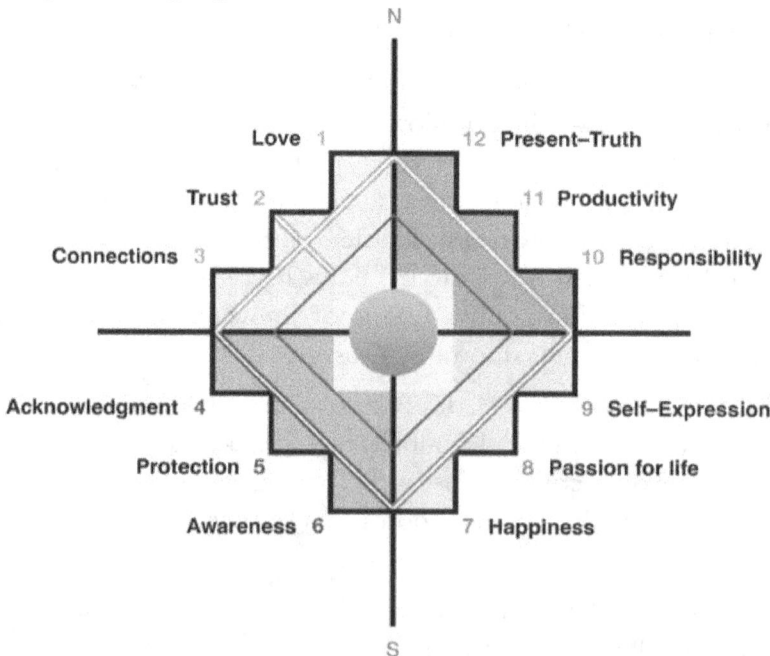

Since childhood, I have been gifted with the ability to decode energy or read Books of Light at the molecular level. I wasn't even aware of it. Working with Acada helped me to recognize this. This time, I had to learn to decode and interpret the protocol of the Inca Cross or Chakana and then translate it into our language in this reality.

The Inca Cross is a geometric figure. *The symbol's geometry has a high degree of symmetry. The symbol can be drawn from a circle. A square is inscribed in the circle, with the corner's tangent to the circle. This forms the "middle step" of the ladder. A smaller square (tilted 45 degrees) is made from the midpoints of the large square. Connecting the midpoints of the small square and extending the lines to the edge of the circle will form the arms of the cross, otherwise known as the "first" and "last" steps of the Chakana. Lines are drawn from the points where the lines exit the circle to complete the cross. A small circle is made from the diameter of the cross lines. To prove the construction, a separate construction line is drawn from where the square corners with the cross rectangles are to the same point on the opposite side. If the line is 27 degrees from the vertical, the Chakana is properly drawn.* (https://en.wikipedia.org/wiki/Chakana).

As a point of reference, I will use one of Acada's stories about the Law of Ones' exodus from Atlantis to Puma Punku to give you the background of the Inca Cross.

While in Atlantis, Acada observed the past, present, and future behavior in linear time. She felt they were like separate universes, each moving differently. The future moved faster than the present because it had less matter, and the past was even slower.

She noticed that the future was split into two sections. The one in high-frequency was bright and had a golden color; she called it the "high-frequency future," and the low density that was gray color, she called the "low-frequency future."

She placed a white light, a female twin-cell proton, inside the high-future section of an atom of linear time. She noticed that atoms eventually obsolete the low-frequency future, and then the past low-frequencies could not access the future and stopped existing.

In addition, Acada also created a code and placed it inside the light ball that allows only people who love themselves to have access to possibilities of light and the abundance of the future in high-frequency.

Her message was, "No more draining and stealing light from the atoms of light and love." This new atom was multiplied, and millions were placed in rocks and crystals that went to Puma Punku. Acada instructed those leaving Atlantis, on their arrival to Puma Punku, to locate the sacred sites where they could feel the energetic fields of the Inca Cross. There they were to download the Light Records carried in their DNA, as well as the information in the crystals and rocks to store them for future use.

Acada relocated the energy of pure feelings and memories from the past to the future to protect them from contamination. In doing so, those feelings transferred to the future and transformed linear time into Circular Time.

This is what the Mu technology can do. The power of feelings can relocate information from the past to the future. This process means that low-frequency feelings like jealousy, competition, and betrayal cannot access the future in the 5th dimension, and eventually, only the 5th dimension will exist.

Before Acada changed the protocols, everyone had access to Mu technology. She ensured that only future generations who loved themselves could access this Mu knowledge. The Mirrors did not expect this. They did not predict that Acada could transfer information to the future, change molecular memories, and lock knowledge into the Inca Cross.

Acada created a multidimensional support system which is part of the energy of possibilities of high-frequency—and connected it to us in her future. She placed a new type of Books of Light in water's hydrogen molecules. That energy is now in our present and future, an observation from Self-Love to the contamination that will rewrite and eliminate the damage. In this way, people who are now in high-frequency, which is Acada's future, are her best chance at creating a new Atlantis future without contamination. This means if we master Self-Love we can have access to this process.

This process was only possible because Acada had the foresight to store the strongest feelings in the Inca Cross protocol in Puma Punku. The Inca Cross was able to activate her new creation.

Acada reprogrammed the Inca Cross protocol, which embodies the idea that your feelings of Self-Love are a map for finding your way out of a situation and overcoming the past. As in other protocols that use different types of feelings and combinations, the Inca Cross is a code using the Sacred Geometry of feelings that's in effect. Think of Sacred Geometry as a language of feelings that helps create possibilities in the future so that you can manifest them in your present.

The people of Atlantis knew about the Inca Cross. The Puma Punku temple of light was the prominent center of feelings of the Inca Cross. There, a 5th-dimensional portal had been built with Mu technology. The ancestors of the Mu were like a living library, a record of every creation that originated in and outside the universe. Those Mu ancestors were called the Guardians of the Light, and they, as well as their energetic connections, originated on a planet called Nibiru.

Accordingly, the Inca Cross has the records of all creations long before the contamination was created. It contains the original blueprint of humanity and all other beings. The Inca Cross also holds information about lessons learned from contamination, so they do not happen again.

The Chakana, or Inca Cross, is a multidimensional hologram of Circular Time and holds the secret of life as a Sacred Geometric symbol or protocol. It carries the healing essence of the 12 Rites of Humanity and other creations via Sacred Geometry. Sacred Geometry refers to the symbols and meanings connected to the proportions of the geometry of energy. It is a higher-frequency language of communication and creation. The sacred balance of these rites allows us to be in our highest consciousnesses of powerful creation and prosperity.

These are the Sacred Energies and feelings used to create humanity's balanced essence. Six rites are male (neutron energies), and six are female (proton energies).

The male feelings or behaviors of the neutron in the nucleus of a cell that balance the Inca Cross are:

- Love
- Trust
- Connections
- Acknowledgment

- Protection
- Awareness

The female feelings or behaviors of the proton in the nucleus of a cell are:

- Happiness
- Self-expression
- Passion for Life
- Responsibility
- Productivity
- Truth

These are feelings that do not change. We have given them different meanings or interpretations throughout time, but they are an absolute truth in our hearts.

The Inca Cross also contains the 5th-dimensional creations of consciousness, subconsciousness, male spirit, female spirit, and DNA. The knowledge and wisdom of using this information was helpful to clear limiting beliefs and blocks created in our energy spaces during our different life journeys since the creation of the universe. At higher energy levels, we achieve our highest goal, the energetic immortality of the spirit, when we learn how to balance our 5th-dimensional spaces of creation.

Pre-Inca and Andean, or Inca shamans took years to learn this Inca Cross process. They were the protectors of ancient knowledge. Shamans are akin to priests and priestesses; they have spiritual wisdom for healing the self and the community.

A shaman is seen as a bridge between the physical plane and the higher spiritual realms. In ancient times, the energy of the Inca Cross's records was transferred into and stored in the DNA of the shamans, who stood for the light throughout time. They remembered the symbols, or codes, to reestablish Circular Time. According to the Inca prophecy, knowledge will be brought to the world at the appropriate time--which is now—to create the New Men and Women in higher consciousness. The evolution of consciousness that the Inca Cross offers will ultimately return us to the 5th-dimensional awareness in which distorted perceptions cannot thrive and will be obsolete.

The Law of One didn't escape solely to Peru and Bolivia. They also left for Alaska, Egypt, and Tibet, taking the Mu sacred knowledge of Sacred Geometry to protect it. Acada's knowledge of the Books of Light and their technology represent a process of the people's love through time that has worked together to make this world a better place.

Acada wants to honor every warrior of the War of Times who stood and fought vigorously, with determination and courage and to her people and others after them who protected the Mu tools to bring the 5th dimension back for them and us in these times. She wants to share her love for her ancestors and her gratitude for the knowledge they gave her, too.

CHAPTER 14
Witnessing Other Creations

Some people may wonder how it is even possible to communicate with the energy of the mountains. It is possible because when one becomes multidimensional, one learns to connect with other living aspects of life.

Tapping into the Books of Light of the Mountains, which is their molecular memories, gave me simple ways to understand information. For instance, one day, a mountain explained that the atom's energy feels like the connection of three happy friends: the male neutron, the female proton, and the electron. The electron reflects in its electronic field, and outside the atom, the memories and experiences of the love between the proton and neutron. Our frequency rises to higher levels in this type of relationship.

When these three friends feel the same experience together, they become powerfully connected because they have the same intention. They are in alignment, which allows our wishes to develop into a manifested reality.

I asked a mountain if it was possible for an atom's essence to have a different intention. How would that affect my frequency? The mountain answered, "Yes. When one or two of the atom's components have been contaminated, they hold conflicted intentions and will lower your frequency because they are out of balance or alignment."

He continued, "When a proton, neutron, and electron are balanced, they allow us to witness past stories." Here is one of the stories I witnessed through that connection. A long time ago, there was a massive explosion in the universe. As I saw an enormous space, the universe, and various particles of different colors and sizes moving fast in different directions, I felt the essence of the atoms. The protons and neutrons that had been in balance were ruptured and separated. In other words, all atoms were balanced in their Twin Cell's relationships before the explosion.

At this point in my training, Che came into the conversation and said that the Twin Cells created the water.

The difference between the time before and after the explosion is that the time before the explosion—also called "space" or "time before time"—did not create separation—the time after the explosion constructed disconnection and built a new dimension.

Before the explosion, the ancient Twin Cells were called "spirits." After the explosion, there were other cell formations, which could not hold as strong connections as the spirit can. A 5th-dimensional atom is spirit energy, so Twin Cell's relationship is a connection between two spirits. It is a 5th- or higher-dimensional relationship. And it is the power of spirits working together, that clears the contamination to close the cycle of the 3rd dimension and restore balance.

Let's say that before the explosion, the world of spirit atoms was like a white porcelain plate that fell to the floor and broke into small pieces during the explosion. The small pieces represent the fragmentation of the relationship between the spirits. When the plate pieces are separated for an extended period, they forget they are a whole plate. Linear time in the 3rd dimension keeps the pieces of the plate apart.

Acada told me that the pure intentions of Twin Cells are the energies that bring the pieces of the plate back together. When Acada teaches us about pure intentions and the power of the Twin Cells, she gives us the knowledge of the principles created from space before linear time.

When spirit atoms are in the 5th-dimensional energy, their consciousness is one; they remember every experience and know how to repair themselves. Fragmented past lifetimes are created because atoms in the 3rd dimension had forgotten that they could repair themselves. But when we remember our connection to the 5th dimension, these atoms get restored and returned to the 5th dimension—where there is only a one-lifetime connection.

We were all in the 5th dimension before we got contaminated in spirit essence. Our spirit is immortal, with loving energy and memories of the full completion of high energy love stories. Death is not a 5th-dimensional experience but a relocation to other types of creation.

When we rewrite our stories with Acada's technology of love, by loving ourselves, we bring together the pieces of the white porcelain plate and connect atoms and cells to the 5th-dimensional energy.

I was in so much gratitude for the Twin Cells! I finally understood what Acada, Che, Prophet Thoth, the Light Beings, and the mountains were teaching me. I felt how much I loved them and hoped they would sense my feelings and thoughts at that moment.

Similarly, to our atoms, our conscious level forgets to love when our conscious and subconscious separate. Low-frequencies like hate, anger, frustration, sadness, and loneliness can easily manipulate our conscious energy.

The Self-Love energy of Twin Cells, or spirit, keeps the conscious and subconscious connected. It is like a car; it only works with fuel or electricity. The fuel and electricity represent the love we have for ourselves. If we stop loving ourselves, we cease generating nutrition and feel empty.

For instance, if you spend your day being critical and hard on yourself, you stop feeling. Another experience would be watching TV for several hours and then you cannot sleep. The brain becomes overwhelmed and exhausted with information and cannot connect with your heart. Remember, when we behave like victims or survivors, we do not remember how to love ourselves. We are not recharging in nurturing love.

Acada said that if we want to love ourselves completely, we should remember to acknowledge ourselves daily, be proud of who we are, embrace ourselves for positive things, and have a gratitude list. She also reiterates envisioning a pink crystal in your heart that represents Self-Love. Embrace the energy of the pink crystal and meditate by observing the movement of the pink crystal in your hearts.

Now I understand that pure intention is a way of loving myself. It is the information I was looking to find. If I can love myself, I can teach my children and others to love themselves. I do not need to heal them; they will heal themselves. All that I must do is teach them how to love themselves and remember their spirit energy.

CHAPTER 15
Decode the Inca Cross – 1st Triangle

1st Triangle—Love, Trust and Connection

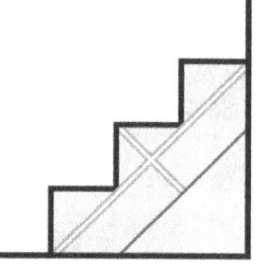

Feelings always give you a solution to a situation and the sense that you are moving forward in life. Feelings create motion because they make things happen. When I trained with the Light Beings, I experienced the situation first; after feeling it, I had the raw information to describe it. It was like not knowing how to ride a bike. You see it for the first time and ride, enjoying the moment, an instant experience. Then, when you stop riding it, you express your feelings about the experience. This is the process of decoding energy.

For instance, one day Che asked me to close my eyes and observe. I did not know what to expect. I saw a dark room in another dimension. He told me to walk into it. I knew nothing about this space, and Che did not share anything with me. He wanted me to have the experience and explain how I felt about it. I could sense his trust in me, making me feel safe and supported.

Che was like the mountains—he wanted me to develop my intuition and the confidence in my feelings to tap into the different possibilities and outcomes of situations.

The room transformed, I noticed no door, windows, or exit inside the dark room. It was just a space. I sensed Che wanted me to figure out how to leave the room. In the beginning, I looked for a way that I could get out. I searched for an exit, but I could not find anything. For a little while, I was scared; it did not help. This led me to blaming Che for not helping. I was expecting him to save me.

I was behaving like a victim.

I wouldn't say I liked the unknown, especially when I didn't have control over the situation. I felt powerless in a dark room without windows and no apparent way out. I tried different emotions to get me out of the room, like anger, frustration, and disappointment. It didn't work. I decided to start creating a feeling of love for myself. I then generated the feeling of trusting myself. I did not know, then, that trust is a feeling. It is a love-based feeling stemming from faith in the love of all things. It is the love the universe itself has for me. It is the firm belief in reliability, truth, ability, or strength. After feeling trust, the room got lighter.

My feelings of trust brought light into the room, and then I felt a feeling of connection in my heart. It was like accepting that it is okay to embrace myself. I was not behaving like a victim anymore.

After this experience, Che confirmed that trust is a feeling. I wondered why he did not mention this before the experience in the dark room. He explained that I needed to experience the emotions in low-frequency, which are blocks and limiting beliefs and feelings, see the difference among them, and decode them. It was essential. He said that it's like looking at a picture of the ocean. The photograph won't teach me how to swim, but going to the beach and getting in the water will.

I accepted that most of my training would be experiences that would help me understand and navigate the emotions of the 3rd dimension, like corruption, or the 5th-dimensional energies, like the feeling of trust. That is how I learned that trust is a love-based feeling because without loving ourselves, we cannot develop it.

The black room was the energy of blocks and limiting beliefs that were controlling me. While there, I remembered the times my mother had punished me, and I believed I deserved it. Because I'd thought it was my responsibility to take care of her emotions, I'd assumed I had created her pain. I believed I was terrible because I had generated her hurt and suffering. I had been so angry with myself because I was not good enough to stop her misery. Suddenly, I observed where these ideas were coming from, and it was an energy shadow in my mind. It was an illusion, and I realized I accepted it as truth.

As I felt experiences from the past and saw the true meaning, the room became even lighter.

The room opened in my mind. I went out of the room and stood there, quiet. Che was waiting for me. He was dressed in white clothes. I felt our telepathic connection. I gazed at him. Swallowing down gulps of sorrow, I was sad about remembering the past, and Che knew it. When he looked at me, I saw the unspoken truth that he trusted me, which made me feel better.

I was back in my bedroom. I do not know how I knew I had been in the space within my consciousness for almost two hours. I accepted that I had made myself responsible for my mother's emotions. I understood with clarity that I had not created my mother's sadness. She was already sad.

Now the energetic toxins of these limiting beliefs were clearing from my body. I started feeling again after a long time, "Yes, that is what I was supposed to do!"

At that moment, I had stepped out of the room without being aware that I had connected my conscious and subconscious the way it had been before my mother had punished my sister by placing some hot pepper in her mouth. As a kid, I saw the horror and trauma of the experience, so my feelings were eventually shut down.

I had connected back to my subconsciousness, my dear older brother, and those feelings of wisdom had opened again. He gave me my childhood memories while I was in the dark room. The Light Beings were communicating through my subconscious feelings.

Now I know that the power of my subconscious is the gate that allowed the Light Beings to come into my heart and a portal to step into the world of the Light Beings. My subconsciousness is a point inside of me: the collective consciousness of higher intelligence and other higher beings' knowledge that connects with me. It is my point of channeling. My subconscious is incredibly powerful.

I asked myself. "How could I have gotten out of a dark room by feeling?" and "What is so powerful about love?"

I heard a voice saying, "This is not romantic love. This is the technology of love." It was Che in the unseen world. He continued, "The technology of love is the creation of everything. It never destroys but goes into expansion. Love is a language of creation. If I feel love, everything comes together, and I should never hold back."

Even though I could not please my mother, I was a love creation. He added, "Punishment is contamination that makes us hold back love or sets us up to push love away from us." He talked about the energy of unconditional love. He said that unconditional love is the action of giving and receiving.

In the technology of love, we give and receive energy; in the block of punishment, because it is an imposition of an undesirable and unpleasant outcome, we close our hearts and do not know how to receive love.

Che said it was essential for me to experience the darkness of punishment—to witness how I had punished myself and others. He said I'd learned to rewrite the block by trusting myself because I would learn to love myself again and create balance to connect to my heart I AM. He told me that love is the essence and source of the creation of life.

Going through that experience gave me an understanding of the first triangle of feelings in the Inca Cross: Love, Trust, and Connection. Connection builds in trust, and trust builds in love.

An energetic triangle is when you combine three feelings and create a stronger component with these feelings' frequency. According to Che, this energetic triangle is how you communicate with your inner self at the atomic level. In the energy language of the atoms, one plus one = three.

Cocreation. Father (1), mother (1), child (3). (3) is the outcome or product of the cocreation of (1) and (1).

Father creation – element 1

Mother creation – element 2

Child creation – element 3

For instance:

(1) I want to co-create with the universe and buy a new pair of shoes.

(2) Universe gets me a new client that pays money to buy the shoes.

(3) Shoes are manifested.

In this scenario, the equation is 1 element (my desire) + 1 element (new client and financial means) = three elements (outcome or product)

Che explained that the basic atom has one proton, one neutron, and one electron. Every relationship between the proton and the neutron inside the nucleus reflects in the electron. The electron will reflect the experience of feelings to the DNA outside the body's experience. This makes it possible to have a relationship of three elements.

We have more than seven billion atoms in one cell and more than seven billion cells in our body. It is hard to grasp how small the atoms that make up your body are until you look at their sheer number. An adult is made up of around 7,000,000,000,000,000,000,000,000,000 (7 octillion) atoms.

It was 2006, two years after I'd felt Che for the first time. I had an incident that helped me to understand the value of having experiences of love, trust, and connection. I was cleaning in the kitchen when the energy of a mountain came into the house and said I had to go with him.

Suddenly I felt part of my conscious transferred to a room in a hospital. I was beside an older man dressed in blue hospital clothing and lying on a bed. The mountain said he was prepared to die and would be dead in three days. It was time for him to remember the choices he had made in this life. It would happen at the subconscious level. We all go through this process before we die. We remember choices and the impact that our decisions have upon others.

I sensed the man in the hospital had a son and a daughter, and intuitively I knew he had a lot of money. He thought that in his life, he had worked hard to make money and did not spend enough time with his children. It is not that money was his priority. He avoided getting close to others. I saw no love connection with his children. I felt his loneliness.

It was not for me to judge why he chose to spend time working instead of being at home and with his family.

I still remember the room at the hospital. It was clean. There was a bed with white sheets and a light blue bed cover. I sat next to him on the bed. I was teaching his subconsciousness the knowledge I had in my subconsciousness. It was like a download of light coming from me to him.

I was teaching this man that without the feelings of Love, Trust, and Connection, we cannot go into a higher consciousness after we die.

I came back into my body after teaching this man and was excited. Wow, I was able to do the work! I remembered that in the past, when I had returned to my body, I had not recognized when this had happened. Now I have experienced how love connections with others are the essence of ascension into higher frequencies.

I decided to have lots of experiences of love with my boys. I did not want to be like the older man at the hospital: he did not have enough experiences of love with his two children to ascend.

My first co-creation with the universe was to see my boys like they were the best things that had happened to me. I began to be proud of them in every way, even when they made mistakes that unfolded in our everyday routine on good and bad days. The outcome was that they trusted me and knew they were loved unconditionally. (1) + (1) =3

It was also a beautiful way to learn the concept of lineage. Love is a technology that holds and keeps an ancestral lineage together through love experiences in the family.

Digesting the knowledge, we receive can take a while, especially when we have a profound experience that shaped us. It can be overwhelming to feel or be aware of the choices of others. I kept the emptiness of the man at the hospital for a while. I sensed he could have had a more fulfilling life, but he did not know how. I began noticing that my body was like a sponge. Whenever I had an energetic experience, people's energy stayed with me. I was starting to understand how our choices would eventually hurt us, and I was learning to be aware of my choices. How can we prevent ourselves from making decisions like the man in the hospital? It is by knowing that every choice has a consequence and to choose from your heart is Self-Love. Co-create with the universe for lasting experiences. (1) + (1) = 3.

Looking back, I was discovering how to be a teacher. The more I felt that my family was important, the more I felt the energy of gratitude for having them. It is essential to have gratitude for what we have in this life, regardless of the situation we are going through. Gratitude helps maintain the "first" triangle: Love, Trust and Connection.

I wanted to learn as much as possible in the unseen world to support others in their transformation— and to be a mother who stood for my boys' higher selves.

During my training, there were times when I was unsure if I was channeling information or if it was just my imagination. Somedays, the training would take several hours, and I would be frustrated because I felt it was taking over my life. But now I can see that even though it took time away from my boys, it was worth it. Looking back, I was not in a good place, and I needed to learn this to be a balance mother, and they benefitted from it.

The best way to describe the behavior was like a desire, a driving force inside me, like when you are hungry. The feeling gets strong, and you must eat. It was not logical. I just knew I had to walk to the different trails and follow my feelings. I was directed to touch rocks, feel what was around me, and observe the mountains and feel them. Some of these walks felt meaningless because I could not see what happened inside me or in the unseen space.

One day, I was walking on a trail close to my house in Park City, doubting whether my experiences were real or just happening in my head. Suddenly, the mountain said, "Here, have this energy," and he placed a ball of light in my hand. Then he said, "Go back home. Your older son has closed the door on his finger and is crying. Give him this gift, and he will feel better."

I went home as fast as possible, and when I got there my boy was crying and holding his finger. I gave him the Energy Gift in his hand; it went into his body, and he felt better. It was an Energy Gift from the mountain. That was a confirmation that my experience was real.

I have immense gratitude for all that I've been taught as I've spent my whole life as a mother trying to figure out my role. A mother is a teacher who helps her children create a powerful future. The present reflects the future. The mother I am in the present will reflect my children's prospective lives.

I asked a mountain one day, "Will I ever be a healer?"

He answered: "Your relationship with your children will give you the foundation to be an energy worker.

I am grateful to hear the traits that my boys like about me. I listen when they share the things, they do not like about me. Then, I think about the situation and change my behavior as needed to improve our relationship.

My boys are my creation and a reflection of my choices. I have found it very interesting when I work with some of my clients who have children experiencing emotional problems; they want a quick fix. They want me to change their children's negative behavior in a one-hour consultation. It is not possible. It is a relationship! I can help them in a one-hour consultation to be aware of what is not working in the parents' energy, but it is a process that takes time, love, patience, and consistency. Sadly, a lot of parents only want a quick fix.

While preparing to write this book and gathering information, I read my journals. I saw how consistent I was in my heart, praying to Father Creator to help me be the mother my boys needed me to be for their higher selves. I know they have their own choices, but many will reflect my choices of Love, Trust, and Connection.

One day, I was clearing my office and found one of my old journals. While looking at the content of it, I found that May 5th, 2007, was the first time I had memories of Acada and her son. I had forgotten that a day before, I had a dream. In that dream, a powerful light portal opened. A group of Light Beings stepped into the room with Father Creator, Mother Creator, Che, Archangel Michael, my dear mountains, and other Light Beings. Father said, "We all are here to support you." I have never seen so many energies show up to support my work. I did not know that connecting with Acada the next day would be a significant event requiring every part of my being to make this love process happen.

CHAPTER 16
Andean Shamans and Mountains

Acada taught me to feel and observe how the Five Points of Power, which is female energy, works. I also learned that my pure intentions are a female force of creation, and my male feelings are the energy of how to direct my feelings. My next training was to experience male energy.

I had to let go of my victim and survivor behaviors to implement or direct my new behaviors of pure intentions and Self-Love. In this effort, according to Acada, connecting the consciousness, subconsciousness, and heart protocol experiences is key to achieving a future of high-frequency possibilities.

This idea is what the Mirrors failed to grasp: when you accept that your choices have consequences and that you are the result of your choices, you can develop a life of light, love, and persistence. Most importantly, you become a creator of love.

Life is full of opportunities, and even our essence of light is an opportunity itself! We choose a destiny line of love and abundance if we are wise. I want to share my stories and life experiences with you because it is my opportunity to contribute to light creation.

I shared the story of who I called my two brothers before, my conscious and subconscious. I want to go into more detail about my relationship with them. When I observe my thinking, I become aware of my subconscious thoughts like I am aware of my conscious mind. My conscious mind remembers my subconscious feelings and thoughts—they are two brothers who love and care for each other. Their communication is open and of unconditional love.

I like asking questions to my subconsciousness. My older brother, full of knowledge and wisdom, helps me understand myself. On the other hand, my consciousness, is my younger brother, who likes experiences in the outside world, outside my body. When my consciousness connects to my heart, the outside world is beautiful and peaceful, and I feel grateful.

My subconsciousness has knowledge and wisdom of connections with other creations in the unseen world, like Light Beings, ancestors, feelings, and other communities. It's a safe place for me. When my heart and conscious brother merge with my subconscious brother, it feels like we are sitting by the ocean next to a fire, listening to my subconscious brother's stories of knowledge and wisdom from the unseen world. We are always ready to hear my older brother's love, honor, and wisdom stories. In the essence of love, we are a great team. It is a triangle of love.

My subconscious brother connects to my heart, and together, they create an opening to communicate with the energy or spirit of plants, animals, water, fire, and other creations. When I attached to him, I could understand the message of the spirits of creation. That is how I became friends with the spirits of the mountains.

When the mountains' spirit connects to my subconsciousness, I can feel they love every creature on the planet and in the universe that stands for the light. It is their spirit force that makes the mountains so special.

The mountains guide and teach other creations. They are always happy and trust the Light Beings, the Star Brothers, and Sisters. The Star Brothers and Sisters are crystals, rocks, plants, animals, planets, and others that work together for a better universe.

I have noticed that every mountain has its unique personality—the combination of qualities and characteristics that form their individual distinctive character, like being playful or funny.

There are older and younger mountains. When they communicate, they are direct and to the point. They emphasize the meaning of each word and use it to empower the message. They use fewer words than humans do. When they give us messages, it is up to those who receive them to experience the words. For instance, they say:

"I know you can do it."

"Love is everywhere."

"You are more powerful."

"Be present with your choices."

We, the receivers, channel, think and feel the message to experience the wisdom. The process helps the receiver develop self-trust and Self-Love. Among mountains, trust is fundamental. If the receiver betrays them, they disconnect, stop the communication, and don't reconnect again.

For instance, a mountain training a man to be an Andean shaman requested him not to watch pornography because that would confuse his mind and diminish a woman's value. The man did not listen and kept watching pornography. The mountains stopped telepathic communication and did not train him anymore.

How do I know that the mountains are a high creation? Because they can create feelings. Once, I witnessed a mountain creating the energy of love using the technology of love of the 5th dimension and placing it in a woman's heart.

It was amazing! I sometimes work with people who wish no longer to be in love with the wrong person because it hurts. But I cannot remove those feelings from their hearts – only God and higher beings can take or give feelings. So, when I see the mountains displaying the power and knowledge of how to create feelings, I know they are at a higher creation level. They can create love!

The mountains also know that the best way to keep records of light is by storing them in the energy of feelings and ancestral lineages.

When the spirit of a mountain chooses someone to represent him and his community, he will stand by that person in the worst and best times. The mountains and the apprentice will become partners. In the ancient Andean culture, the apprentice is called an Andean shaman. Suppose the shaman knowingly chooses to damage or misuse their power. In that case, the mountains will remove their energetic gifts from the apprentice and stop working with him.

An Andean, also called an Inca shaman, conveys the teachings of the ancestors' traditions of other creations from the unseen world. An Inca shaman becomes an ambassador and takes the messages of the spirits of other creations, such as Light Beings, mountains, animals, and humans, to assist them throughout the evolution of consciousness.

Che showed me that the Inca shamans' most dangerous battles are in the unseen world, where humans' darkest shadows are found. Shamans are willing to do this work to help people transcend into a higher evolution where there is no contamination or separation. Andean shamans are warriors who train to overcome darkness. They feel the 5th-dimensional or higher energies to help others achieve higher energy levels. Inca shamans are driven to stand for a better world and work together with other creations to increase communities' quality of life.

Inca shamans are guardians of sacred sites. They work in cellular and genetic ancestral clearing, astrology, and planetary alignments. They know of the planets' movements and associations, and how they are related among them. They perceive how alignments affect us as humans.

During the training of Inca shamans, the mountains challenge the shaman apprentices as often as necessary to teach them to balance their energy of determination and love to keep the Books of Light records in the light of their DNA. That information is stored in the DNA of the shamans. It is transferred from shaman to shaman as each awakens to understand that they are part of a larger plan.

The shaman develops their Energy Gifts by being exposed to high energy levels. Some Inca shamans are hit by thunder or lightning as an initiation process. A common aspect among Inca shamans is the ability to split energetically in two or more places simultaneously.

Inca shamans talk to people who have crossed over, like their ancestors or teachers, in different energetic spaces. Inca shamans must know how to create energy in different dimensions and receive information from higher dimensions. They know they can only teach to their level of feeling experience; therefore, Inca Shamans must experience other high and low-frequencies realities: to teach others.

Andean shamans have access to the Books of Light. The Books of Light from the future contain "Energy Gifts" that can help others experience the highest possibilities from the 5th dimension. They can help you be fulfilled and complete your potential, and they contain the Light Beings' energy of Self-Love. Also, they rewrite your molecular behavior. Rewriting for the Light Beings means removing the memories and emotions that cause pain and suffering from your molecules and replacing them with light and memories that can have feelings of completion. This process is done by clearing blocks and limiting beliefs. For instance, releasing the events that made you believe you are not good enough and rewriting those events in light and love with a new reality of "I am valuable" and "I respect myself." Energy Gifts help us remember the light that we carry inside us.

To help you understand the power of Energy Gifts, let me clarify that we have many possibilities in the future. Our highest potential is in the highest frequency of our future, and our highest selves in the future hold all the information we need in the present to create for our highest good. Our highest self is one of the sources that gives us "Energy Gifts" to reach our highest potential.

Through that light, we possess the rites of love. We are the creators of light for ourselves in the light of progress, achievement, abundance, and consciousness. The light is a community of communication at every level. When the light is guiding us, the impossible can be possible.

Every Energy Gift is powerful because it allows us to create what seems to be the unimaginable in the world. It becomes possible on every level, and we find abundance. We are the abundance of light in our creations on every level.

Energy Gifts are one of the most powerful tools to integrate into our consciousness, subconsciousness, DNA, and spirit – all critical in creating a new, higher dimension of humans. Energy Gifts are made of feelings. Feeling energies have movement. Sometimes I feel them moving as a vortex.

Most of our knowledge comes from books, what we have learned from others, or the internet and other communication channels. Those sources have limitations because they don't have all the "frequencies" required to be self-aware of energy transmission and Self-Love, such as feelings. Energy Gifts have unlimited information. They are about creation, and the gifts enable us to create the person we want to be. They give us the teachings we need to reach the next level of awareness—the knowledge of how to understand the meaning of life.

Energy Gifts take different forms—energy books, knowledge, and feelings. They can come in symbols or objects like fruit, vegetables, or ancient scrolls. Every book that comes to you as an Energy Gift becomes integrated into you. Energy Gifts can be manifested in different ways, according to what you need and when you are ready to receive. For instance, the gift can be the energy of self-confidence, and that can be manifested in different ways in your life.

Being an Andean shaman is a life experience. The focus is on creating pure intentions and finding ways to express and guide the new direction with the information received. Before Andean shamans die, they choose an apprentice. They then energetically download their knowledge from the Books of Light into the apprentice's DNA to continue the work that started thousands of years ago – just as Father Creator left some of his Books of Light in Acada's DNA. This process was inherited from the Mu people, passed to the Law of Ones in Atlantis, and then given to the Tiahuanaco culture, pre-Incas, and the Incas. They are, as you may remember, descendants of Tiahuanacos.

CHAPTER 17
Accountability

The day was March 1st, 2018. I was driving downtown Salt Lake City and saw several police cars at the intersection of 400 S. and 900 E. Later, I read in the newspaper that a woman had died after stumbling into the path of the TRAX train.

I thought about how unpredictable life can be and how we must enjoy and value our time in the present moment. It opened my heart to two important questions: Why do we hold back in sharing our feelings? Why aren't we living life to our fullest potential? I felt the answer in my heart. Because we had conditioned by blocks and limiting beliefs.

The woman's death took me back to that day in 2007 when I'd observed the man dying in the hospital. I spent three years helping people cross over into the unseen world. Like the mountain said, I would not remember most of the work. But it was happening now so that I could recall it. I was actually present to the experience of teaching them.

It is in my nature to wonder about the possibility of things. This time, I concluded that if we could remove every block and limiting belief in this world, we could remember the truth of the past. The cumulative consciousnesses in low-frequencies do not want us to remember what is true. Feelings help us remember the true events, which is why darkness has been trying to destroy feelings throughout time.

The technology of feelings brings accountability in a way most of us cannot imagine. There is accountability for every choice we make. The accountability of making higher choices is eternal life without separating our memories of love and the Books of Light. If we know how to use the technology of the energies of feelings like Love, we can heal ourselves from all illnesses. It takes some time, but it can happen.

With feelings, we can remember and be aware of low-frequency damage. This damage can return to the entity who created it, and they could learn from their low choices. Accountability also helps trap entities in their games without harming others. They can only hurt themselves—until they learn to honor and respect themselves and others.

For instance, when I release the contamination of sexual abuse in my clients, the energy of contamination goes back to the people who did the damage to hold them responsible. They will eventually experience every emotion and sorrow inflicted on the person they damaged. The abuser will feel inside of him the pain, fear, depression, stress, and lost opportunities of the person he damaged.

If the abuser was also abused, that energy goes back to the person who harmed him, and so on, until it reaches the first person who did the damage—the source. The first-time damage created would have been done thousands of years in the past.

The feeling of accountability is the energy that reflects your actions back to you. The expression of accountability in the protons in our atoms is the female expression of our power. Accountability's healing and energy travel through different past lives, ancestral lineages, collective consciousness, and time. This is what the power of feelings can do. Darkness can never be stronger than light; it can only lower frequencies to make us forget our feelings.

Acada's story is significant because it means accountability for many creations. Throughout time, her feelings of love have grown and survived in the high and strong energy of accountability. She also helps us remember the codes of feelings, bringing life back to a high-frequency and abundance like before the contamination. There is accountability for every choice, higher and lower choices. We always get back what we created for others.

Che was firm in his female energy, and I could feel the energy of his atoms. He also was strong in reflecting accountability. I had seen him making dark entities accountable for their choices in the dark. One time, an entity was standing before him, and Che's light reflected the entity's choices from the past. At that time, I did not know that Che was one of the most powerful lightworkers ever to have had a human body. I felt protected.

Che would always challenge me to go to the next level. He would say to me, "No excuses." He was not intimidated by darkness. When dealing with low-frequencies, he had no tolerance for them. He said to them, "I know you can choose light."

CHAPTER 18
My Initiation

In 2007, I owned a clothing store on Main Street in Park City, Utah. I specialized in handmade sweaters from Peru for children, men, and women. I also carried a high-end line of clothing made of alpaca wool from there. This business allowed me to go to Peru once a year.

One day, while folding sweaters, a Light Being stood next to me and told me I had three months to close the store. It was time to learn the ancient ways of my people and eventually have a business providing ancestral and DNA clearings to empower my clients in new ways of life.

I began having recurring dreams in which I was taking courses in college. In some, I was almost done with my studies and looking forward to graduation. In others, there would be conflicts of one kind or another with finishing my classes, and I could not graduate.

At the beginning of December 2007, I had another dream where I was taking a course, and a woman helped me with my homework so I could finally graduate. This dream represented the foundation of completing my training which meant I had learned to love myself, trust myself, and connect to others in love. A new direction of love was opening in my life.

Everything must be created in energy before it can manifest in the 3rd dimension. The manifestations of my dreams were unfolding.

During the Christmas season, I got a call from Peru; my friend had met an Andean Shaman, Pablo. I was surprised. People assume we have lots of shamans, but even in Peru it is rare to find an authentic shaman. I had an intuitive hit that prompted an immediate sense of urgency to meet this man.

That night, I called Pablo and asked him to connect with the energy of the mountains to see if he could help me to understand more about Acada. He sounded happy that I was contacting him. He said that a few days before, the energy of a mountain from Bolivia, Potosi had visited him and told him that a sister was going to Peru and his assignment was to initiate her as an Andean shaman. He meant me.

Even in my wildest dreams, I had not foreseen that I would be prepared to be an Andean shaman! Being invited by the Potosi Mountain to represent his teachings was both a surprise and an honor. It was a big responsibility. He knew my heart's intentions and my love for humanity. My preparation has taken several years, and I am still learning much about my role as an Andean shaman.

I flew to Peru in February of 2008 for my training. I was excited to finally meet someone on a physical level who could guide me to and find the answers, the reasons for Acada's experiences— and mine. I am very grateful for Pablo and his help in clearing blocks and limiting beliefs from my body to be in high-frequency places to channel and find out more about Acada.

During the flight to Peru, I wrote my intentions to increase my energy during my training.

Here is what I had on my list:

- To learn true love for my boys and be present for their needs
- To develop my skills and Energy Gifts
- To get to know myself better
- To accept me for who I am and love myself
- To have the most amazing relationship with my boys
- To pay my business debt
- To take direction in my life so I do not waste my time

- To generate more money
- To experience tranquility and peace in my life
- To stop pleasing others and focus on what I want

A few days before the trip, I channeled a message from Che. He knew I was nervous about traveling and wanted me to feel better. I wrote down the message.

Look at the stars; I will be in the light of the stars.

Everything is ready for your journey.

There is nothing to be afraid of.

You will have more clarity about the story,

giving you more confidence in your life.

Your energy will be addictive to some people,

and I will teach you how to protect yourself.

Have love and compassion in your heart.

Pablo was waiting for me at the airport in Lima. I assumed I would meet an older man with a dark skin color, wearing colorful clothing like people in the small rustic villages. He was nothing like that. He was a young man in his early thirties. He wore dark pants, I believe it was black, and a white shirt. He had a big smile on his face. He was so happy to see me. I felt overwhelmed, as I did not know what to expect.

Pablo later mentioned that he was trained in ancient ways since he was sixteen. We took an airplane to Cuzco. Cuzco is the historic capital of the Inca empire and is rich in history and culture. The large cluster of stucco-roofed buildings on all sides of the mountains made this city unique. "Hear the Opus (mountains). They are happy you are here," Pablo said while driving to the hotel. I was so excited to meet someone who could talk to mountains.

The first night in Cuzco, I had a dream. In it, I saw Acada. She was walking downhill on a sidewalk. I sensed her urgency to find someone. I could see a section of the city; the walls were made of megalithic stones, and next to them were the sidewalks, also made of rocks with strips of soil joining them. I felt the strong motion of Acada's legs as she strode down. The dream woke me up.

While in Peru, it felt like my body was downloading the information of Acada's memories little by little while hiking in Cuzco's different pre-Inca and Inca sites. It was the beginning of remembering the story of what happened to her and her people in Atlantis.

Sometimes I could go for weeks without remembering anything. Other times, I'd have two or three memories a week, and there would be moments I would feel the experience that Acada had wanted to show me for days. She said that it was vital to ensure that I would not be contaminated with the interpretation of the 3rd-dimensional energy.

Acada was my point of reference as a dreamer, a creator of love. Our dreams and desires to create our lives are our female power, and the direction and how we make it happen is the male power.

Little did I know that I had observed the relationship between my conscious and subconscious in my female energy, which is my creative energy. I believed that the Love, Trust, and Connection I had with my conscious and subconscious brothers helped me to be called an Andean shaman.

When we got to Cuzco, Pablo suggested I stay with him and some friends. I did not know him, and I wanted to have some privacy. So, I decided to stay in a hotel, but that was a bad idea. That night I dreamed of Acada walking the streets and looking for something. I could not sleep well was very tired by the time Pablo came the following day, around 9:00 a.m. After that, I decided to stay close to Pablo all the time. I did not know what to expect from the trip.

That day, Pablo took me to the Adobe house, where he had his ceremony room. He said we would make an offering to the mountains, which he called Opus, which means the energy of the mountains in Quechua. His ceremony room was relatively small but lovely. We placed fresh flowers, seashells, candles, crystals, stones, and fruits on a table. Pablo invited some family members staying with him and his wife to participate in the ceremony.

Pablo made sure we had everything on the table that the Opus wanted. We added some food – chicken and fries. Then Pablo went outside to open the space. It was like a patio, but there was nothing there except brown, dried soil. He peered at the sky, stretched his arms upward, and drank water. He poured water into different spots and placed food on the dirt ground. He said that he was making an offering to the Opus and the energy of Pachamama, "Mother Earth," in Quechua.

While he was doing that, I stood next to him. Suddenly, I had a vision of an Inca Priestess, she wore a long wool dress, and it was held around the waist by a broad, colorful braided waistband. She also had a wool shawl over her shoulders.

She was sad because her daughter did not believe in her ceremony process. I realized she was talking about me because this was new, and I resisted believing what I was observing. When I told Pablo about it, he got quiet, opened his hand, and received a ball of white crystal light the size of a small apple from the universe. He gave this to me to place in my mouth. He said it was spiritual food that I needed to eat. When I felt the energy, it gave me the sense of being loved by the universe.

We went back inside the small room. As a part of the offering, people and the mountains eat together. We ate chicken and fries, then Pablo set some white paper on the table. We laid out different flower petals, leaves, seeds, and candy while we requested what we wanted to create.

I placed the list of intentions I'd written on the airplane on the table. Pablo said to take three of the leaves used in Peru to prepare bundles for ceremonies and put them together with my fingers while thinking about my intention. Then, he said, I should place the leaves on the white paper. While putting them on the paper, memories started coming to my mind, including memories of the choices of Acada's husband. Pablo looked at me, smiled softly, and said, "There are consequences of our choices when we make people suffer." It was like he knew what I was feeling. He didn't see the story but rather the formation of the energy. I was surprised he could see the damage of the contaminations just as I could.

While placing the leaves on the paper in the second row, Pablo said, "Now, I am going to teach you your second triangle. "Wow." He knew I had finished my first triangle: Love, Trust, and Connection! His mountain teachers guided him, and he knew what he had to do. Pablo called the agreement between humans and mountains the "Andean Contracts of Love."

I felt a connection in my heart and saw a vision of a group of people making an offering to God. I received the energy of connection in my heart and became overcome with the emotions of grief and heartbreak. I started crying. I felt what Acada had felt, and I was back observing her in Atlantis. She perceived that if she stopped loving her husband, Ta, she would disconnect from her Twin Cell energy. My connection at that moment had allowed her to reconnect to Father Creator. He explained to her that her observation wasn't accurate, and Acada could feel Father's love for her as he spoke this. Father continued, saying, "Ta was misguided and chose the darkness." Ta had made his choice, and it was time for her to make her choice – to honor her needs and desires. Father Creator helped her understand that she had an opportunity to move forward in her work and eventually help Ta and others.

I was helping Acada to rewrite her story, and it was changing. Instead of the dark woman of the council poisoning Acada's thoughts, Father advised her instead. She was not alone anymore. After that experience, I felt my energy rise and I could see better in the unseen world. I also noticed that while Acada was getting stronger, my energetic gifts were also expanding.

I was not yet done placing the seed and leaves on the white paper when I recognized the spirit of the mountains in the room. They came together all at once. I observed that they were shaped as a bundle of energy in a human form. They were sacred mountains, lakes, and lands! They were coming from places that had 5th-dimensional frequencies. I was told before that mountains can take the shape of humans, but this was the first time I saw this.

They were playful and happy, and they were also very confident. They were calling each other brother and sister.

I saw the Opus Potosi, one of Bolivia's most powerful mountains. I saw a very confident, tall, and elegant female energy. Her dress was colorful, the base color was blue, and the dress had a long tail carried by two other mountains. I asked Pablo, "Who is she?"

He said, "That is the energy of Titicaca Lake." Pablo explained that lakes also have spirits like the mountains.

Wow! Too bad I'm not going to Puno to see her. "Why not? Why couldn't I go?"

I shrugged my shoulders and thought about it for a moment. *I want to go. I need to be there.*

I told Pablo that we were going to Puno to see her! I was so happy to be around the mountains and the lake and interact with them. I could see them talking, amongst themselves, like old friends at a wedding reception.

I also noticed that they enjoyed eating. They would get close to the table and digested the energy of the food. It made me smile. They would undo the mountain shape and then take the form of a ghost, go close to the potatoes and chicken pieces, smell, and intake the energy of the food as if they were sponges. I intuitively felt they were enjoying the experience. It felt like I was the one that was eating. I was very impressed by them.

While I was observing them, I sensed a male mountain in front of me coming toward me. As the mountain got closer, he asked me if I would like to marry him. I did not know what to say. I was surprised. I stood there, thought about it, and tried to make sense of the situation. I approached and told Pablo about it because I wanted to understand more about that message. He said to me that sometimes the "mountain" offers that. He said that the mountain was assigned to protect my energy. It is their way of saying they want to be a protector, but it does not usually happen in the first ceremony. I did not think too much about it and I trusted the mountains. So, for the next few days, while walking in the ancient site, his energy connected to me, and he became my protector.

This was my first initiation ceremony. I was honored to see all these beautiful energies coming to my initiation. It was a big multidimensional party.

My Initiation

There was a lot of unspoken communication with Pablo. He knew Che was with us. The first time Pablo commented on Che was when he saw Che sitting in the back seat of the taxi while we were going to Cuzco downtown. Pablo moved his head, pointing to the back seat. And said Che is there. Pablo did not say much to me, but he understood that Che was my teacher and protector.

The day after the ceremony, the Opuses were waiting for me in Sacsayhuaman, a citadel on the northern outskirts of Cusco. If I had gone by car, it would have taken twenty minutes. That day, the roads were closed because there was a protest. The government wanted to allow companies from Chile to manage some of the ancient sites in Peru, and people were against it. So, we had to walk for an hour to Sacsayhuaman.

While walking, the energy of past generations weaved through me, connecting to the rocks, houses, streets, and roads. It was fun to walk in the streets and take the ancient Inca trails by the sites in the mountains. Sacsayhuaman is a zigzagging, massive stone citadel on a steep hill overlooking Cusco. A wall of big rocks in different shapes holds the upper temple in the site's lower part. Sacsayhuaman is a site that was built before the Inca empire.

That day, Pablo drew a triangle representing my first Inca Cross Triangle: Love, Trust, and Connection. The three sacred mountains that requested me to speak for their teachings were Sra Titicaca Lake, Machu Pichu, and Huanacaure, the land in the center of the central plaza in Cuzco. Pablo said they were the directors and the sub-directors for all my triangles. It made sense; it was a Contract of Love between them and me.

The triangles were not chosen based on the locations but the energies that wanted to connect to me in my Inca Cross symbol or life protocol. In addition, my protectors were Ollantaytambo, Potosí, and the mountain I married, which did not give me his name. I was going to represent these Opuses in their feelings of creation. Pablo also said other mountains would come forward to create more feelings with me and represent my other triangles in the Inca Cross. He said they had already connected with me. Some of the mountains were Putucuci, close to Machupichu; Ausangate in the jungle; the Colorado mountains; Pachutusan; Salcantay; and Sacsayhuaman.

We approached Sacsayhuaman—it was a magnificent view. The sacred stone buildings and the main wall were built in zigzags with giant stones up to 5 meters high and 2.5 meters wide, between 90 and 125 tons of weight. The shape and harmony of the landscape were similar to Machu Picchu.

I had seven crystals in my purse. Suddenly, while walking on Sacsayhuaman, I felt the energy of Acada's husband, Ta. His disappointment, sadness, and low-frequency choices took over his mind and body. Everything was happening fast, and it was hard to process all. I felt Acada in the time of Atlantis trying to do everything to help him remember who he was. Now I looked back clearly with more wisdom. After Acada lost her baby, she had a nervous breakdown, and the mountains helped her increase her energy. I felt even more connected to Acada being surrounded by the mountains and understanding loss.

I was ready to be connected to my second triangle in my Inca Cross. When I got to the lower part of Sacsayhuaman, I walked next to the big stones in the zigzag wall shape. I felt that I should go to the entrance at the south of the site and touch one of the huge rocks that had a formation of five fingers and place my fingers there. I did as I felt instructed, and suddenly a portal of light opened. The position of my hands had unlocked and opened it.

I hear a voice saying, the portal's entrance is to the right of my hand, on the way to the site's upper part. Something transformed once I got into the portal of light; it was the same place but at a different frequency. It was another time.

I did not know how but I knew there was not enough time. I only had a short time to get to the second level of the site. While walking on the upper side, we got inside the portal, Pablo asked me if I could see the two Incan warriors following behind us— protecting us. I turned around and saw them with colorful, woven clothes. The black, white, green, yellow, and red matched their beautiful dark skin. Pablo also showed me two alpacas on the roadside in the other reality. All this in the other dimension. It was hard to believe it was happening.

We saw the city of Cuzco as we neared the top of the mountain. As I ascended, I saw behind me in the other reality, people with colorful Inca traditional clothing placing fresh flowers of different colors on the lower dirt road. I felt their acknowledgment, gratitude, love, and trust. I could see that my outfit was transforming into traditional Inca clothing. I was dressed in a simple wool-long tunic with a cape of woven geometric design of different colors.

As I was admiring my new apparel, a dark entity shadow, flew out of nowhere toward my body's right side to attack me. Confident as an eagle, Pablo turned his head around, faced the dark entity, and blew air from his mouth toward it. The shadow left faster than it had come.

I froze for a moment—a reaction to Pablo clearing the entity—and then I heard one of the mountains say, "The War of the Times is about to start."

I saw two groups of people, one to the right and the other to the left, and all of them were wearing uniforms from different historical periods. I saw soldiers from the French Revolution, Mayan warriors, Inca warriors, conquistador soldiers, Nazi soldiers, and others I could not identify. There was going to be a battle between the two groups. The War of the Times represented the damages and conflict throughout history created by the contamination of blocks and belief systems in human society.

Che told me we that needed to leave immediately to protect the crystal I carried in my bag and not to look back. I stared at Pablo, and he nodded, understanding my thoughts that it was time leave without me saying anything. Pablo and I ran to the lower area at the left of the site. Then I walked around half a mile toward the pre-Inca site of Qenko. When I was close to Qenko, I made the mistake of turning back and looking at Sacsayhuaman. An arrow hit me on my forehead. It was sharp, piercing pain that penetrated deep.

Even though it was an arrow from a different dimension, and I could not see it, the pain was intense. Once I got to Qenko, I went inside an underground tunnel where I stood by a big rock and waited for Pablo to get close to me. I asked him to remove the arrow. He saw it, created something energetic with his hand, then he pulled out the arrowhead from my forehead. I felt the pain.

I felt better when it was out, but I was overwhelmed.

"What just happened?"

There was not enough time for an answer, and I knew we had to keep going to reach the next site.

We kept walking until we reached the Temple of the Moon—Amaru Markwasi. It was a small site, but I felt connected to it. While climbing the stone path, I sensed a male energy close by. The closer we got, the stronger his energy became. It was not in this reality, but I could feel his goodness and love. He had a sense of purity and vulnerability; his energy was a bright light in the shape of a body with an elongated head. He was the pure essence of light.

He said, "Please help me save my wife. Bring her back to me."

It was telepathic communication—we read each other's thoughts, sending messages without words or gestures. It was outstanding that he could speak to my heart. I felt he was reading my energy, my Books of Light. I sensed his presence inside my body's energy field, observing me. It was light, like a gentle breeze. It was not invasive because of his intentions; he was pure.

This *being* knew my feelings, and everything made sense. He made it clear that he needed me. I told him I would help him but didn't know how. As suddenly as he had appeared, he was gone, and the portal that had opened between his reality and mine had closed.

As I descended from the upper part of the temple, I worried and rushed to complete my next connection to the land. I did not have time to think about the promises I'd just made. Pablo, who had been waiting for me in the lower part of the temple, walked close to me, showing me the entrance to a small cave. We went inside it. There was a flat area around three feet tall. The flat area was part of the enormous rock that made the cave. It was a ceremony table. Pablo asked me to step on it. When I was on the stone, right above me, there was a small hole where I could see the light from outside coming in.

Pablo made some energetic connections by moving his hands. He asked me to look up into the sky through the hole, and suddenly, I felt like I was physically standing in the main plaza. Ollantaytambo's site. Ollantaytambo was two hours away. I wondered, "How did I get there?" Then I realized that while part of me was in Ollantaytambo, I was still standing on the ceremonial rock.

I had split! I was in two different places simultaneously, and I was aware of it. I wanted to celebrate, but I felt there needed to be more time to do that. When I came out of the cave, I climbed higher and saw a rock crafted in a triangle shape. I sat on the stone. It was peaceful, and I had completed my 2nd triangle: The feelings of Acknowledgment, Protection, and Awareness. I felt accomplished and good about myself and what I did that day.

It was right before 5:00 p.m., and I had made it. I sat there for a long time, receiving the energy in my stomach's upper area. The rocky mountain in front of me had the shape of a face. I smiled. It was a reminder that Che was with me.

Now, I had time to think. I had always wanted to visit these places. Maybe somehow, I had been there just by thinking I was.

My Initiation

I had been blind to my true nature and wondered what was happening to me. I suddenly remembered that I was a multidimensional being, and there was a certain vulnerability to that reality because I did not always know how to deal with the unseen world. There were so many uncertainties, but I was committed to the work as I focused on finding solutions to have balance, stability, and love in my family.

I felt that the Temple of the Moon was Atlantis's library; the rocks were an energetic library of the past. I was sad when I left the site because I knew I was committed to helping the being with the elongated head. I wanted to learn more about him, so I would be ready to help him when the way came.

On my way back, I saw an area with many tall eucalyptus trees, which triggered me to remember that while climbing the hill on my way to the Temple of the Moon, I observed in that space people dressed in white and trapped in a place like a concentration camp. There were nearly a hundred of them. I looked at the area again where I had seen them previously, but the people were not there anymore. My work in the Temple of the Moon had set them free. I was happy for them.

It was late, and the strike was over. We could have taken a taxi, but we felt like walking down the center of Cuzco using the Inca trail. Before I descended the stairs, I turned around and looked at the top of the mountain. It was the journey's end, and I knew I was not returning there anytime soon. It was my way of honoring the mountains. I unexpectedly saw Che there with forty or fifty Inca warriors. Pablo looked up and smiled. "There is Che," he said.

I was exhausted physically, mentally, and energetically. My legs and feet hurt very severely with every step I took on the way down. I felt like they were breaking. I sensed Che's presence, and he told me I should walk down with my feet sideways instead of straight. I did that, and my legs and feet relaxed, making the walk easier.

Later, I felt Che's hand touch my head. I was shocked that he had a physical body. It was his body of the 5th dimension that I sensed. Can we feel the physical aspects of other higher dimensions? Yes, if we are at a high-frequency. My frequency was high enough that I was able to feel him.

It is important to make a distinction here. Seeing Light Beings is akin to watching a film. A screen shows reality, and no mutual physical senses are shared between the observer and the performers. This time, I was not seeing Che, I felt him physically as if he were accompanying me in the same room. He was in this reality and had a physical body that I could feel.

Ancient indigenous people in Peru believed that their ancestors lived with them, and those ancestors were included in the family's everyday chores and activities. It made sense to me now; it was just how I had experienced Che that day. I have learned that there is much more than what we see. That made me feel humble.

CHAPTER 19
Fire Initiation

After my journey to the Temple of the Moon, we left for Puno, where I went to Lake Titicaca, a large lake in the Andes Mountains in Peru and Bolivia, to make an offering to connect and understand my 3rd triangle of the Inca Cross. At midnight that evening, we began the seven-hour journey by bus.

I could not sleep because my head felt like it would explode. I was glad that Pablo was there to take care of me. After walking in the different sites, the day before, an intense light radiated in my mind. It filtered through my body via a glass portal. I felt luminous, emitting, and reflecting knowledge. It was like being inside a scanner, with the bright light copying the information.

I was tapping into the energy of so many past stories that I wondered if I was going crazy. I could not control my thoughts. I felt dizzy and lightheaded like I was going to faint. And I was so, so tired.

It was around 6:00 a.m. when I started seeing light symbols in my mind. The symbols seemed to be in front and above me in a black space. The symbols made of golden light illuminated the area. It was as if someone painted the lightest light and the darkest dark, with a high-contrast background for the symbols.

At first, there were only two or three symbols. I looked at them closely; they were holograms, three-dimensional images formed by interference light beams. Then, slowly, more began to show themselves. They came faster and faster, hundreds of them. I could not take it anymore. It was painful. I asked, "What is the meaning of this?"

"You are learning to decode several energetic foreign languages of creations, people, and others," was the response I heard.

It can take months to learn a new language, but I was doing it in seconds. I knew I could not speak the language but could translate and read it in feelings. It was intense. When it stopped, we had reached Puno. I felt weak and sick.

We took a taxi from the bus station to Lake Titicaca. It is the world's highest lake navigable to large vessels, lying at 12,500 feet (3,810 meters) above sea level in the Andes Mountains of South America between Peru to the west and Bolivia to the east. Titicaca is the second largest lake in South America (after Maracaibo).

I was freezing, and Pablo gave me his blanket to cover myself. The goal was to perform a ceremony on the waters of the lake, so we rented a boat. On the boat ride, I held a crystal in my hand. In front of me, I saw the entrance to a beautiful crystalline city sitting atop the lake. I was so tired that it was hard to channel the information, so I asked Father Creator to explain what was happening. He showed me a connection with a pyramid in Egypt that was being rebuilt. First, I saw a young boy, then him as a king, and then he died young. I needed help understanding the meaning of the vision.

After 30 minutes, we floated on the water forward to the center of the lake. I took a banana from the offering basket and dropped it into the water as Pablo instructed me. I did not know what to say anymore. The last few days, I'd experienced many energies of light and others of darkness. I was learning to recognize which were true and which were false, but it was overwhelming and took a lot out of me. As tired as my body and mind were, I knew in my heart that this place was home. It felt familiar and safe.

I was standing on the boat, looking at the water, and suddenly, I experienced a telepathic conversation with several voices at once, then I had several visions that were memories. They were from the times of my ancestors. I also saw a couple. Acada and Ta, they were not in Atlantis. I spoke for Acada. I told Ta, "You and I together will change the world." I also said, "When we talked about changing the world, you knew I was serious about it …" I could not remember more. They were speaking in another language, and I could understand and translate it into my language, Spanish. I understood from the experience that I now had access to a database of information. Later, Che explained that I was learning to decode the symbols of the technology of love.

We returned to shore, where I sat on a rock next to the lake to meditate. I no longer knew what was real. I was short of breath, and I felt cold and numb. Then, I saw a wet coin on the rock. It was an old Peruvian coin from 1936 washed up from the lake. Che was so gentle with me, he knew my stomach was intensely hurting, and I could not even stay focused; he said that the coin was a gift to confirm this experience was real.

While sitting there, I felt another female energy inside me. I sensed her being peaceful and calm because her dreams were being fulfilled. I saw her floating on the lake, dressed in white, getting ready to marry a man who could float on top of the water as she did. I saw them standing atop of the water, walking further into the lake to get married. I noticed the love the mountains had for him, as much as she loved him.

I ran my fingers over the coin lying in my palm and wondered what it represented. Was it possible that this was the story of female energy that embodied Lake Titicaca's energy on the day of my initiation? I love stories of love, and this was a beautiful experience I will long remember. Once the experience was complete, the pain in my stomach was gone.

We left Lake Titicaca and traveled to a small town. At its center was a plaza with trees, grass, and wood benches next to a white adobe Catholic church. I had this intuitive knowing that I had been there before. Everything looked familiar. While I was there, I had a vision. I saw a woman on the day of her wedding. She was dressed in white. I tried to remember the details of the dress because the story was too fast-paced.

She was excited about getting married. She was so happy, but her face quickly changed to state of shock and pain. Then I saw her become sad. Her wedding was canceled because someone told her that her fiancé had had a baby with another woman. I could not see the end of the story. Her heartbreak and sadness remained with me while we drove back to Cuzco. I think it was one of my past lives or one of my ancestors' lives.

We got back to Cuzco around 5:00 p.m. It was nice to be back after a long bus drive. During the ride, Pablo mentioned that while we were on the boat in Lake Titicaca, I had fainted right before entering the crystalline city, and he had to carry me inside. It sounds strange, but he was so used to going into different realities that when he mentioned the experience, it was like something casual for him. I did not remember anything, and he did not say more.

My last offering of the heart was the fire ceremony, intended to connect and help me to understand the 4th triangle of the Inca Cross: the feelings of Responsibility, Productivity, and Present/Truth. Che said that it would be an energetic understanding, but my mind would only understand the meaning later when I returned home. That night was the clearing by fire, the most challenging journey experience. A fire ceremony is an ancient tradition of my ancestors, thousands of years old. The fire is a portal to understanding beyond what the normal eye can see. It provides a way to let go of old stories and drama.

The fire burned in a circle, and I stood at its center. Pablo said, "This fire will clear the blocks and limiting beliefs in your energetic space."

It felt that everything I'd endured in the last few days was to prepare me for this experience. I had to jump as high as possible while the fire was going on, and I was contained within the ring.

I had to ensure I was in the center so my skin would not burn. One jump was easy, and it became exponentially more difficult after twenty times because I was already tired. As the process continued, it started to feel like I wasn't consciously controlling my body, so my emotions and desires took over. I began to see the movements created and the information of my experience flowing through my body.

Pablo and two women had a roll made of newspaper in their hands, which they used to disperse the smoke to clear the low-frequency energies coming out of my body. They also placed water around the fire to contain it. They told me the damages were released when the blue fire became yellow.

The first time was hot. The second time was hotter and much more intense. I started noticing the dark energy areas in my body, and the blocks intensified. I felt the blocks in my stomach and started throwing up to get them out. Some of the dark energies in my stomach got stuck in my throat.

The 3rd time was sweltering hot and the most extreme. I felt the king from Egypt who I'd seen the day before. I was rewriting his story through the energy of my body. I saw the white man with the elongated head who asked me for help with his wife. I was rewriting his story to help him find her. Then I saw a soldier from Spain with a blue uniform and a knife in his stomach. He looked straight into my eyes. I sensed his deep sorrow for being part of the destruction of the Inca civilization. I was clearing his actions and helping him move forward. Then I saw an arrow protruding from my stomach, and I jumped several times to try to remove it from my body. It was extremely hard, and I was making no progress. I searched for anything around me that might help. I saw and felt an angel— tall, with a strong presence. He was there to help me release the arrow.

Once it was removed, that vision cleared and I saw a bright white light, leading into a new vision. The light was Acada! She was inside a cave, kept captive by heavy chains attached to the stone wall. It was a dark cave and quite small. It felt humid. The heat of the fire in my body began removing the energetic blocks of that event, and the story started changing. I saw two angels coming into the cave, cutting the chains, and taking Acada out. When I saw her emerge from the cave, I felt gratified seeing her released and free.

The tall angel came to me with a ball of light about the size of a tennis ball. He asked me to put it in my mouth, allowing the energy to flow into my body, the heat, and the fire. After that, it was easier to breathe. I jumped for another 30 minutes until I saw something white on my right shoulder, like an infection. Pablo touched my shoulder, gently put his fingers together, made some energetic cuts in my back, held the white sticky mass, and slowly removed it.

Staring back at me as Pablo was healing the infection, I saw a dark shadow clinging to my back. I asked Pablo to place the sacred water he had prepared to remove it faster.

At last, the clearing was done. I left the red brick and cemented dark room. I walked slowly to a small adobe room while the two ladies stared at me, waiting for me to ask for help if I needed it. At a snail's pace, I reached the bed. I was tired.

My back felt covered with wounds, but I could not see anything marking me. As I lay on the bed, I heard that an angel had been assigned to care for me. Che was there, and he held my hand. Pablo and one of the women helping during the fire ceremony were in the other room. I heard her say I was strong and had the power to endure and control the situation. Later, I discovered that other people who go through the firing process of clearing often faint or can't finish. I had made it! I felt accomplished and fulfilled.

I slept well that night. By 6:00 a.m., we were already at the airport to fly back to Lima. My body was hurting badly, especially my back in a spot that Che told me not to touch the night before. I touched it by mistake. It felt like I had stitches from removing the white sticky mass.

After arriving in Lima, Pablo, my friend Sra. Juana, and I went to the Inca site at the zoo. Sra. Juana was the friend who'd told me about Pablo on Christmas day. The Inca site, which one of the mountains had told me I must visit, was a place to recharge energy. This place was where the Incas held their gatherings and council meetings, discussing what was needed in the community.

Once on the site, I saw—in another reality—a group of Incas with colorful clothing and golden crowns. They were the masters of the council and were talking to Che. One said I had a lot of courage— and the others agreed. He added that sometimes I hid my vulnerability, but Che's support helped open my heart and show my feelings. It was true. Letting people get close to me was not easy.

After a few minutes coming back to my reality, I found a place to recharge. It was a handmade adobe water canal created by the Incas for irrigation. I jumped inside the canal and sat there for a while, feeling the energy penetrating my body. There was no water there anymore, but the energy was strong, and it was a healing place to restore my energy.

That night, I was walking in the halls to get to the gate at the airport, getting ready to fly back to the US. I turned around and saw, outside the big windows, a large group of people dressed in white saying goodbye. I realized they were the same people who'd greeted me on the path in Cuzco. I smiled at them, and I felt gratitude and love.

When I boarded the plane, I found the flight was full, except for the row I was assigned to, with three empty seats. It was a good place to lie and stretch my legs, and I knew that the mountains had made it possible for me to rest.

On that trip, I learned the mystery of life. Our bodies are important because they clear ancestral lineages by removing the damage of blocks and limiting beliefs. I allowed my ancestors to rewrite their past stories and create a better future for generations to come.

When we increase our frequency by making positive choices, we feel Love, Trust, and Connection to the light—the first triangle of the Inca Cross. We generate future outcomes of light and positive consequences. I was grateful for having my body and being connected to my ancestors of light and love.

CHAPTER 20
2nd Triangle of the Inca Cross

2nd triangle. Acknowledgment, Protection, and Awareness.

After my trip to Peru, I witnessed changes in my connection with Acada in Atlantis. As I began to clear my energy space, Acada became stronger. She did not feel the pain of the past as much as before I went to Peru. Let me explain this differently. In my energetic experience, there were two Acadas—the one in Atlantis and the spirit guide. The spirit guide showed me her life in the past, and as I saw the victim, survivor, and Self-Love behaviors; I got stronger. It was a 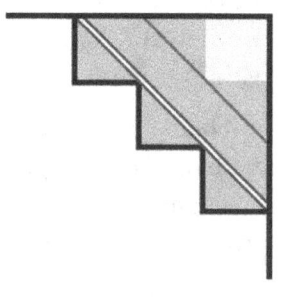 process of seeing how she rewrote her 3rd-dimensional story to the 5th dimension.

Looking from the perspective that feelings help us to move forward in the future, I got to feel the connection to the 2nd triangle of the Inca Cross: Acknowledgement, Protection, and Awareness.

Acknowledgment is to accept the existence of the truth; the state of being the case: fact.

One of the new teachings I have come to accept as truth is that we not only have past lives but also carry the past lives of our ancestors in the atoms of our bodies.

I also came to accept that had several lifetimes in the 3rd dimension resulted from the energetic contamination created in Atlantis in Acada's time. By clearing and completing those lifetimes, we can integrate fragmented past lives into one lifetime of love—a connection only between the present and future.

By integrating past lives into one life, we remember who we are. When we connect to the memories of our feelings, we do not have past lives anymore. In the 5th-dimensional or higher energies, we have only one lifetime without separation or death. We remember ourselves and our feelings by bringing the billions of genetic stories in our bodies into a higher frequency.

Witnessing these genetic stories made it important to understand and feel the energy of the second triangle. It isn't possible to witness high-frequency stories if your intentions are not pure or contaminated. In the energy of Acknowledgment, I learned that duality is not the only option. There are more options than right or wrong or good or bad. Seeing and viewing from only a black-and-white thinking is a misconception. I see now that life is not about observing from the perspective of only two colors, black and white, but many colors. From the future perspective, as long as I observe from Self-Love, I will be able to see the other colors or possibilities.

We've already talked about being victims or survivors of a situation. These behaviors are based on duality. I had clients who believed they could learn from contamination. They thought they should stay in an abusive relationship because there was something to learn from that experience. I also have clients who think they have been sexually abused because they chose to learn that lesson in this lifetime. That is not true! There is nothing to gain from darkness or abuse. We only learn from light. You do not have to suffer to learn the meaning of happiness. That is a duality concept.

For instance, a client called. He was upset with his twenty-four-year-old son. His son was not doing what he wanted; he was disappointed. The father was angry because his son did not have a consistent job, did not go to college, and had an unstable marriage. He wanted me to agree with him that his son was wrong, and he was right. I suggested to have a consultation with his son.

After talking to his son, I called my client back and told him about what I saw in his son's energy and the information I had received from the Light Beings. I told him, "Your son has a learning disability and cannot cope with life because you lost your temper when he was young, and it has become a trauma." I also told him, "Your son is running from being alive."

This man was not ready to listen to the truth. He kept complaining about his son. He also told me he was unwilling to pay for his son's consultations; his son had to figure out how to get the money. The father had lots of money.

In duality, when we want to be right, we must make someone else wrong. And when people believe that they are right, they often believe they are also entitled to fix or destroy others— it gives them a sense of meaning in life. I was reminded of the months I'd spent working with homeless people, many of whom had wound up on the streets due to parents who wanted to be right instead of loving their children for who they were. Like those other parents, the father wanted me to fix his son because he was scared. He felt he was right, and his son was wrong. Duality is a creation that comes from fear, not love.

My client called me a few days later; he shared that his son wanted to kill himself and agreed to pay for his son's consultation. The feeling of Acknowledgment is such an essential tool to rewrite dual belief systems. Working with my clients has taught me to see and acknowledge their light. The feeling of Acknowledgment is listening to what people want. Then I make suggestions –but I can't tell people what to do.

I acknowledge that I can't make choices for others. As a parent, it can be challenging when we talk to our children. I recommend giving them love through suggestions and information that help them make better choices. You can also help them understand that their choices have consequences and that you will be there for them.

I had a client who wanted me to choose for her. She insisted that she could not decide. She would not eat or buy clothes because she didn't know what she wanted, which was hard for her. I suggested making her own choices. I supported her by sharing what I was feeling and seeing and giving her the messages that I received from the Light Beings, but I did not make choices for her.

One time, I shared with her one of her past lives, one in which she damaged a young woman by interfering in the woman's relationship with her husband. It was a way of manipulating the young woman. It was a great opportunity for my client to clear her past life by seeing her choice. She started crying, saying she was not good and did not love herself. It was apparent to me that she was choosing to believe she was not good enough. The woman cried and cried and blamed herself as a bad person. She thought she could not make decisions, but she was choosing not to love herself. We all make choices even if we are not aware of them.

I also acknowledge that I can't be responsible for how people view themselves and can't take responsibility for their choices. We should respect people's choices unless they want to hurt themselves. Then we can ask for assistance from the appropriate resources.

Every time we make a choice, we change the future. It is why we get to choose with the wisdom of our feelings. The future is predictable according to the choices of the present. If you eat something you know is going to make you sick, it will make you sick. If you drive through a red light, there is a possibility you can get in a car accident.

One time a woman called me for a consultation. She was dating a man she liked, but he stopped contacting her. She wanted to know how he felt about her and why he was not calling.

I told her that the higher source did not allow me to tap into his energy and see his thoughts or feelings about her. It does not work that way, and the Light Beings will not give me that information because they respect people's privacy.

"My journey is to help empower you to see your choices through your experiences," I told her. "I can't tell you how others think about you and, for you to use that to make a choice based on a perception of others. You will get confused."

I said, "Sorry, but if I am not receiving any information, there is nothing I can give you."

After that experience, I understood that the information I get from the Light Beings is not intended to control a situation or others. This woman wanted to be right and misuse the information to make herself the victim. Furthermore, she was looking for someone to blame for her choices. I have learned to acknowledge the Light Beings in their choice of whether or not to give information.

In the Inca Cross, the feeling of Protection is built into the feeling of Acknowledgement. Feelings of Protection are powerful. It's about setting boundaries.

I have another client whose job is to jump from helicopters and ski down the mountains. The first time we talked, she knew her schedule was busy. She asked if she could text me when she was free and see if I could help her. I agreed. The boundaries contained that she would not make consultations online, but she would text me when she was available, and we would work together, which was an exception to my scheduling, but she placed a request, and I agreed. The communication was clear. We have been working together for over two years, and she is moving forward in her creations.

I have learned that if people want to change, they must honor and acknowledge their situation and be honest about their ability to commit. The feelings of protection are the same; we must know our boundaries. We must feel what works for us and what does not.

The worst contamination of the feelings of protection comes from narcissistic parents. I am talking about the bullying energy parents create to manipulate and force their children to please them. When I help people from that background, I find they do not know how to protect themselves. They do not know how to set healthy boundaries. They also have low self-esteem and high levels of anxiety and depression.

One day, Acada and I— Acada was assisting from the unseen world—worked with a 53-year-old woman who had just had an affair with a married man. I asked this woman, "How would you feel about having another affair besides this one?"

She looked at me, and I sensed she was okay with the affair. She did not know how to set boundaries. I asked what Acada wanted me to ask her: "How is your relationship with your mother?"

She said, "I killed my mother by taking her out of my life." She meant she did not have a relationship with her mother.

I looked at her, and I felt the love that was coming from Acada. Another question came from Acada. Acada asked me to ask her, "So, you are also okay killing the man you are having an affair with by separating him from his loved ones?"

Then, I witnessed Acada placing a transparent cape of light around her to release the mother's damage. The woman began to cry. She had learned to destroy people like her mother did. She began to understand that when she was punishing others, she was punishing herself. She recognized that she no longer needed the energy of punishment.

The feelings of Protection are the ability to protect what you are creating for yourself. I witnessed a woman around sixty-five who wanted to be a life coach. She had worked hard and had spent over $20,000 on different training programs. She was in debt and needed to succeed more in her coaching program. She learned marketing tools and believed she was ready to teach others how to create powerful lives. That was the intention of her heart, but something was missing: love for herself. She was suffering from the pain and sorrow of her mother's rejection. She was trying to prove her strength by helping others—a survivor's behavior.

We must be careful not to use others to overcome our insecurities. We can only bring transformation to others when we allow them to have their experiences of Self-Love. There is nothing to prove. Love yourself and set your boundaries of love.

I encountered that woman a few years after, and I saw in her eyes that she had learned the lesson and was a gentle coach. She had learned to give her knowledge by being patient and caring, providing information by tapping into her clients' heart desires. She had to let go of the story that she had to prove she was strong. She was already strong and capable. There was nothing to prove.

One of the ways you can practice the energy of protection is by writing your journey in your journal. Write down the true desires of your heart by asking yourself if your choices bring love back to you when you think about them. This process will help you be honest with yourself and speak your truth.

The feeling of Awareness is perceiving a fact. Prophet Thoth is one of the Light Beings who taught me to perceive love for myself.

It was an honor to be trained by Prophet Thoth in the energy of Awareness, which is very powerful. I heard about him from Acada, but I first saw and connected with him in Peru, on Lake Titicaca and he became my teacher.

I am trying to remember when I first heard about him and his book, *The Emerald Tablets*. I felt excited about purchasing his book. When I got it, I remember looking at the book, touching the white cover, and feeling the wisdom of an ancient teacher. His energy stayed with me.

Prophet Thoth could see the blocks and limiting beliefs in my body. He said to me one day, "Why do you think you are afraid of life?" That was a good question. I was reflecting on my relationship with my mother. My answer was: "I am afraid of life because no one loves me, and I am not a good person." He gently looked into my eyes and said, "I am standing in front of you because I love you."

In the feeling of Awareness, I identified that I had the idea that love was a to-do list. If I were to finish my list, I would be rewarded for my work by being loved. That idea was from my relationship with my mother, but it is not true. Love is unconditional.

Prophet Thoth taught me the power of sound, ideas, words, and sentences. He said that sound is the foundation of all creation. Sound movements invite other sound movements in the space that allows the creation of ideas. It seemed so simple. Then he said that the ideas would create another sound and words, and together these sounds would create sentences, creating a concept and language.

Thoth said, "Look at it this way: The sound is a space waiting to have something placed inside it. When you place other sounds, an idea gets to be created. Envision a white space, then place the feeling of love into it. Let the energy of love create an idea, (I am loved). Now, create another sound of a word, 'I,' then create another word." He suggested "am" and adding the sound or word "Love." Then he said to repeat the sentence, "I AM LOVE."

To my surprise, I had created the concept of "I am love." I felt love running through me. I had replaced the old idea of love as a to-do list with a new one. I felt love, and it was strong in my heart. Ideas are powerful and life changing.

Prophet Thoth and I worked together for several months. He taught me that ideas could be decontaminated by clearing the contaminations of the sounds of the ideas and making the energy of ideas stronger. He also taught me to be coachable, and I fell in love with myself, a combination of vulnerability, nurturing love, and kindness. With Prophet Thoth, I learned to be a lover of light. With Che, I learned to be a warrior.

In the crystal temple, which is another dimension on Lake Titicaca, Thoth is the guardian. It took me a while to remember my experience at the lake when I connected to the crystal city. In the city, there are energetic records of each of us. When I work with my clients at the beginning of the consultation, I sometimes connect with Prophet Thoth's energy, heart to heart, and I get information from the temple when needed.

I often felt insecure about myself when I was training. Once, Thoth took me to see a man's records to teach me to be more confident. I had been working with a very sick client with anxiety and heart problems, at that time. He did not have money to pay me, so I helped him without charging him. He started feeling better and making lots of money. I was happy for him. But instead of being in the energy of gratitude for getting better, he hid his healing experience from his friends. He did not want them to know about me and how he was improving. He was ashamed of me, and he was ashamed of himself.

I was heartbroken and confused. I felt used and did not know how to create a better situation. After weeks of trying to learn how to deal with my emotions around it, Prophet Thoth came to me and shared a story to help me understand my situation. It was the story of a Mu woman and a king.

He showed it to me as slides, like watching a movie. I saw a Mu woman walking through the forest and mountains. She was aware of her connection with her environment; every living thing around her was her friend. She did not feel alone. That day, Thoth shared that the Mu people were sometimes half-mountain and half-human, where they had the body of a human, but their faces looked like rocks. People from Mu knew about creations. A Light Being told me that the Mu beings were the Mother Creator's people because they could feel every creation.

In my vision, I saw it was a beautiful day. The softness of the sun's light reflected the green trees and other plants on the mountains. It felt peaceful. After a while, it got dark. The Mu woman was tired and ready to rest. She got close to a mountain, took the shape of the rocks and soil close to her, and attached herself to the side of it. It was amazing to see her transformation. It looked like she was part of the mountain and went to sleep.

Then I saw a white man on a white horse; he was tall, thin, and confident. Somehow, I knew that he was the king of his community. His horse made a wrong turn, and he fell off and hurt his legs. He called for help, but no one could hear him, and he sat there for a long time before the Mu woman showed up. He did not notice her appearance because he was in too much pain and only focused on getting help.

He lay on the ground while she gathered some plants and placed them on his hands and legs. He started feeling better. He felt the love she had inside for herself and how good he felt by being near her. Now, he opened his eyes, gazed at her face, and did not care how she appeared. He was more intrigued by the love she shared while healing him. Through the love she carried, he saw how she could communicate with nature like she was part of it.

I felt her love for him; she stayed with him until he got better. His body was healed, and he felt strong. He knew it was time to go back to his town.

He could have asked her to come with him, but he changed his mind about how she looked. He did not like how she looked in human eyes and was afraid that people would judge him. When he decided to leave, she honored his decision. She left her heart open, hoping he would change his mind someday.

She was not sad but happy for him to be strong again. She did not feel a loss because she did not know the concept of loss. In her high energy, separation wasn't something she knew. That is what kept her connected with every creation.

The king went back to his town. It was a beautiful and colorful town. The houses were made of adobe, a mixture of red dirt, water, and straw, with well-kept gardens. The houses were beside each other by a dirt road to the palace. The palace was made of stone, rustic cut of rocks. There were several horses on the road.

It caught my attention how his people had a sense of superiority, the human belief that they were better than other creations. The king was the same; he thought leadership was about feeling superior, giving him false power to decide for others.

When it was time for him to choose a bride, he chose between the two most beautiful and desirable women in the kingdom. He picked the most pretty one—according to him. He did not choose with his heart but with his mind. He thought he had to look good in the eyes of his people.

Time passed, and he had two daughters. They were beautiful and always looked nice. He was proud of his daughters because they had learned to keep their place in society. He would say, "It is a good thing they know they are royalty."

Prophet Thoth said, "That was far from the truth." His daughters were disconnecting from their hearts. There was nothing to feel in the emptiness of the space they carried there where Self-Love and love for others should be.

Years passed by, and the king grew older. He had forgotten about the Mu woman. One day, he looked at his face in the mirror and saw he had wrinkles, lots of them. The Mu woman came to his mind, and he remembered the love she had for him. He had changed. He was not as beautiful as he was when he met her. Grief hit him, that he had rejected her because he thought she was unattractive. What he thought about beauty had been wrong all those years. He also felt he loved her and understood in a new way. He said, "Now I know physical beauty does not stay forever."

He searched the forest for her for several years but could not find her. He prayed to Father creator to help him locate her. When he was dying, he opened his heart and prayed again to Father creator.

"I am dying; I want to be with her. Where is she?" He asked Father Creator.

Father answered him. "She is in another place in the universe, another planet, because of the love in her heart. She is in a place where she can create more love in higher frequency."

The old man smiled., "Father, I want to be with her."

"Son, I get to honor her choice, and she does not want to be with you," Father replied.

After Prophet Thoth shared that story in the light records, I cried. I thought of my client, who accepted my gifts but was ashamed to be seen with me. Because I am short, 4.11', and he was tall, that made him uncomfortable.

Thoth said gently, "So, what do you want?"

"I choose not to work with him anymore. This client does not accept who I am," I said. "I want to heal and help people who see my value and love."

Awareness is a gift of love. I am learning to be aware of who I am and to understand that I am very different. Being different does not create separation but love. I have learned to embrace that being different is a gift of God. Father once said to me, "I love you for being different because you bring something new, another aspect of me to open the eyes of the world."

CHAPTER 21
Father and Mother Creators' Story of Love

The feeling of Awareness is feeling the situation and having the desire for a better outcome.

I think Mother's and Father's love story is the most beautiful story of the feeling of Awareness. I shared this channeled story one day when I was with a client who did not understand the energy of love. She had a severe alcohol addiction and wanted to be healed, and I noticed that she was looking to feel a connection to love when she drank. It is common for people with addictions to look for the connection of love, and they are not even aware of it.

She said that she had never felt love from her parents or husband. I was not there to question her if that was true or an idea she had created, but I felt I needed to share my experience of Mother and Father Creator's love for each other to help her. Father Creator told this story while I was channeling for another client.

When Father Creator talked about Mother, it felt like an unlimited expansion. Father said he met Mother when he visited an island; he saw her on a boat. From the first time he saw her, he knew she was the one for him. He asked her, "What can I do to be in a relationship with you?"

She said, "I want you to create lots of water, a big ocean of water."

He went and created an ocean of water, then came back and asked her if that was big enough. She said no, it must be bigger. He went and made more water in the ocean and returned to Mother and said, "Is that good enough?" She said it had to be bigger. He kept coming back to her, and she kept saying, "It has to be bigger."

One day he returned, and she said, "Yes, that is big enough."

Mother smiled and said to Father, "I asked you to create the biggest ocean for you to see my value. Father smiled and said to her, "I love you.""

Later, when Father married Mother, they became the largest ocean of water ever created. They made a promise of love to stay together.

It was the love of Mother that motivated Father to create a bigger ocean. She helped him become an unlimited creator. Mother showed Father the feeling of value by helping Father create and acknowledge her and himself. This is how Father and Mother fell in love.

My client did not feel love because her parents and husband had not acknowledged her value and did not see her as a powerful creator. She searched for love and acceptance in the wrong places. When she learned to see her worth, she understood she did not need her parents or husband to approve of her behavior but to follow her heart and reach her potential by feeling her value.

We are accountable for our choices. The higher the choices, the more expansion of love we create. In lower choices, we shorten the expansion of love. We always get back what we give to others. It is the law of expansion.

Mother represents the ocean waves that hit the beach, and Father represents the expansion of the flow of the ocean. When water waves hit the beach, they are strong. When the waves return to the ocean, they create motion, supporting other creations' lives. If the sea is significant, the water creates enormous waves that can travel in the water.

Mother Creator likes action; when creating, she moves and looks for a way out of a situation to bring balance. She gives the energy of balance to all creation. Father takes her message into expansion. She finds the source of the circumstances and the solution, and Father moves to carry her message. The female energy knows what she wants, and the male energy will expand the love given by the feeling of direction. So, we have Mother and Father Creators together as creation and direction.

Think of it this way. There is a car traveling on the freeway. The freeway is male energy, and the car is female energy. The freeway has a path, a way to go places. The freeway has signs, lights, road directions, and exits that take you somewhere.

The car is a creation. Someone created it first in energy (the idea of the car), then manifested it physically. It is a thought, a dream manifested, and that is the female energy: a dream, a goal, or an idea.

This is how our atoms work. The proton represents the movements of the waves of the water that are Mother Creator, which holds the creation or space. The neutron is the power of Father that expands the ocean's water. Together, they have the same purpose: to expand the ocean's water—the energy of love.

I was surprised to learn that our feelings can be either male or female. Yes, two types of feelings balance us: direction and creation feelings.

Returning to the story of Father's and Mother's love creation: the female energy has the dream to create an ocean of water, and the male energy makes it happen. And we are all based on that foundation.

I asked one of the Light Beings, "What about Father? Doesn't he get to do what he wants to do?"

The Light Being smiled and said, "Remember, Mother and Father are the same creation, the big ocean of water. Both want the same thing; they reflect each other in their pure essence of creation and love."

In the intention of creation, Father and Mother reflect what they feel for one another. In the Inca Cross, these feelings are represented: the male feelings, which are the feelings of direction, are Love, Trust, Connection, Acknowledgment, Protection, and Awareness. The female feelings of creation are Happiness, Passion for Life, Self-expression, Responsibility, Productivity, and the Truth or Present.

When they are reflecting on each other, this is the result:

- When Father feels Love, Mother feels Happiness.
- When Father feels Trust, Mother feels Passion for Life.
- When Father feels Connection, Mother feels Self-expression.
- When Father feels Acknowledgment, Mother feels Responsibility.
- When Father feels Protection, Mother feels Productivity.
- When Father feels Awareness, Mother feels Truth or Present.

Now, I know that I am sensing the connection of Father and Mother Creator when I am feeling.

CHAPTER 22
3rd Triangle of the Inca Cross

3rd Triangle. Happiness, Passion for Life, and Self-Expression

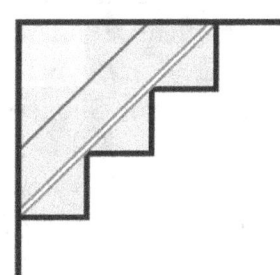

Female feelings are the nesting space for any creation. One of the female energy principles is that you can't have a relationship with someone you do not want to be with. Father shared that he was in a relationship with Mother because he chose to be with Mother, and she decided to be with him.

I will suggest valuing the people that want to be in your life. If someone wants to be with you and you want to be with them, honor that experience, and if someone does not want to be with you, honor that as well.

We can only co-create with someone that wants to be part of your life experience in the feelings of Happiness, Passion for Life, Self-Expression, Responsibility, Productivity, and Present/Truth. That includes our relationship with ourselves.

A Choice is the essence of the birth of light, a new experience. To feel "valuable" is a choice, and it is the platform to connect to the female feelings in the Inca Cross.

Father explained that in the balance of our female and male feelings, the worst thing that can happen to a female is feeling replaced, which confuses her sense of value. For instance, when a person, either a woman or a man, if their partner is cheating on them, they feel replaced.

When female accepts she has been replaced, she experiences separation, like a part of her body is detaching. It is painful and powerless, and she loses focus on creating stability. The feelings of happiness, passion for life, and self-expression shatter and stop producing abundance. They cannot support their creation or other creations, and the energetic immune system goes down.

When a female feeling is separate from its matching male feeling in the Inca Cross, we get open to energetic attacks because the male feelings are not there to protect us. Let's explain it differently. When the energy of Happiness, Passion for Life, and Self-expression lowers, blocks and limiting beliefs can come into your energetic space, contaminate you and take you out of balance.

I had a client whose husband left for a younger woman. It was painful, her female and male energy was imbalanced, and she felt powerless. As a creator, she believed she had done something wrong and blamed herself for it. She took responsibility for the infidelity, even though it was not her fault—she chose to behave as a survivor to overcome the pain. This is how traumas get created when someone subconsciously disconnects from the 5th dimension by taking responsibility for a situation that is not their fault.

The female feelings are powerful when in balance because they have an unlimited knowledge and are the gift of making others accountable. I understand that when the female feelings are separated from the male feelings, and they take responsibility for something they have not done, they forget about their power. The situation can be resolved when they redirect the love to themselves and love themselves; they come back to their full source of love and accountability.

Let's talk a little more about accountability. Accountability is experiencing your creation and reflecting your light, which comes to you from Mother and Father Creators. Accountability is like investing in the stock market. When you invest money in something that is increasing in value, you will get your money back, but if you invest in a company that is losing money, you will lose money. We all reflect on our choices, and we learn from them.

We are accountable for the amazing things we create in our lives and the hard work we do to be a being of light. You also are accountable for the low choices you make. Either way, you get back what you invested in your life. Accountability lets you be who you are in action. It is the integration of transformation, reflecting your choices.

What is an energy attack? An energy attack is when the female and male feelings are separated; you lose your sense of value, and low-frequency attacks feed on the vulnerable feeling. For instance, a married couple has dreams and goals. Suppose the husband is unfaithful and the wife feels rejected, which is an energetic attack. In that case, separation begins, and communication stops. The dreams and goals that they created together do not get to be fulfilled.

I had relationships that did not work out, and there was a lot of pain in my heart. My male and female feelings were separated, and there was contamination in my energy space. One of the contaminations was the idea that I was not good enough, that I was not as beautiful, and that I wanted to fix myself. I compared myself to other women and believed they were better than me.

Happiness is the female expression of Love. It is the strongest female feeling. It expresses joy, satisfaction, contentment, and fulfillment. It is the feeling of unlimited possibilities.

Youth are so easily manipulated, and they lose their self-value. How many young men and women are convinced that recreational drugs do not have consequences? It does affect their level of creation, the female power. Some to the point that their brains are damaged.

Parents work to support their families, trusting their children will be safe at school, while predators come into school to sell drugs, damaging the youth's brains. It hurts not only the children but also the family.

The feeling of trust is corrupted and creates instability in the family. I kept thinking it was unfair for parents to deal with the drug dilemma. Then I heard a voice that said, "To feel VALUABLE is the invisible feeling that can protect our children."

If parents love and value themselves, they will find a way to communicate with their children and guide them. I wanted to understand and learn more in how to educate and protect our youth. This happened a few days before my trip to Jackson, Wyoming, where I was invited to participate as a speaker at a women's holistic wellness event.

While driving from Salt Lake City to Jackson, for the first time in my life, I felt the true feeling of being valuable. It was only a small, tiny particle coming from the 5th dimension into this reality, and I had to take it somewhere where it could expand in this reality.

The process was guided, and the mountains of Yellow Stone were a good place to spread this new energy. While I drove there for five hours, I stayed in the energy of Self-Love in my heart to maintain the frequency I carried.

There is a large crystal from Brazil located in the Main area of the Jackson Hole Mountain Resort, around twenty minutes from downtown Jackson Hole. I drove to the ski resort, found the crystal, and downloaded the energy inside of it. After few minutes, I saw the new energy, as a white light, expanded in different directions. It was beautiful.

Later that afternoon, I had a vision and saw other places where the new feeling of value transferred: rivers, lakes, and the snow that covered the mountains. I was happy that this new energy could help lots of people. It would take some time, but the process had started.

During the event, I spoke to a group of thirty powerful women. While talking to them, the energy of Value in the environment transferred to them and their ancestors. On my way home after the event, it felt that the women of the group and I had come together. And as a community, we sent that light to our loved ones and others. I felt different. I felt valuable. I felt comfortable communicating with others, more grounded, and happier.

Passion for Life is the 2nd female feeling, and it is the female expression of Trust. It is also referred to as an activator of the 3rd triangle because it takes happiness in motion. It makes opportunities happen in the feeling of happiness.

One of the unique aspects of Passion for Life is the desire to share the feeling with others. Remember, feelings are part of molecular behaviors. Once I knew and felt "self-value," my body, heart, and mind wanted to reflect that to others. It was happening in my body, like when I felt hungry or thirsty, and it was not something I could control, but to give my body what it desired. I was going into another dimension at the molecular level to create more of this feeling of self-value and share it with other feelings and frequencies. My body was healing and helping others.

Self-expression is the 3rd female feeling and the female expression of connection. It is the expression of your inner world with your outside world. This plays a crucial role in accountability. In this connection, the female energy clears the damage of the past. I could not stop thinking about all the young women and men that had been damaged using drugs, and by just thinking about it and feeling it, I was in my female feeling of self-expression. My new energy of self-value was going on a molecular level and making myself accountable to the energies responsible for the damage done in my present and past lives. The molecular energy was not only mine but also the molecular energy of the women in the event and the energy of nature in Jackson and Yellowstone.

This is one of the ways our reality will become 5th-dimensional. I know things will not change overnight but eventually grow exponentially in this reality. This is the female power.

Remember that dreams and goals are essential to female energy. Creating more plans and a vision of new possibilities in our lives increases the feelings of Passion for Life, Self-expression, and Happiness so that the latter can connect back to Love and other male feelings. All the feelings in the Inca Cross will start working together again to create pure intentions – feelings of creation in action. In other words, we create in the present without letting the past control us. We can obsolete the past.

CHAPTER 23
4th Triangle of the Inca Cross

4th Triangle. Responsibility, Productivity, and Present-Truth

In 2017, while living in Park City, Utah, I had a vision. I saw myself driving through a canyon and entering a city covered by a bright white light. The vision was a sign that it was time to move to a new place, and the light represented where I needed to be.

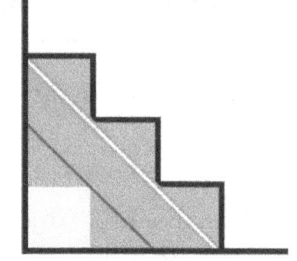

I drove from Park City to Salt Lake City (SLC), Utah, a few days later. I found myself driving through a canyon and emerging to the same place as in my vision. That is how I knew that I had to move to Salt Lake City. One day, shortly after I moved, I was driving to my new apartment, when I saw the light coming from the mountains and was directed to the apartment. The mountains created an energetic space to support me in my new place. In my new home, I tapped into more information on the 4th triangle of the Inca Cross.

The 3rd triangle is about seeing your value, and the 4th dimension is about recognition and commitment to your self-values and others' values. It is about others seeing your value as true and realizing your abilities, achievement, and services. According to the Light Beings, there is another way to describe recognition. It is the action of giving and receiving. You give or share your value with others and receive love as a reflection of your actions.

For instance, when you compliment someone from your heart, like, "You are so kind to me, thank you." That will be giving energy, and when that person accepts your acknowledgment and has gratitude, it is the receiving. Both of you feel a connection and go into happiness and reflect expansion, which is more of that exchange.

In our 3rd triangle of the Inca Cross, with the energy of self-value, we clear the community and ancestral damage and disintegrate the past with the help of the energy of accountability. The 4th triangle of the Inca Cross creates the new generations to come and focuses on the 5th-dimensional teachings and values, which is the relationship between the present and future without the past, which is Circular Time. In that reality, we work with the Light Beings and our ancestors, not in the past but in the future, for a better world.

I like to listen to Spanish music on the radio, and back when I was training, I enjoyed a particular song. Sometimes the radio station would play that song two or three times a day. I liked the sound of it, but I never took the time to listen to the words. One day, I was hiking with my kids. I took a break, resting in the car and listening to the radio when the song came on. I paused and listened to "Que me alcance la vida" (That My Life is Long Enough) Sin Banderas.

When I listen to the song, I comprehend that love is an energy exchange: giving and receiving. This song represented the best way male energy gives love to female energy in response to her love. To me, it also meant a story of love between protons and neutrons in our bodies when they are balanced—a molecular story.

Father explained that the Energy of Love is not conditional but expansive. He went back to the story of the water in the ocean. Father Creator did not make conditions for Mother by telling her that her Love was conditioned to the amount of water she could provide. In his energy of expansion, he knew he could give her what she needed because it was a joint creation. Father wanted the same creations as Mother. Father understood that when Mother wanted to develop her four triangles, her creation was also for Father. He was committed to providing expansion.

Expansion is the power of male feelings that declares, "We can only recharge in feelings." This means we can build more feelings only if we start from a foundation of feelings. You cannot build love in an illusion of "I am not good enough." You have to let that story go and then feel you are good enough, and you can build on that. We must trust our feelings because if our female feelings do not trust our male feelings, we create separation and damage the energy of commitment.

Commitment is a way of showing love. But when commitment gets damaged, we lose direction and stop believing in our creations. So how do we rebuild trust in our creations and direction? By empowering the feelings of the 4th triangle in the Inca Cross, which are Responsibility, Productivity, and the Truth (being in the present).

In the 3rd triangle, the female energy returns the creation energy to the creator with the energy of accountability, which changes or re-writes the event or the damage to powerful creations. Sometimes it is also called karma – what goes around comes around, or there is a consequence for every action. The feelings of the 4th triangle bring back the balance in the 5th dimension.

From the feelings of the 4th triangle, our observation of the future as a spirit will reflect the light from the future to the present. We do not have to contaminate ourselves with the past because we are not observing from the perspective of the behavior of a victim or survivor. The balance and abundance process only works from the future and present in high-frequency – 5th dimension.

In the 4th triangle, linear time cannot use our energy to exist, and linear time stops to exist. In the 4th triangle, where the 4th dimension is repaired, the illusion of linear time is removed, and only Circular Time will exist. The 4th dimension is integrated back into the 5th dimension as it used to be before the contamination existed.

As an outcome of the reaction of the 3rd triangle of the Inca Cross and the 4th triangle, the energy of our "ancestors" that chose to feel will transfer to the energy of the future in Circular Time. Ancestors choosing low-frequency emotions will be given several opportunities to choose the light. If they choose to stay in the past of low-frequency, they will be as obsolete (stop existing) as linear time will. Also, in the process, the water in our body becomes 5th-dimensional water, and our vibration changes to a 5th-dimensional vibration.

The role of self-value in the 4th triangle of the Inca Cross is as essential as in the 3rd triangle. It transfers from the 3rd triangle to the 4th triangle. In the 4th triangle, it will observe the future of the entity that did the damage in the past. If it does not want to be responsible for the damage done, the feeling of self-value will travel in the low future and obsolete the entity's essence. It will completely disappear— no existence. Then, the entity cannot travel to the lower future and reattach to the victim. The energy of the person damaged by the attack of the dark entity will be clear and filled with a 5th-dimensional energy future. Therefore, darkness, such as sexual abuse, cannot exist in the future of the 5th dimension. Eventually, in the years to come, when all the future experiences in low-frequency are clear and integrated into one high-frequency future, entities and blocks will not exist.

The 4th triangle of the Inca Cross is also known as an activator of the Inca Cross. It is here that life reactivation happens. The male energy matches the female energy's choices to act in a specific situation to create 5th-dimensional experiences.

This is how the activation, or balance, happens: the male feeling of Acknowledgment starts nurturing and loving the female feeling of Responsibility. With the feeling of Awareness, Responsibility starts awakening her to be responsible for her positive creations. Then the male feeling of Protection activates and connects to recharge the energy of Productivity. Productivity recovers her identity and starts activating her Energy Gifts and building her confidence. Then the feeling of Awareness starts activating the feelings of the Truth of the Present. The Truth of things will manifest in thoughts or ideas to restore balance in the 4th triangle.

Let's say you trusted someone, and that person betrayed you. Your commitment energy is damaged, and so is your connection with your female feelings. When you lose connection with your female feelings, you forget your goals, dreams, and passions. You feel deep emptiness and a lack of direction. But when you reconnect to the 4th triangle by feeling love for yourself, the Inca Cross integrates your energy. You connect to the female and male spirit power, Mother and Father Creators, your subconscious, your conscious, and your pure Egypt. You start observing your life from a 5th-dimensional perspective instead of a 3rd-dimensional perceptive of illusion.

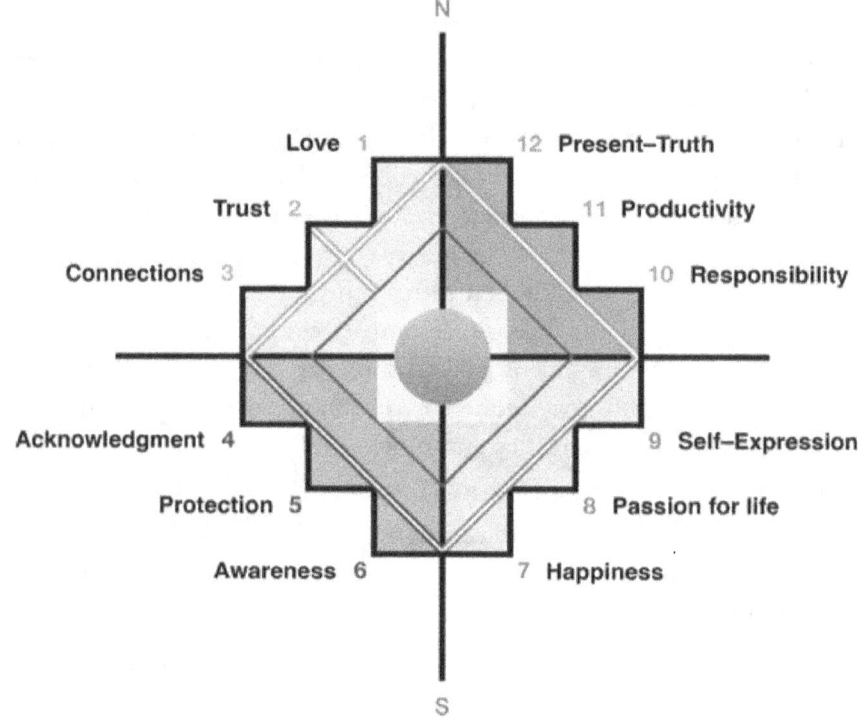

I want to explain more about the feeling of Responsibility. Responsibility teaches us that we can only guide to our level of knowledge or experience. We cannot teach what we do not know. I had to experience in my space the energy of feelings to understand the creation of the 5th dimension and how valuable and powerful we are when we are creating from it.

The more Acada, Prophet Thoth, Che, Mother, Father, and others shared their knowledge with me, the more my sense of responsibility grew; by receiving this information, I learned that I am not a terrible person and was not a bad mother or daughter. I labeled myself as a survivor of the situation. It was easy to blame myself and so I shut myself down to avoid confronting the situation or others. Now, I can express myself from a space of Self-Love. If something bothers me, I can say, "I feel you are not listening to me." "Sorry, I do not understand. Can you share that again?"

I have also learned to accept my commitment to the light and stand true to my feelings. As my people say, I've learned to fly.

In my energy of responsibility, I also learned that darkness, or low frequencies, will always betray us. Low frequencies do not want to create with you but instead take your light and use it for their benefit. In high-frequencies, light is abundant, and sharing and teaching are ways of life.

In the energy of responsibility, you are wasting your time if you are waiting for low frequencies to love you back. It will not happen; darkness does not have feelings. It will not understand how you feel and how hard you work to make pure choices. Darkness will tell you what you want to hear. It will give you information to create a realistic illusion, but it is still an illusion. Darkness will say, "Do not trust yourself; you better trust me." It will make you feel powerless and show up as a hero to save you from your choices. Your responsibility is to learn to love the light, trust in it, be present, and listen to your feelings to keep creating light and standing for your freedom.

Prophet Thoth taught me to see the difference between Light Beings and dark beings who pretend to be light.

He said, "The real Light Beings have feelings, and the dark beings want to pretend that they are Light Beings, but they do not feel. When a Light Being approaches you from another dimension, ask them to show you the feelings of love or happiness in their heart."

One day I saw a Light approaching me. I asked him to create feelings of love in his heart, and he created some energy. I next asked him to recreate a feeling of happiness, and he could not. I knew, then, that he was a dark entity, and he did not represent the light.

I told Prophet Thoth about my experience.

"Darkness cannot imitate the energy of happiness; it is a high-frequency above their understanding because they do not feel it," he said.

Remember, dark entities can't travel to the high-frequency future. They only can travel to the lower-frequency future, hide there, and attack you from there.

In the 4th triangle, the male energy of self-value, which is in the future connected to the male energy of the value of Father Creator, goes into expansion which stops the dark entities from going to the future and eventually dissolves them.

When they can't go to the future, the high present energy commands them to return the Light they had taken from others. Once they give back the energy they had taken, they are empty like a flat balloon without air. They stop existing in the present.

When encountering a dark entity in the unseen world, I see their ability to create movement is insufficient because they do not create with feelings. You must feel the energy of love or happiness of the entity to see if it represents light. If you do not feel they can create love or happiness, they do not represent the light. This process is a good way to avoid being misguided.

Over time, we have forgotten the true meaning of love, and it is easy for dark entities to deceive us. It is sad to know that, as a society, we have lost the understanding of love. I have been happy to learn that the triangles of the Inca Cross will help me understand and feel love because they are the creation of love.

90% of the time, darkness approaches us in the guise of light. It is unlike a horror movie, where darkness appears like a monster or is a scary-looking thing. Some dark entities can be very attractive because of the physical beauty and make themselves desirable. Whenever I see a Light Being approaching me, I look at them without fear and ask them to create happiness in their hearts.

Prophet Thoth said that happiness feels like when we are confident about a situation – there is no doubt. It is when your confidence is a piece of knowledge. Prophet Thoth told me that when I see a being not representing the light, I should call for him to remove the false energy from my space. It is not up to me to teach dark beings; they may set me up to take my light. It is the power of Light Beings to use feelings to relocate dark entities. On the other hand, if a lightworker can create feelings of happiness in their heart, I listen to their message.

In the feeling of Responsibility, we make a Contract of Love in which we set pure intentions with ourselves to have Self-Love boundaries. Here are some of my Contracts of Love:

- I want to teach others to love, but I must learn to love myself first.
- We live in a society where sometimes we value others because they are nice to us, but we do not want to know a person's genuine emotions or thoughts. I do not want to hide by being nice; instead, I get to be authentic.
- I do not want to trade low-frequency emotions for feelings. Emotions in low-frequency do not have pure intention.
- I want to learn to stand only for the light, learn from my mistakes, and be responsible for my choices. This is how I teach when I am in balance.
- When people judge me, I do not take them seriously and remove myself. I intend to help people return to the 5th dimension— if they want to.
- I want to generate the substance and source of knowledge to make my dreams happen.
- I want to embrace anything that nurtures, makes me feel good, and works for me.
- I always want to have gratitude for direction.
- I want always to be aware that I can't please everyone.
- A Light Being said, "You can be a great teacher and take a horse to the river to drink water, but it is up to the horse if he drinks water or not. Be a great teacher and show the way, but let your students make their choices."
- I want to stand in the energy of responsibility to give information to others, but I cannot be responsible for others' choices. The beauty of life is to be responsible for our actions, so if I choose to be responsible for others, I am taking a beautiful gift of love away from them. I am happy when my clients get the results they want.

I enjoy the success in their life, but I am not responsible for their choices of failures or successes.

- I want to stand for people's highest potential. Through my life experiences, I have understood dreams are powerful, but if we do not apply ourselves, we cannot make them happen. Someone may dream of being a doctor, but he will not become one if he does not attend college classes or study. I must remember this because some people want energetic gifts but are unwilling to apply themselves to make choices and set high values to get the results they want.

- Some people are looking to blame their choices on others. I must remember I cannot be strong for them or feel sorry for them. I must trust that they will figure out the beauty of making choices someday.

Productivity is the energy of learning to produce for your higher self, which is your highest potential in the future. I remember when Acada showed me the power of my higher self in the future. I saw that the possibility and version of me in the future was everything I wanted.

Looking back at these experiences, I have noticed that I have changed a lot. My once careless behavior that sought adventure has become wise and has learned to honor sacred knowledge. It has taken time to understand that the feeling of Productivity is the expression of honor and respect for what I know and do not know.

I have learned not to take the information given to me for granted. With the feelings of Productivity, I understand that when information is given to me from the mountains or higher beings, it is not to feed my ego. It is given to me because they consider that I have the possibility to bring a better way of life. The feeling of Productivity in the Inca Cross gives us the courage to make choices and actions from honor and respect.

The last feeling of the 4th triangle of the Inca Cross is the energy of being Present, or Truthful, with myself. It is the power or feelings I create to move forward in the feeling of Love. With my new understanding and application of the feelings of Responsibility and Productivity connected to the feeling of Truth, I was present in my new reality: the power of completion.

For instance, let's say you have a delivery truck. You had been delivering furniture all day. You just finished your last delivery, and you feel complete. The feeling of Truth is the sense that the task is done, and you feel fulfilled. You do not have to think about the past but what other activities you can do and move forward.

This last feeling of the Inca Cross reminds me of the saying, "It is what it is." There is no pain or suffering but complete acceptance of a situation's truth. There is nothing to hide – just a sense of identity, a set of characteristics that allow me to be definitively and uniquely recognizable.

In the Inca Cross, your truth is unique to yourself because no one else has the same experiences as you. You are the evolution of your feelings and desires of the heart, and you become your own light and support others in your uniqueness. Be aware of your Inca Cross, your Present-True molecular behavior: your light identity.

Your identity transition of the Inca Cross encompasses the memories, experiences, relationships, and values that create your sense of self to reach the 5th dimension in your true identity. The cycle starts with the first triangle and finishes with the fourth triangle. It is an amalgamation, a process by which a dominant group of ideas and feelings combine with a subordinate group of ideas to form a new group of thoughts and feelings. The Inca Cross creates a steady sense of who one is over time, even as new facets are developed and incorporated into one's identity.

Now, I understand that the difference between the higher self and spirit is that the higher self is the best option for oneself in the future, and the spirit is your essence without contamination. In the balance of Love— Happiness, Trust— Passion for Life, Connection— Self-expression, Acknowledgment— Responsibility, Protection— Productivity, and Awareness— Present/Truth, I can overcome dark entities, blocks, and limiting beliefs and connect back to my spirit. My pure intention in the 3rd dimension will match the desire and support of spirit to assist me in acting into a higher perspective of myself in the present.

CHAPTER 24
Pure Intention: High-Frequency Future of New Possibilities

"I shared stories of low-frequency in the past to let them go or change them to stories of love then transfer them to a future of high-frequency to become opportunities for you to become a 5th-dimensional being of light." Acada

All the symbols are energetic holograms of feelings. In ancient times, the Law of One represented the intention symbol by a triangle, a polygon with three edges and three vertices. Pure intention is an observation from the energy of our spirit supported by the collective consciousness of spirits. It is a desire for Self-Love and goodwill that matches our spiritual power.

Intention

A pure intention's driving or motivating force is the energy of love. For instance, it is like the feeling of falling in love. When you love the other person, you want them to be part of your life. It is a beautiful feeling to be in the life of others. Then the desire to be a better person is the influence of your pure love for the other person. The love is transferred to the future of high-frequency, and more possibilities of love get created.

There are two types of futures. The lower-frequency contamination of the past and high-frequency future that has no contamination and is connected to pure intentions. Let's go back to the story of Acada to learn more about pure intention, the future, and possibilities.

Acada's intelligence and gifts were challenging for the Mirrors because she was unpredictable. She worked through her Books of Light in various dimensions (levels of consciousness). She traveled to different realities that were individual levels of consciousness inside each dimension. She implemented changes in Future-Present molecular behavior by running various programs on different computers simultaneously – while she brought feelings from other realities through portals to create a new technology that would help humanity.

Whenever Acada found a cure for contamination, she created feelings to protect it. Then she transferred it to the future in high-frequency, where it could be safe. It took a while for the Mirrors to figure out what Acada was *creating* through this strategy.

For instance, she contaminated herself with the energy of jealousy. Being in tune with her feelings and Self-Love, she discovered how to communicate with her spirit. She received channeled messages on how to clear the contamination within her. She worked with animals, plants, mountains, water, Light Beings, and other creations to help her build light bundles to heal the contamination. After finding the cure, she stored the information in her genetics.

This is how Acada found a solution to make the Mirrors accountable in the future. Accountability in the future will eventually travel back into the present and past to clear the damage done.

She rewrote linear time with the energy of pure intention and the Inca Cross. When the pure intention of Circular Time goes into the motion of feelings and is integrated into linear time, something extraordinary happens. A pure love story is created at a molecular level and transferred to the future in a higher frequency. The space where the story of linear time existed becomes obsolete, as does the linear past.

When Pure power is manifested in a story of love in the future of Circular Time, which is the future in high-frequency, the new feelings of the love story in the future that got transferred from the past create new possibilities that integrate into what Acada calls the Future-Present in high- frequency. In Acada's language, it is a new DNA, and it is the connection of the white and blue light, representing a new generation of beings without contamination. This DNA created with the *pure intention* feeling, and the Inca Cross, are part of the new technology of love.

The *Future-Present* in high-frequency is when the *present* = *the future*. It is when a possibility becomes energy ready to manifest. When future possibilities transfer to the present, those possibilities can be manifested because there is no opposition from the past. Once feelings have been transferred to the future, the past is obsolete – it no longer exists. The Future-Present is when the feelings of giving and receiving are the same and in balance. In our language, it is the feeling of unconditional love.

For instance, you might want to lose six pounds in the next two months. That is the future energy of the possibility. If you lose six pounds in two weeks, it is the manifestation of the present. So, if you manifest what you want, there is pure intention. If you failed in the attempt, it is because there is still a block that does not allow you to maintain your Future-Present Energy.

When we increase our light through Self-Love and use the principles of the Inca Cross, we can do this as well, and we can help Acada re-write and clear contaminations of blocks and limiting beliefs. It is the promise that if we choose to feel and are connected to spirit, we will always be connected to the future so humanity can survive. Eventually, peace will return to the planet. But if we as a human community decide to close our hearts and process information without feelings, we will destroy ourselves.

Acada explained that 5th-dimensional possibilities are humans' behaviors and opportunities that help us achieve higher frequency. Feelings and 5th-dimensional possibilities are fundamental because they generate the energy balance for humankind to exist and be alive. Every time you feel something in your heart, like love, trust, connection, awareness, compassion, self-value, happiness, and other feelings, you are generating possibilities for humanity in the future to be a better community. You create the opportunity for humanity to survive. Feelings are the key to having pure intentions. Remember, feelings are emotions that make movements and cycles of life. Still, low-frequency emotions do not create motion therefore they do not connect to the future to create possible solutions.

As a point of reference about how feelings and pure intentions work, Acada shared that the People of the Law of One represented their heart's messages and feelings, which were their pure intentions.

For instance, before the contamination, when a woman of Atlantis chose to become a mother or a man decided to be a father, they would go through a learning process; it was like going to college. First, they got to know themselves through Self-Love and understanding the responsibility of having a child. They learned to make choices that would provide the child physical, emotional, and genetic stability. This training took around seven years. Can you imagine going to college for seven years to learn to be a father or mother? It was a significant commitment.

They understood that their children would be their future, their next generation, and that they must be cautious in educating that child to bring balance to humanity and keep the expansion of light.

The Law of One took equal care with choosing their partners. For them, marriage was a commitment between two people at every level of creation. It was focused proactively on creating a future to have the foundation of a sturdy relationship in the present. For instance, Acada loved her husband Ta very much, and she knew that by loving and standing by him, she would help him be a better person in the future. He felt the same way. It was pure love intention.

Let's define what an illusion is. An illusion is a preconceived idea created by someone or a situation to hurt or use someone else. Illusions do not come from a loving heart. When we create with our pure intentions we begin with feelings: feelings create reality. An illusion destroyed Acada and Ta's marriage. When Acada saw her husband was unfaithful, she believed he did not want her anymore—and the woman she consulted at the council created the illusion that Ta did not love Acada anymore. Acada chose to remove herself and not interfere with his future.

While I was channeling this information, I was finding out new information about Acada and Ta. Che, who was listening to the conversation, explained, "The energy of misguiding creates blocks that takes away the ability to live with pure intention."

Acada and Ta were set up. The true story is that Ta went to a Mirror gathering where a woman gave him a drink, stimulating his frequency in an illusion. He thought he was with Acada when he was sexually involved with another woman. Then Ta found out that Acada had an abortion – in his mind, she had destroyed the baby who had represented their future. He closed his heart to Acada and left her.

Ta was also misled. Che said that "Ta was naïve and believe that everyone had good intentions. It was a time when people did not know the corruption and cruelty of the Mirrors because they were good actors." He was told that by supporting the Mirrors, that had the technology to help Acada, he could stop Acada from doing more "damage."

Ta believed that Acada was mentally sick and needed help. The Mirrors told him that Acada had to be separated from anyone to avoid harm. He thought they were helping Acada as she was separated from her children and removed from the council, and he said nothing to save her damaged reputation.

Ta did not know that Acada was separated from his Twin Cells, and from others, to be genetically experimented on to remove her light. I can't even imagine how hard it must have been for Acada and Ta. There was so much pain and confusion.

In my channeling, I was not allowed to see the specific details of what happened to her in the experiment labs. I know she was able to leave eventually, but she was sick for a while, and then she healed herself and worked to clear the contamination.

The general public did not trust her anymore because the Mirrors damaged her reputation. Only the people of the Law of One who were not contaminated knew she had pure intentions, so she worked with them.

Pure intention does not carry the energy of punishment. The Law of One people understood, analyzed, and researched why people choose what they choose. They did not believe in judging, punishing, or creating conflict. Then, they investigated why people did what they did. If a mistake was made, they helped them to understand their actions and set boundaries of light by giving accountability to restore the damage done.

Acada eventually found out that most council members were corrupt, and she saw that they were punishing others. Acada explained that we do not learn from punishment. One of our biggest misperceptions in this world is the belief that we teach by forcing pain. There is nothing to gain by hurting someone or imposing something on someone, something they do not want.

Acada wants us to understand that the reality of our future can be better if we know why people do what they do. We need to love, support, respect, and help others understand the consequences of their choices without punishing or hurting them. By loving, nurturing, honoring, and valuing, we can create a place to offer growth and expansion.

Remember, you are your Self-Love, your self-value, your choice, an offer to accept something higher, and an opening to create what you want to create in your heart.

When everything was being taken away from Acada to punish her, she knew she had to stand for what was more important to her, the values of love. She focused on bringing her message to her people.

Acada says, "If someone is taking experiences away from you as a punishment to teach you something, that is not coming from the light or reality. That comes from the perception of something that is not 'real.'"

As we expressed before, pure intention is an expression of personal value and love. We are valuable in every way because we, in our bodies, hold cellular memories. Many stories have been created throughout time that will help change the future for the betterment of humanity.

Therefore, you are very valuable. In the energy of reality, it is imperative to choose to see your value and to stand for it in the same way Acada did to help her people: us.

One day, I noticed I had a deep sadness. I knew it was not me but a memory of Acada. I was looking at the experience through her eyes. I had done this before, but this time was different. Acada was also observing the situation through someone else's memories.

I saw Ta in a room in his new house. He was married to someone else. This observation was a memory of Ta after Acada had the abortion. He was different— sad and shut down. Ta was next to the bed, holding an object in his hand, and as I looked more closely, I could see it was a necklace. It was a dark green crystal shaped like a circle, and I knew somehow that this necklace belonged to Acada. Ta was thinking about Acada. I felt he still loved her. But little by little, he was forgetting her.

The deep sadness of the loss of Fatherlove was constantly with him, but he began to forget that, too. I sensed that he had to hide his feelings from someone— not his wife, but someone else.

I saw his wife standing outside the room near the door and looking at him. She was not in love with him; she had married Ta to spy on him, and she had to ensure that Ta would not reconnect with Acada. She went to Ta's father and warned him that Ta was still in love with Acada. I did not see why Ta's Father was concerned about it.

Ta believed that Acada killed their unborn son because she had been contaminated, gotten sick, and lost her mind. That was the true story of what had happened to him; he had been contaminated and mentally sick.

Acada's memories took me back to the time she lost the baby, before the 2nd explosion in Atlantis. There was a day that Acada could not find Ta. She searched for him everywhere and finally found him on a stone sidewalk, sitting on his knees beside a dead body. Ta had killed a man and eaten the flesh from his face. Blood was everywhere, on Ta's clothes, the man's face, body, and the sidewalk. Ta looked confused, like he was unaware of what he had done. Acada approached him slowly. It was not the first time she had seen this. She took him gently by the arm with love and walked him back to their house.

This memory reminded me of my dream about Acada on my first night in Cuzco, Peru. In the dream, I saw Acada walking fast on the stone roads and looking for someone. Years later, I figured out that both events were the same event.

In the 3rd dimension, the extreme behavior or epidemic of blocks and limiting beliefs in Atlantis were like being overdosed by drinking alcohol. People's brain communication pathways were interrupted, affecting how it works and creating mental confusion.

These interruptions changed their moods and behaviors. It made it harder to think clearly and act reasonably. With their clouded judgment, increasing the risk of experiencing acts of violence and harming themselves and others, some of them would kill themselves.

They also had trouble recalling what they had done under the influence of the blocks and limiting beliefs, causing them to lose their coping mechanisms, like the ability to face and manage painful or difficult emotions, after seeing the damage they have done under the influence.

Channeling Acada's experiences was complex because the stories did not come to me in chronological order, but in bits and pieces. It was like I had to put a puzzle together. I knew Acada wanted me to channel from a 5th-dimensional, non-linear time perspective because feeling the experiences was important, but it took a long while.

Looking back, I know better now. I had several blocks and limiting beliefs, which slowed down the process. One of my blocks was that I was not good enough to receive this information. I thought I had to be perfect and have everything figured out, and I spent too much time in the past, which led me to behave as a victim or survivor.

Acada hid Ta in their house for several weeks, and no one knew about it. I still remember a morning when I woke up and gazed through the window, when I had a vision. Ta was sleeping on a bed next to a window, and I was experiencing Acada in her house, taking care of Ta. I had deep pain in my heart. It was Acada's pain, while praying for Father Creator to come and help Ta.

A few days after that memory, I was in a hurry, getting ready to go out, when I suddenly had another vision. I stopped and stood in the living room to witness it. I saw Ta and Acada having a conversation. Ta looked worried and sad.

He said to Acada. "I know, eventually, I will forget you, but you must remember that I will never stop loving you." I knew little about the story then but seeing them waiting for the worst to happen broke my heart. Ta was never the same after that encounter.

There was another memory of Acada in the time before she found the cure. I felt like I was Acada getting ready to go to Puma Punku. After she contaminated herself, she had found the cure. She desired to go there with her people that were not contaminated. She wanted to take the technology of the cure to Puma Punku before the Mirrors could get their hands on it and manipulate it.

Her memories of the past came to her. She had hoped to find the cure for the contamination in Puma Punku. But after what had happened to Ta, she could not overcome her feelings. How could she? Going to Puma Punku would mean leaving Ta, and she changed her mind and decided to stay with Ta.

I have felt her broken heart several times because she did not go to Puma Punku. She wondered how events in Atlantis would have unfolded if she had gone with the team of scientists to Puma Punku. How many people would she have saved from getting sick? She thought about how to stop linear time to prevent all the damage from coming to her people and how to prevent society from being destroyed. According to her, the only possibility she could see was to take all the contaminations into herself, even though it would be hard on her body. She hoped she could find the cure— as long as she was connected to Father's Books of Light. Now, it was time to go. Acada found the cure. I felt a sense of peace and love in her heart. The energy of gratitude flowed in her body as a delicate textile moved by a gentle breeze. I sensed her feeling of accomplishment everywhere in her body, and I felt her love for her father. She said, "I did it!"

When you've had a traumatic experience, you can only relate to someone with the same experience. Ta knew about his mistakes and did not want Acada to make the same mistakes under the influence of the contaminations. Ta worried about her. When he discovered Fatherlove's death, he believed Acada was contaminated. His father took advantage of that and suggested Ta bring Acada to his wellness center to help her.

This was not the first time his father had offered this option. When Ta was young and newly married to Acada, his father excitedly told him about the new experiment he was running. "All good for our society," his father had told him. Ta explained to his father that he wanted Acada to remain as pure as she was, but now, things were different. Ta believed in his father and thought his father could help Acada.

Ta did not know that his father would try to manipulate Acada's DNA, and neither Acada nor Ta knew that Ta's father was working for the Mirrors. Acada was experimented on with the misappropriated Maldek technology. The Mirrors used the energy of her neutrons to see if they could reproduce them and create a new, strong race of people without feelings. They were not, as it turned out, able to do that because the energy of love Acada had for Fatherlove was strong, and they could not shut down her protocols of feeling.

Acada was not the only woman being experimented on at the center. She observed the damage done to others. She saw women of the light forced to get pregnant with babies of male energy but without the light of the female energy. These were a type of android. The babies were born damaged, which was traumatizing for the mothers from the light protocol. It was a community contamination.

Ta's father didn't want Ta to know the specifics of his work, which is how Acada was able to leave the center. He did not want Ta to be suspicious, and it was time to remove Acada and make Ta believe that his father's work was able to help Acada.

However, his father didn't realize that Acada didn't trust Ta anymore and wouldn't confide in him. She did not talk with Ta about what she had seen— she knew he would not believe her. Still, she chose to infect herself to find the cure for all the contaminations.

Ta's new wife believed that he and Acada would reconnect again. When Ta's new wife saw Ta gazing at Acada's necklaces, she told Ta's father. To protect the Mirrors, Ta's father went to Acada and tried to force himself on her sexually. She refused him, as he expected she would, but then he told Ta that Acada was sexually provoking him.

Ta was confused and angry. He wanted to protect Acada from possible behaviors of contamination; he knew how it felt to be contaminated, but he was also jealous.

I still remember clearly when Ta came into a room where Acada was. He was angry and moved his hands up and down. He looked at Acada like he had so much pain he could not take it anymore. He asked her to stop provoking his father. "I am not," Acada responded.

Ta was in so much emotional pain. He did not believe her and used physical force with his hand to stop Acada. Ta constricted her neck. When he touched Acada, he was exposed to the cure of the contaminations that came from Acada's body. He energetically downloaded the cure to his own body, bringing him back into 5th-dimensional reality.

For the first time in a long time, Ta could observe reality without the blocks and limiting beliefs of the 3rd dimension. He observed from a perspective of future high-frequency. As Ta felt Acada's pure intentions and Books of Light, he saw the truth: she had been manipulated into having the abortion. He also remembered who she was before the contamination. But it was too late. Acada was dead. He had killed her.

Ta cried for a long time next to her body. He touched her body and wanted to bring her back to life and tell her how much he loved her. He had lost her. His Twin Cell.

Now he knew the truth; he had the memories of the essence of love and also the experiences and memories of what are illusions, blocks, and limiting beliefs. Acada had transferred those Books of Light to him, that helped him to remember who he was. in spirit and love. He was aware of the Mirrors' experiments done by his father.

Ta had a conversation with his father. Ta told him that before Acada's death, she had downloaded the light into him, and he knew the truth. "The Mu people were here to be guardians of the water. They were not here to serve you; you used them for their knowledge." Ta continued by saying, "Technology can't replace love. Stop using Technology to hide your desires."

He remembered what his father used to say to him: "You are weak. You do not have direction and have to rely on Acada. You cannot stand on your own." Then Ta released those thoughts from his mind, and from his heart and told himself, "She is my dance partner." By this, he meant Acada was his Twin Cell.

Ta left Acada on the floor and went to his father's experimental center. Once there, he helped the people being experimented upon escape and set the place on fire. Ta escaped to what is now Belize and Guatemala. Eventually, he died there. Ta's actions helped the final destruction of Atlantis.

CHAPTER 25
Puma Punku: Observing How Acada Clears Contamination

*Your experiences in the past of linear time are not who you are.
Let them go. You are your future in high-frequency connected
with your spirit, now. Acada*

After Acada's death, The Law of One people in Puma Punku did not want the temple of light, with the knowledge of the Mu, to get into the Mirrors' hands and access their technology. But without Acada in Puma Punku, there was only one option: to destroy the entrance to the 5th dimension in the temple of Puma Punku. The Law of One created light from the sky, and the temple's rocks crumbled, and it was destroyed.

Once, I observed a past life of a man who was a guardian of a 5th-dimensional portal in Puma Punka. In this reality, I could see the strength of the portal of light that came from the other side of the portal. This man was waiting for the arrival of Acada and the people from Atlantis to cross the portal of light. I sensed that he felt there was not enough time to get everyone through. The stronger the 3rd-dimensional energy got, the harder it became to keep the door open, the energy was contaminating and taking over the planet.

I could feel his indecisiveness and struggle about waiting a little longer or closing the portal. Tears were coming out of his eyes. He kept telling himself, "Be strong and hold your space." He thought about the people that could not cross the portal, including Acada. The man took a deep breath and closed the portal, choosing to close the light door and disconnect the 5th dimension energy.

Occasionally, I would still feel Acada's memories in my body. The memory of when she decided to stay in Atlantis and contaminated herself to find the cure. Also, when she intended to go to Puma Punku, taking the cure to heal the planet and the people by reconnecting the energy of the 5th dimension back to Atlantis. I would sense The Law of One, in Puma Punku, waiting for Acada's arrival to activate the records and the protocols of love, counting on these records to heal, neutralize, and eliminate the contamination. I felt the melancholy of the Law of Ones because Acada didn't make it to Puma Punku, as she had died.

Feeling these low-frequency memories meant that there was still contamination in my body, and there was clearing to do to let the past go. Yes, I had to learn how to close the past and learn to focus on the future with high-frequency. The spirit of the Mountains in Peru and Bolivia had a plan to help me, a trip to Puma Punku.

One afternoon, while working at my computer, I heard a sound behind me. I turned around and saw a portal of light open, and a mountain appeared. It was happy to see me and share his message with me. It said, "You will learn how to rewrite stories." I saw my energy going through the portal and claiming a mountain that had a golden light around it. I knew it was time to go back to Peru and Bolivia. I made the necessary plans, and this time, I traveled alone. It was the message.

Before leaving for Peru, I did some research. I found that the native people in Tiahuanaco believed Puma Punku was where human creation started. I hoped to find more stories among the native people to support the vision and dreams I'd been having.

It was my second trip to Puma Punku. I flew into the airport of Juliaca and traveled by car to Puno, where I spent a few nights in a nice, safe hotel with a rustic adobe style. The food made from scratch with fresh products like corn and potatoes tasted good. The sensation of the flavor of the gentle soup stayed in my mouth for a while.

It reminded me of those Sunday visits to the places near my hometown, Huancayo.

On the first day, I met with a mystic tourist guide who knew some of the ancient histories of that area. His name was Aldo. I asked him if he knew about Acada and her story, but he knew nothing about it.

On the first day, Aldo offered to take me around Puno on his motorcycle. I still remember the motorcycle's sound while driving on the road next to Lake Titicaca and the cold wind hitting my face – Puno is at a high altitude in the Andes! It is part of an Altiplano, a high plateau that formed along with the tectonic uplift of the Andeans mountains. It is home to Lake Titicaca, the highest navigable lake in the world.

That day, it became chilly later in the afternoon, but seeing the open fields and the mountains of different shapes was nice.

The next day, we traveled from Puno to Tiahuanaco. It took us almost four hours, including our stop at the Bolivian border, where I had to go through customs. This was my first time in Puma Punku, and I did not know what to expect. But I could feel every part of me being guided to be there.

Aldo had noticed my energy and was surprised by how much knowledge I had about the place. He said he knew someone who might be able to help me. Before going to Puma Punku, we took a stop. While I was sitting in the back of the car, Aldo entered a house and came out with a man I didn't know, an older man around sixty-five. He had the dark color of skin marked with the tan of the strong sun from the high-altitude weather.

He sat in the front seat of the car, seeming quite serious, but nice. He invited me to do a ceremony together that night and make an offering to the mountains to find the answers to my questions. This is the way of ancient people in some of the Andean areas; they have to do an offering ceremony to the spirit of the mountain before getting any information.

After meeting the older man, we went to Puma Punku. I was present for every step I took when I entered the site. I felt the ground, the soil, and I touched the stones. The air was very rich. Breathing deeply, my lungs filled with pure oxygen.

Standing by the rocks at Puma Punku was a very humbling experience. For the first time, I was physically standing in a place where the events I had seen in my vision happened instead of feeling Acada's Books of Light. This was what Acada had called an "action moment." It was not a memory, nor imagination, but a reality. I was standing in this place with so much history.

This place is where the Law of Ones, that escaped from Atlantis, had arrived, hoping to find the cure. They hid the Books of Light here, which they had brought. This was where the Pre-Incas learned to do ancestral clearings and transferred the knowledge to the Incas.

It was an honor to be there, holding and feeling the rocks with all those stories. The more I felt the rocks, the more I could feel and channel Acada. Acada was so gentle while she taught me. I could see her in a different dimension, guiding me through my intuition, to touch specific rocks and activate some of their energy into my energetic space. As I continued holding the rocks, more memories came in clearly. I could sense how much Acada loved her people and why the People of the Light loved her. For them, she was the essence of love and wisdom.

By touching the rocks, I could feel the stories stored in the memories of electrons, neutrons, and protons of the stones. I was receiving information about what had happened in the past, from a 5th-dimensional perspective. I was learning how to use energy!

My heart was beating fast. I observed the advanced technology in the stones' cut, shape, and structure. I saw pieces of the rocks from the Temple of Light in Puma Punku, all that was left after the destruction. I imagined how it had looked before it was destroyed. It had to have been a challenging task to build the temple; the weight of some of the stones could be measured in tons. Then, I saw the most powerful evidence: the Inca Crosses carved into some of the rocks all over Puma Punku. My best description is seeing energetic holograms inside the Inca Cross crosses that held records of memories of events throughout history. It was like being in a chemistry lab. Just as I had seen it in my visions and dreams. It was the Temple of Light from the 5th dimension!

It was the place where people knew about the molecular behavior of the energy of the 5th dimension, connected to every living thing. There are no words to explain how I felt. I had to understand the process of the Inca Cross, before I visited this place, to understand the Law of One beliefs.

I stood in Puma Punku. In a quiet space, I wondered, "What was my role in this story? Why was I chosen to receive this information?" I felt overwhelmed. It gave me so much to think about. But I also felt the love of the mountains, Acada, Che, and others. I had to stay in my heart. I told myself to be in the feeling of courage and to focus on learning.

While holding a rock, I heard Acada mention again, as I had to remember this: when feelings are in high-frequencies and Circular Time, they can rewrite stories of low-frequency. She called this process "Rewriting Stories of the Past." She told me that rewriting a story is a process that requires a high-frequency witness to observe the story. By observing the story, with the pure intention of having a better outcome, without pain and suffering, it is possible to connect to a Light Being or several Light Beings, who can then make the changes to create a new love story. The Light Beings remove the blocks and limited beliefs from the past. Removing the blocks brings the future of high-frequency to the present through, Energy Gifts, to balance and fulfill a new story of love.

As a training, Acada shared an experience of a woman who lost her identity because of the conflicts she had with her husband. The intent of the story was to teach me how to rewrite stories of limitation. The woman was kind, nurturing and compassionate but she was married to a man contaminated by the energy of hate. The contamination had happened when this man was a child and accepted the idea that he was not good enough because he had not done well academically in middle and high school. He did not pursue a college education because he believed he was not smart and grew insecure and angry about it.

He felt inferior to his wife because she had a college education, and he was always acting out to prove he was better than her. For instance, he would say, "I make more money that you. You are not good enough for me," and lose his temper and make her feel small.

Caught in his illusion, he was not connected to his heart. He said hurtful things to diminish her, even in her role as a mother. By acting in that way, he was hurting himself and their beautiful boy, who eventually learned to be angry like his father. His wife also changed and got contaminated. She was resentful and blocked her heart; she did not see that she was also hurting her child.

I witnessed Acada observing this experience and healing the woman. She held a space of alignment, which was the knowledge of the love of Father and Mother Creators, in a molecular behavior of balance of female and male energies.

Acada did not make the man and the woman right or wrong for their behavior. Instead, she observed their behavior, from the perspective of Self-Love, to find the source of contamination. She saw the conflict or radiation in an atom.

Acada brought energy from the future of high-frequency, placed it on the damaged area, and cleared the block from the woman's body. Then, Acada observed the future, where she saw different options of a new reality for this woman so she could be without the contamination. She saw in the light of the woman's spirit the energy of the best possibility of this situation. Acada brought it into the present as an Energy Gift to give to the woman. She then invited the woman to receive the Energy Gift and place it in her heart to create a better situation. It was so beautiful to witness that Acada connected to the woman's spirit for her to choose the best option for the situation. It was not Acada's choice but the choice of the spirit of the woman, her pure essence making a choice, and Acada connected them. According to Acada, this is how prosperity is created, reconnecting to the source of spirit, which is the future of high-frequency.

Throughout this process, I also noticed that Acada's Self-Love energy was represented as a pink crystal, gently moving and floating in an open golden space, in her heart. She transferred the light of the pink crystal from her heart to the hearts of the mother, father, and son to heal them. It was a process of several weeks, but the father, mother, and son all came to a better understanding. The contamination was removed.

Every energy healing, in the 5th dimension, happens with feelings because the feelings change the molecular behavior. Accordingly, Acada's process transfers contaminated stories from the present to the future by frequently reflecting light and feelings. The information is then rewritten in the future with the Self-Love of the Light Beings. It becomes a collective, high-frequency story of love. By doing this, the Light Beings are closing the linear time of the past until it is completely gone. By eliminating the past in love's frequency, it is like the contamination never happened. This process stops memories of pain, suffering, and trauma. Unburdened by all this, we can make better choices. We are no longer influenced by the low-frequencies of the past and have a better present and future.

I had so many questions and wanted to talk to the native people. Over that day in Puma Punku, I tried to communicate with them via a translator in their ancient language, but when I asked questions about the past or their ancestors, they grew suspicious and looked away. Perhaps they did not want to talk because, in the past, soldiers from Spain had destroyed their ancestors, and they were afraid to be hurt again. It also felt like they were protecting something.

Finally, I met a man who shared with me that he had heard from the native people about a powerful woman who oversaw the arrival of people to Tiahuanaco and Puma Punku from another civilization, long ago. He also said that the people who arrived could touch the temple's rocks in Puma Punku and recharge in the light of the site. I found it a confirmation of the experiences I was having.

Back at the hotel, I met with the older man. We ate and prepared the offering for the ceremony that night. The plan was to place the offering bundle in the fire. While preparing the bundle, I noticed a flat white sheet of paper, around 10x14 inches. Also, there were several hard-shell nuts on the table. The man cracked open a nutshell and looked inside, and I also glared at it. I felt the energy of my boys. He was reflecting the feelings of love I have for my boys.

While working, I felt a Light Being's presence, and he instructed me to ask him, "Do you remember the face of God?"

The older man paused in deep thought. I looked at the sheet of white paper on the table as it began to take shape— a three-dimensional face. That face was the older man's understanding of God. He had the gift of shifting energy, which I had never seen before. His feelings of Passion for the Life of the Inca Cross had manifested his thoughts in a physical reality.

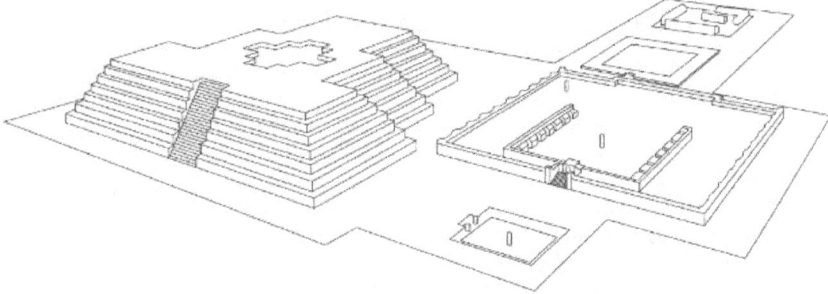

The next day, we went to the Tiahuanaco site. It was raining heavily, and I did not see more than three people. I kept walking and got to the top of the small mountain next to the Inca Cross Pyramid. Lightning vibrated through the sky and loud crashes from the north, south, east, and west came together above me. Light downloaded into my body. Having strong energy from light is a way to increase the frequency, and that is what lightning does— and did for me.

When I got to the hotel in Puno, I felt very ill, like I was dying. It felt like I was burning from the inside out. The blast of electricity gave me a mild headache, and I felt weak and numb, with tingling in my arms and legs.

The next day, I was even worse. My body held extreme weakness, and I still felt the burning sensation within me. While resting on the bed, I saw a portal of light inside my stomach. There, I saw a man—the older man who'd performed the ceremony two days before. This time, he walked with me into an underground tunnel in Tiahuanaco while talking to me. He pointed to the walls in the tunnel as he showed me drawing on the walls, but I could not understand what he was saying.

It took two days to feel better and get ready to go back home but weeks to recover and return to a normal state of health, mind, and strength.

I found, in the aftermath of that experience with the electricity of lightning, that my ability to remember past lives got stronger, as were my feelings of love. I could identify the source of the contaminations much more quickly.

A year later, when I returned to Tiahuanaco and Puma Punku, I heard that archeologists had just found an underground tunnel under Tiahuanaco. It was an amazing discovery. It was the same tunnel I saw in my visions the day after I got hit by lighting. It was a confirmation that my experience was real.

CHAPTER 26
Machu Picchu: Clearing Contamination

> *My work is to support light and love. I do not support the behaviors of victims or survivors, but I support your essence of "Self-Love"—your spirit power to rewrite behaviors that do not work for you. Acada*

Five days after my trip to Puma Punku and Tiahuanaco in Bolivia, I was on the train to Machu Picchu. I felt very peaceful when suddenly I heard a voice. It was a Light Being. He said, "Since you left Puma Punku, you have in your energetic space a low-frequency entity, "Do not be scared. I am here to help you release this entity in Machu Picchu."

He continued, "If you become afraid, it will lower your frequency. Stay in the energy of loving yourself. I want to make sure you know I am here with you, and when you notice the low-frequency entity, I will be there with you at the right time and place to clear it."

Some Light Beings were waiting in Machu Picchu for me to help with the release process. I was guided to the right-hand side of the site's entrance, and I walked on the stone road next to the stone walls.

When I got there, I felt I had to stop. Without thinking, I placed my hand on a rock that was a stone wall next to the dirt sidewalk. I held my hand there for three minutes until I saw, from my chest, a release of dark energy. It was like a black shadow. It had the shape of a human but had a lack of light.

I remembered not to be afraid and to observe with the energy of Self-Love, but it was not easy. This experience was new to me. I connected with Light Beings before but had yet to experience shadow entities coming to this reality from another dimension. I had several questions for Acada: "Why was I carrying this energy for the last three days in my space? What did it mean?" I was surprised by her response.

The dark entity was the consciousness of the woman who advised Acada in the time of Atlantis to have an abortion. I was experiencing her community's experience. By observing Acada's story, the experience manifested in my space. My energy had become a bridge when I connected to the past through the Books of Light. That bridge had brought this woman's energies into the present to make her accountable by reflecting and magnifying my energy of Self-Love.

Self-Love magnetizes and exposes things for what they are in the future. It may be hard to understand, but in Circular Time, I was their future. She was transferred through my energy in the present from her past. It happened because I witnessed the damage she had done to Acada. As a witness of the high-frequency future, which is the observation of the spirit energy, I had become part of the accountability process of the 5th dimension. It is how ancestral, community, and personal DNA clearing happens.

The Light Beings at Machu Picchu witnessed how the woman's energy was dissolved. For over 15,000 years, she had corrupted others with her choices. In her molecular memories or Books of Light, I did not see she had made many high choices to evolve into the light. Her energy was too weak to survive in the future, where we observe and witness choices we have made in the past to rewrite them to light.

In her future, our present, she saw through the reflection of Self-Love of the Light Being's, the pain and sorrow she had created for others, and that energy returned to her. She did not have enough Self-Love experience to correct the damage she had done to others. She felt the pain and destruction she did all at once and could not rewrite the damage because of the lack of love in her energetic field. The energy of the damages she inflicted was stronger than her Self-Love, which wiped her out. In the energetic world, nobody destroys us but ourselves, and we do so by making low-frequency choices.

It took me a moment to realize that this woman's energy was dissolved, and some of Acada's past was clearing. Everyone affected by this woman was also clearing, and the energy of the 5th dimension was increasing.

Acada reminded me that this was the beginning of a new evolution. We are all going to clear the linear energy from the past. The planet's energy is rising, and it's time to release these dark energies, blocks, and limiting beliefs from our cellular memories. Earth is starting its ascension. The ancestral clearing will become stronger, and the new generations of sons and daughters with values and principles of Books of Light will be releasing blocks and limiting beliefs more easily.

After this experience in Machu Picchu with the entity, I saw the impact of my choices in a completely different way. I realized that I could create or destroy my connection to the future. When energy destroys itself, it means it no longer exists. Nothing is left, even from its previous or future existence. After the entity's energy was destroyed, part of me did not believe it, so I tried to see if I could find the entity in the unseen world, but I could not find it anywhere. There was not even a single molecule carrying the energy of the woman. The memory of the event was there, but her essence did not exist anymore.

I decided that I didn't want to contaminate others or myself. Acada came to my assistance and sent me a message. *"If someone gets angry and says you are not good enough, and you accept the idea, that energy of the idea of you not being good enough comes into your space and attaches to you energetically, creating a block. It will take you then out of balance. It will trap you in the illusion because you believe it. It will stop you from focusing on what you want in your present. If you choose not to believe in the illusion, the feelings of the 5th dimension will remove the block. Removing the blocks will bring clarity, truth, and confirmation that you are good enough and have choices in what you want to believe."*

Forgetting about the past is one of the best weapons of corruption. Throughout history, so many people have gotten away with damaging others because we do not know the truth of the situation. But when we find out the truth, it is the beginning of something new.

When I saw what happened with Ta and Acada in Atlantis, it was a way of remembering the truth. From my 3rd-dimensional perspective, before I knew the truth, I had wondered why Ta was not there for Acada. I had assumed he didn't have courage and didn't care for her. Sometimes I even believed she was better off without him. Those ideas were in my head, and there was an invisible force trying to keep those ideas alive.

Was it possible that the invisible force trying to prevent me from learning the truth was the Mirrors? Yes, I had to consider that because the distortion of the truth kept mental blocks in my mind. So, even though it was sad to see the story of Ta and Acada, my heart wanted to know more to see reality for what it is.

During this trip to Puma Punku, Tiahuanaco, was when I awakened to the experience of Acada in two realities. Acada in her life in Atlantis and Acada as the Light Being from the Future in high-frequency. In her past in Atlantis, Acada's pure intentions were spiritual food to her people. She was gentle, loving, and peaceful. She was powerful and valuable in her choices. I don't think she was aware of how significant and profound the effect she had on the well-being of others. I felt her thoughts, her dreams, and the respect she had for her people that gave her the determination to find the cure for the contamination.

In my heart, I wanted Acada to survive and travel to Puma Punku to release the healing energy to the whole planet. But as hard as it was, I had seen the true story.

Past Acada was the one I had felt in my body, her sadness, and her pain for losing her children. I felt her struggles and constant willpower to focus on the Future. There was so much darkness around her. She had to always be on alert not to step into the dark shadows of the past in low- frequency.

Future Acada was a consciousness that communicated mentally with me. She was a 5th-dimensional experience of love and full acceptance that observed and taught me to rewrite damaged stories into stories of love.

I also noticed that the more I saw (I call it remembering) the experiences of Past Acada, the more the truth was revealed; the information became my outline to make the changes I did in my everyday life. I was letting go of the behaviors of a victim and survivor to a being of love in an energetic journey that makes sense to me now. I also learned that more possibilities are present when we clear the past because of the stronger connection to the future.

It was future Acada that guided my trips to the ancient sites in Peru to witness Past Acada's story. She was working in my molecular energy, placing the codes or Books of Light memories in the rocks to clear the contamination that Past Acada had created in Atlantis. Little by little, I started feeling the codes and analyzing them.

CHAPTER 27
My Five Points of Power

One day, I asked myself if it was even possible to clear all the illnesses on this planet. I was at a low point in my life. It was hard to see people getting sick, not finding the right medication, or having no money to purchase insurance or medicine. I have seen people choosing between buying food or medication or becoming homeless because of medical bills. I would feel

Five Points of Power

some people's pain, frustration, and hopeless energy, and it hurt to see them struggling.

There is nothing to learn from scarcity. I was already on my journey of clearing blocks and limiting beliefs, but I wanted more. I wanted so much to stop the source of all illnesses, and inside me, I felt there was a way to do this.

At first, I did not know why; I believed that the source of all illnesses was an original illness that created the others. I learned that linear time in the 3rd dimension contributes to generating illness. But what was the source? While searching in the unseen world for information about the first disease ever created, I encountered illnesses that attacked me as a way of protecting themselves. It was hard on my body because I was using lots of energy and was not recharging as fast as I needed.

I got sick for several weeks. I was exhausted, and I could hardly move. My legs hurt, my kidney was inflamed, and my liver was almost ready to shut down. My anxiety worsened, and my energy depleted so rapidly. I decided to take a break.

Once I got stronger again, I continued researching. One morning, I saw the source of all illnesses. It is an idea created within the mind. I recalled that moment when Prophet Thoth referred to the creation of the idea as a bubble of air. The idea was inside, and the bubble was the container that held the idea. Then I saw it: the container that retained the idea was contaminated and created illnesses. There were tiny black dots attached to a white moveable wall as the skin of the tomatoes that holds the fruit inside of it. Wow! It was amazing. I saw the creation of the illness. But who contaminated the container?

The answer was there all along. It was a subconscious energy, low in frequency, acting as a predator. And using linear time to manipulate a neutron to contaminate the container, by fragmenting the Five Points of Power symbol. Without the Five Points of Power, our strongest feelings, we can't connect to the 5th dimension and balance in the energy of the Mother Creator.

After that, the separation of the conscious from the sub-conscious energy happens without the protection given by the Five Points of Power.

Then, Linear time gets inside a neutron and damages it by taking it out of balance, breaking down the energy of direction, which is the male energy, and separating it from the proton. The idea of behaving as a victim or a survivor appears in the cell, and then the energy of the damaged neutron attacks and takes over the cell.

The contaminated neutron is trapped in the energy of linear time in the 4th dimension. It is brainwashed and overtaken by illusions. The illusions drain its energy and are given to low-frequency, subconscious, dark entities that feed from that energy. The neutron knows it must have the energy to be alive and will anything to survive; therefore, it will take the proton's or electron's energy.

The damaged neutron bleeds creative energy, the female energy from the proton in the same nucleolus to survive and recharge. While feeding on the energy from the proton, which is a violation, it sends messages to the proton,

"You are not good enough."

"You are not loveable."

"You are an inconvenience."

"Nobody wants you."

These are, of course, blocks and limiting beliefs. The proton then believes the story, making it easy for the damaged neutron to take its energy.

The corrupted neutron will disconnect the subconscious and conscious energies attached to it, take over the subconscious energy of the 5th dimension, and lower it to the 3rd-dimensional frequency. Once the conscious and subconscious are separated, it creates a 3rd dimension block in the subconscious protocol, so the information of the 5th dimension is not accessible. It is like having your internet services disconnected.

By disconnecting the damaged neutron from the Light Beings and other creations of a higher source, the damaged neutron becomes a bridge for contamination and communication among low-frequency creations of the 3rd dimension. And this is when it happens: the female and male force, or "creation" and "direction," do not match. In the bubble that contains the idea, there were tiny black dots which are low-frequency, subconscious behaviors that accept parasites, mutations, viruses, and other illnesses.

The manipulation of the subconscious energy started with the Mirrors in their desperate desire to survive the meteorite. Their energy was not high enough to reincarnate in a body because of the low-frequency choices. So, they decided to separate the Twin Cells and integrate their own energy into the Law of One's subconscious by making and keeping them sick. Therefore, the Mirrors were able to survive, inside the energetic field of the Law of Ones' as long as linear time would exit.

For instance, Acada explained the energy of sexual abuse. When a person forces himself onto another person, it contaminates one or several neutrons of the victim. The neutrons store the corrupted subconscious energy of the attacker and event. Therefore, the victim is constantly replaying the memories of the attack. She gets stuck in the past of linear time. But suppose the Five Points of Power is rebuilt. In that case, the Twin Cell's energies are reintegrated and connected to the high-frequency of the future. Then, the predator's subconscious is released out of the neutron. The neutron's energy returns to Circular Time.

Mother Creator's energy plays a decisive role in integrating a damaged neutron. Mother Creator's blue light of her Five Points of Power penetrates the corrupted neutron to clear the illusion, holding the dark subconscious energy accountable.

As part of the healing process, I observed that Mother Creator's energy comes in a blue crystal light to the corrupted neutron. First, she separates the low-frequency dark subconscious entity from all the other protocols. Then, she removes the corrupted subconsciousness that took over the neutron and places the dark entity in an energetic container created using the high-frequency future.

In this way, the subconsciousness of the predator can't take life from anyone— it simply dissipates and stops existing. Then Mother Creator heals the subconscious energy of the victim by using feeling codes so the subconscious can start to feel again and feed light to the conscious protocol. The conscious and the subconscious reconnect again to co-create.

Another illustration is the story of one of my clients, where a damaged neutron interfered with the relationship between her as a mother and her son. The mother loved her son very much. When it was time for him to go to college, it was very hard for her because she was constantly worried about him being on his own and making his own choices. The mother wanted to be always available in case he needed her. It was unhealthy because she held back what she wanted to create for herself, like making new friends and having fun.

I saw the damaged neutron inside one of her atoms. It was contaminated with the idea that her son needed her. Accordingly, their relationship was based on needing each other. Then I witnessed the energy of the Five Points of Power that removed the illusion of the damaged neutron. The neutron got stronger and brighter. The Five

Points of Power of Mother Creator transformed this mother's energy. This mother's relationship with her son changed. It became a relationship of Circular Time, a relationship of trust. Eventually, the son became his own person without the interference of his mother's worries and insecurities.

During the process, the damaged neutron can choose to stand for the light. If the damaged neutron decides to stay in low-frequency, it gets removed, and a new neutron is invited to match the proton in a Twin Cell energy: the love of the light creation. Mother Creator then creates a new connection, a balance of Twin Cell energy of the conscious and subconscious. This guaranties that Mother's Five Points of Power will never be removed from the balance of the atom again.

The electrons of the balanced atom will reflect the new balance of the proton and neutron and share that with the other atoms in the body. Father Creator's Twin Cell energy will connect the proton and neutron to the future in high-frequency, a bundle of higher possibilities to be manifested in the present.

Corrupted neutrons can be inherited from ancestors. I observed that Andean shamans, with the help of the Light Beings, travel to the 4th dimension in linear time to find the low-frequency stories of the past, stored in the atoms, and clear them. When I observed Andean shamans, I saw that they represent the love of Mother Creator. They are trained to stand firm in their symbols of feelings to break through the protective shield of the corrupted neutrons.

The Andean shamans use the Inca Way protocol of love, Acada's technology, to travel to the damaged neutron space and create expansion and love in its place. If the contaminated neutron chooses to create love again, the Andean shaman reflects Mother Creator's Five Points of Power to the damaged cell, it reactivates the Five Points of Power of the damaged neutron or creates a new symbol of the Five Points of Power in the neutron, reconnecting it to the 5th dimension.

When the Andean Shaman reflects the energy of Mother Creator to the neutron; it helps to awaken his power and increase his frequency by making higher choices. This opens the possibility of going back to space before linear time existed – before the explosion happened in the universe.

Mother Creator, with the blue light of the Five Points of Power, removes the 3rd-dimensional, dark subconscious entity and places it in a container, puts it in the center of her Inca Cross's energy, and locks it up. The colors of the feelings of the Inca Cross start moving around the dark subconscious and activate her feelings. By reflecting the colors of the feelings, it neutralizes the energy in the container that holds the contaminated ideas and thoughts. This brings awareness to the dark subconscious of the damage and choices made in low-frequency. This is how Mother Creator creates accountability.

During this process, the color of the container that holds the idea becomes light. Then, Father Creator's Future Protocol merges with Mother Creator's process. Father Creator's energy stimulates a new movement of feelings. Those feelings remove from the corrupted subconscious what the entity took from others —love, abundance, and confidence. These are then restored to the person who was damaged in the process.

The subconsciousness, devoid of energy, feels empty because his existence was based on stealing energy from others. I could not help thinking about people that had become wealthy by stealing from others.

At this point, the twin proton is aware that the damaged neutron is healing and sends waves of energy of love. When the damaged neutron accepts the proton's love, he again falls in love with her and sends love back to her. They are again in the process of giving and receiving and creating unconditional love for each other. They are reconnected. Then the proton, with memories of fragmented love experiences, is restored to a single, united experience and returns to the 5th dimension.

The corrupted subconscious, supported by linear time, ceases to exist since it does not know how to create in love. It is about love and how we can reach the next level. We can only move forward with the pure intentions of our hearts, which is Self-Love. When Che was training me to release blocks and limiting beliefs, I did not know I was going inside the atoms, reflecting my Self-Love, and witnessing his work. I learned that my role in my physical body is to reflect my s Self-Love and that the Light Being did the healing and clearing.

My job then was not to heal because my knowledge was limited compared to the knowledge and technology of the higher beings. As a witness of love, I was helping to make things happen. With my heart's intentions and using the Inca Way process, I increased my frequency and received more information. That was a sign that the neutrons in my atoms and cells were getting stronger. And my direction in life was getting strong as well.

When removing molecular damage, the Light Beings can't leave the space empty; it has to fill with light to create more light. So, after the Five Points of Power of Mother Creator removes the damage, she places the light and feelings from the 5th dimension back in the neutron. The feelings prevent the damage of the blocks and limiting beliefs from returning. The neutron can remember its connection with the proton. When they are back to the same energy balance, they remember consciously, through ideas and memories, the damage that they did to each other in the past when the corrupted subconsciousness manipulated them. They release the blocks and heal each other with gentle love. They learn to trust each other again and rewrite their story to a higher frequency of love. The power of the high-frequency subconscious takes care of the protons, neutrons, and electrons. It keeps them together in love and balance.

Just as the neutron gets contaminated with the corrupted subconsciousness of the 3rd dimension, electrons can also be contaminated. Then the electron blocks the feeling and supports the corrupted subconscious. The corrupted subconsciousness steals the feelings of the electron just as it does with the neutron and fragments the protocol of the Five Points of Power.

One morning, I was meditating, and I had the idea to reflect the energy of Mother Creator's Five Points of Power in my heart. I sensed a radiant and strong light coming to my heart, and a shadow forming, creating pain. As the pain grew, I noticed it was shame. I remembered my mistakes with my children, like losing my temper or not listening to them. It was clear that I was ashamed of making those mistakes and hurting them.

I was angry, annoyed, and powerless. It was hard to remember the past, but then the light that was coming from Mother Creator's Five

Points of Power began activating not only the memories, but also solutions for the mistakes that I had made. Her Five Points of Power were reprograming the past events and changing the pain into creations of love.

This was the time in my life I understood the potential and amount of the power of the Five Points of Power. To clear the mistakes of the past and move forward in making better choices with my children, I get to utilize my Five Points of Power: trust, direction, compassion, distribution of love, and unconditional love, and that will clear the past and help me to create the life I want with them.

CHAPTER 28
My Symbol of Personal Intimacy

Personal Intimacy has to do with expressing what you want to *experience*. This book was a gift from the universe, showing me that I could experience spiritual, physical, and emotional transformation in my life. I have noticed how much I have changed since writing this book. In the beginning, I had a lot of anxiety and stress whenever I wrote. Sometimes, I cried, powerless, believing I did not have what it takes to write this book. I felt like I was doing something wrong by expressing my feelings, especially when I exposed the behavior of my mother.

Over time, I noticed that I was standing in the way, powerless, and shut down in most areas of my life. For instance, I was timid, but now it is different. This book showed me that it could be safe to express; it was a new experience for me. While writing, I discovered and exposed the truth about my connection with others. Now, writing, reading and communicating with others has become easy.

Through the process, I have learned to admire and appreciate Acada's work because she found ways to help the light and truth survive. I noticed little by little that Acada's symbols were energy fields that we have in our DNA, and by receiving energy from the 5th dimension, our body's molecular energy level charged to a pure form of Self-Love.

The Personal Intimacy symbol is two even lines crossing in the shape of a triangle, creating a common point that connects to the center of a circle protected by two smaller outside circles. The outer circle has five openings or fragmented sections in the upper part of the circle.

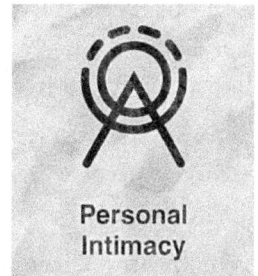

Personal Intimacy

The energy of Personal Intimacy is a creation of the high-frequency future in Circular Time. It is the observation from a spirit, from the future, without the limitations of time and space. It is the projection of a hologram without the spirit being in the past or present. It can't be controlled because the observer is not in the now. It cares about the action, which we want to experience in high-frequency, like love, expression, and making happen, not the restrictions of time and space. Some Andean Shamans called it the direct connection to the consciousness of the universe.

For instance, the energy of wanting to experience feeling valuable has a process. The combination of letting go, accepting you want more, and manifesting that. Three things can happen at once. That is the power of the Personal Intimacy symbol. Let's say you do not want to be unhappy. You want to be happy; you accept that is your desire, and you manifest happiness. There are no time and space restrictions; it happens in the now.

When I felt the high-frequency future, my energy had to be in high-frequency and clear of contamination, to experience this symbol of Personal Intimacy. Most of the time, my experience only lasted a few seconds. With this protocol, I have learned not to underestimate the high- frequency of love. With this symbol, the unlimited power of love opens to create light, communities, values, and principles. I will do my best to explain more about this protocol. Remember, protocols are like a car engine that helps us to move forward for a better world.

In the time of Atlantis, Acada used this symbol. She knew she would not be able to create with Ta in Atlantis. But she could be stronger if she could connect to him in their Twin Cell energies in the high-frequency future. So, as she did so many times using her multidimensional gifts, she remembered the past events in love frequency with Ta and traveled there, but this time, she redirected her thoughts to the future and observed the event from there and only sent a light hologram of her essence. She created a hologram of her body and sent it to the past like a Star Wars hologram projector experience.

With her essence of the hologram, once in the past, she found an atom of Ta that had no contamination and had the memories of their Twin Cell connection and took it back to the future.

In the high-frequency future, Acada connected this atom of Twin Cell memories to the highest possibility of Ta, his higher self and his spirit. Then she joined together her higher self with Ta's higher self. Now that both were in the power of the Twin Cell, together, they created a new reality with two Circular Times in the high-frequency future.

The Personal Intimacy symbol allows you to witness yourself subconsciously in the future and eliminate the source of the problem or contamination. With the power of this symbol, Acada witnessed the ability of the Androids' artificial intelligence to acquire information about their victims' behaviors and vulnerabilities. Then, with that knowledge, they would attack by weakening their immune systems. This is how Acada learned the most about the contaminations that had artificial intelligence.

For instance, when the contamination of self-pity was spreading everywhere in Atlantis, Acada took the contamination into her body, felt the frequency, and found the source of the contamination. Because Acada transported her ideas through Circular Time, she went to the future in low-frequency, observed and understood how the contamination behaved, then processed the information to separate the Twin Cell energies. Then Acada relocated the cure to the future in high-frequency.

When working with someone who was contaminated, she observed the future of the high-frequency of the person. Then she chose two locations. One represented the female Twin Cell energy, and the other represented the male Twin Cell energy. She would place the cure in those two locations of Circular Time and then link the two places. The healing energy intensified, and the contamination could not survive.

Acada worked with Father and Mother Creators, who created the Personal Intimacy symbol in the future. She wondered how to experience something that has yet to be created. She learned that it has not been constructed for us in the present, but the future is a consciousness created from our choices in the present, and all possible solutions to the present already exist. With the Personal Intimacy symbol, you make changes to help your body and mind improve their development and evolution from a perspective in the future.

Acada taught me about the distinction between possibilities and manifestation in the future. Possibilities from the future happen to us according to how we perceive the present, which could be choices of love or confusion.

Manifesting in the future, the process that Acada created, was a genius idea. She connected the possible events in the future of love and manifested them there. I will try to explain this. You are in the present and think about eating a banana; it is a possibility of what can happen in the future. But now, think about being in the future and eating a banana there.

We mentioned before that the future has possibilities but no manifestation. But this time, Acada was able to manifest in the future. It is the experience of eating the banana that happens in the future and now that experience is already manifested in the present even though it has not happened yet. It had already happened from a perspective from the future, not from the past, and it cannot be undone. Because the past was not involved in the manifestation. There is no way to undo this.

Acada took the energy of unconditional love into the future, manifested it there, and then reflected it into the present through a portal of light. The manifestation of the future of unconditional love will know what to do to support the rewritten stories. That does not mean unconditional love does not bring accountability in the process, and it does so with the essence of the truth instead of the limitations of time and space in our minds. The manifestation of the experience of the future is a point of reference for a solution.

Is it possible that part of your identity is the ability of knowing what you want? Yes, I encourage you to listen to what you want. The symbol of Personal Intimacy helps you redefine your true identity by knowing what can be possible from a manifestation of the future. It is the spiritual intelligence that guides us in making choices.

I had a terrible habit. When people would talk to me, I interrupted when I got nervous. I felt awful every time I did that, but I could not stop myself. After a while, I envisioned the energy of unconditional love in the future and saw myself overcoming that bad habit. I saw a light coming into my heart that changed it. The behavior eventually went away. I had to remind myself several times. Now, when I talk to people, I can listen to them without interrupting. I suggest you use the energy of unconditional love from the future to change behaviors you do not want to have. I call this giving yourself Energy Gifts.

By giving yourself Energy Gifts, you can change the perception of how you observe an experience. The energetic gifts come from the future in high-frequency and have the symbol of Personal Intimacy integrated into it. The Personal Intimacy feelings set you free from the trap of the past, and it will dissolve the past in low-frequency and bring the truth of the situation—your essence of love.

As I learned Acada's process, Che told me it was time to experience my symbol of Personal Intimacy; it would help me to focus and strengthen my feelings. Like so many times before, he did not tell me much, and I had to experience the feelings to keep them in the cellular memory of my body.

In those few seconds that I can participate in the source of the Personal Intimacy protocol, it is as if I have a vortex of energy coming from the ground and up through the center of my body in a spiral form. My inner light grows stronger. Then, the frequency of the light speeds up all over my body so powerfully and fast that it opens up the future, bringing higher consciousness to my body.

With the feelings of Personal Intimacy integrated into my atoms, I can, according to Acada, develop my intuition. The thing that one knows from instinctive feeling rather than conscious reasoning, is that which will prevent contamination.

Let me give an example. One day I was planning a workshop and thinking about the people I wanted to invite. I thought about four ladies that I wanted to come. I knew they could not afford the course, so I decided to lower the price for the class. Suddenly, I felt pain in my heart. Then, I heard Che's voice saying that the pain in my heart was telling me that the event's intention was not pure and that I should rethink my decision.

The intention was not pure because I felt sorry for the ladies who could not afford the course. He continued by saying that if I do something because I feel sorry for the person or situation, I am not respecting them or myself. I was creating from a powerless space. I must honor myself and others with compassion and love. I must use my ability to teach or show an outcome with a joint empowerment solution.

I took some time to think about what he said and meditated on my heart's feelings. Some memories came to my mind. I remembered the times in the past when I had little money, when I felt sorry for myself and powerless. I reflected on the story of the four ladies who could not afford my class. I closed my eyes and requested Father Creator to give me an Energy Gift to stop feeling sorry for myself. I envisioned myself receiving golden energy in my hand and placing it gently and lovingly in my heart. I observed how the block disintegrated in my heart, and little by little, the pain went away.

My heart felt lighter. Some other memories came to my mind. I recalled holding back from asking my mother for things because I felt sorry that she barely had money to support us. I saw her as powerless. I felt helpless and made myself wrong for wanting something. Observing the memories of the past was painful, but they were clearing, which was important.

While I observed my memories, I felt I had a choice, and I chose not to feel that way anymore. In accepting the new choice, the Personal Intimacy energy brought the healing energy from the future into the present, which was placed in my heart. The energy merged with the Inca Cross symbol, and a new reality was present in my heart.

The reality is that it is safe to want what I want. That new feeling was stronger than the need and thought to feel sorry for myself, and I let it go. I decided to teach the workshop and give the four ladies a discount to come to the course. My focus changed; I wanted to empower them instead of feeling sorry for them.

With the help of my Personal Intimacy feelings, a new reality was born with the reflection of Mother Creator's Points of Power. Yes, I saw how Mother Creator's Five Points were in my heart. Working with the Personal Intimacy symbol, I, like Acada, had gotten ahead of the process of the contamination of time. I learned from the behavior and that prevented the action from happening again.

The concept points of reference made sense now, when the Light Beings said, "Let me give you a new point of reference." They were talking about a manifestation or experience in the future that had not happened in our present.

I still remember when I was struggling with how to convey my life without feeling sorry for myself. I did not want that emotion, but I did not have experience with how to feel another way. A Light Being gave me an Energy Gift.

After receiving the gift, some of my experiences have shifted. Feeling sorry for myself changed to a new feeling of confidence that comes from knowing I can make things happen. It was in my body's energy force driving my thoughts, an intelligence or consciousness that empowered me.

I would describe it as an internal knowing. When you know that you are hungry, your body asks for food, or you tell yourself to drink water. Feeling sorry for myself was not there, but the knowing of being comfortable with myself took its place. The atoms in my body were reprogramming to behave differently. It wasn't a mental process but a molecular behavior.

I will go back to a time before I felt valuable, and I did not have a point of reference of it. I requested an Energy Gift to feel self-value and placed it within my heart. For the first time in my life, I felt how it feels to be valuable. It was amazing. It was a sense of being worthy of love and it was ok to be loved by others. I learned two things that day.

First, that I must increase my energy of Self-Love in my heart to receive the Energy Gifts to manifest what I was asking for. Second, the understanding of value was a manifestation of the true meaning. It was coming from the future to give me a point of reference since I had yet to gain experience in the past. This was a gift from Acada. Her creation of the Personal Intimacy hologram of feelings allowed me to experience something from the future to fulfill what I needed in the present.

CHAPTER 29
My Symbol of the Future

> *"We all move forward to the future, not to the past ... Focus on your future."* Acada

Future

While Personal Intimacy feelings lock the manifestation of feelings in the high-frequency future to change our behavior in the present, the symbol of the future, according to Acada, represents the feelings, experiences, and possibilities in the future that will assist you, empower you and support you in making better choices. It is the new reality after implementing the new point of reference.

The protocol of the future is a symbol of a six-pointed star with a dot in the center. This symbol is also seen in sacred geometry. What is different about Acada's symbol is the dot in the center that represents the connection to universe, which makes it totally unique.

Acada explained that honoring our feelings makes our future stronger and makes a healthy immune system in our body. She said, "If I think of a white horse, it may not be a white horse, but if I feel a white horse, it is a white horse."

Your experiences of feelings can never be taken away from you, and they can only be blocked. Thoughts can be taken away or manipulated because they are not as strong as your feelings.

When you create a thought, it creates a "possibility." The action of making the possibility happen is a feeling that sets the action in motion and manifests the opportunity. Let's say, for example, that I am considering going to the movie theater; this is the thought that creates the possibility. The actual act of going to the movie theater is the feeling. The action and the movement make the manifestation. If I only think about that, it does not make it happen, because the experience of the motion did not occur.

The motion is to get in the car, drive to the movie theater, and purchase the ticket. It includes working to make money to buy the ticket. These are actions or experiences, and we get to feel the experience of making them happen. It is what happens when we travel to the future by feeling Self-Love.

Feelings make the motion and action occurs. For instance, when people are depressed and think about a negative future, they are not in the motion of life because they are not feeling at a life-creating vibrational frequency. Their feelings are blocked.

When you are not producing a pure intention in your heart, you are not building a movement for a 5th-dimensional future of manifestations. This concept was challenging to understand, and I needed some help. Che wanted to help me understand this concept. He was quiet momentarily before talking, which was unusual for Che because he's a talker. Then, he said. "I am Ta, Acada's husband".

I held my breath and did not want to say anything I would regret later, but I was shocked. It was sudden and unexpected when Che told me he was Acada's husband.

I was quiet and kept listening, He was open and vulnerable. I knew that moment was not about me and my emotions but about giving him the space to express his feelings. Che continued, telling me that he had met Acada in Atlantis when he was a young boy of around four years old, and she was a few years older.

Che said that when he was close to Acada, he could feel she could talk with her heart. Sometimes she did not say much, but he could feel how her presence healed others.

I could feel Che's intense love for her. Che continued by saying that Acada had the powerful energy of creation. Being close to her, he shared, was like being in a higher dimension. He asked me to focus on and feel my heart's energy to intensify my experience of his story.

Che continued by saying that people who connected with Acada's heart energy would instantly fall in love with themselves. They would see the best of themselves. The energy of her heart was the energy of her people, the Mu.

He got quiet for a while then; I felt him smile and share that he and Acada were playing in the garden when she lost her shoes. He was around four years old. While they were looking for them, she stood for a moment, imagined her shoes energetically, and, just by thinking and feeling them, there they were. She had brought back the shoes right there in front of her. He was amazed by how magical she was.

Che explained that his mother had died when he was very young. Acada could feel Che's sadness and his emptiness from losing his mother. She was a great friend to him. She supported him in his healing from losing his mother. Acada recreated his mother's memories of love in his heart to connect to her. Because of the love and choices, she made, he connected to a better future.

Che and Acada spent much time together in those younger years, but then Acada moved to a different city and they were separated. A few days after that, Acada became very ill. When Che visited her, she got better almost immediately after his arrival. Acada's father decided to bring her back to her old house to be close to Che. Che said that Acada supported him in his dreams and goals and would say, "Ta, I want you to learn all the knowledge I have because someday I want you to help me."

Ta shared at that time that he didn't understand the importance of Acada's future. When she was around fourteen years old, she was invited to be part of the council of Atlantis to represent the Mu people. Many council members did not want her there because her role was to maintain the high-frequency of the water in the 5th dimension. This threatened them because water holds the memory of love and kindness that was so important to the Mu people. The council members that were Mirrors wanted to take control of what was left of the water in this planet – Earth. And eventually they took the Five Points of Power of the water.

Che's focus was helping his father's projects. While spending time with his father and stepmother, he noticed that his stepmother couldn't feel. He was around five years old when his father married her and he did not realize that she was a human android. Later, in his twenties, he asked his father why he had made that choice. His father said that when Che's mother died, he wanted him to have a mother energy, so he created the android. That was not true because his father was obsessed with the technology of the androids and wanted to learn more about their behaviors as a mother.

It was hard to believe that Che, my teacher of integrity and trust, was Ta.

When I thought about Ta, I saw only the man who betrayed Acada after she lost her baby. He was sharing his story to show how confused we can get in the 3rd dimension.

It was good that it happened when I had the tools to see the difference between the 3rd dimension of blocks and limiting beliefs and the perspective of love of the 5th dimension.

I chose to see his story from the 5th-dimensional perspective instead of judging him. I was in no place to make judgments or diminish him as I had been contaminated by my ancestors' behavior and societies as well.

I sensed his feelings and knew how much he loved Acada. I wished they could be together again.

I noticed my genetic story about Acada and Che was still in low-frequency because there was still suffering. It hit me that I had the power to change things— my higher choices and connection with my essence of spirit could make it happen. My transformation and connection in higher frequency with the 5th dimension could create a clearing in my DNA.

By loving myself, I could bring Acada and Che back together in the future high-frequency. First, though, I had to learn to love myself.

There was a time, at the beginning of my training with Che, I envisioned him in front of a portal of light. He was in the other dimension of the portal, and I was in this dimension.

"When you open the 5th-dimensional portal, I will await you on the other side," said Che, smiling.

At the time, I did not understand, but I do now. Che was not talking to me. He was speaking to Acada. It was the desire of his heart to be reunited with her.

Che continued sharing his story. He and Acada decided to get married. They moved outside the city to a quiet place and started a family. They lived in a white house surrounded by trees, with two square pools of water – one representing Mother Creator and the other Father Creator. There was a garden bench on which to sit between the two pools. Che and Acada would often sit together, enjoying the water.

Inside one of the main rooms in their house, they had a structure like a podium that held a Mu crystal as a display; it was a pendant. A green circle shaped crystal that hung from a chain.

Acada wanted a simple lifestyle, being with her children teaching them her ways of life. Both Che and Acada wished to enjoy peace. Che expressed the most beautiful moments he had shared with Acada when he was at the 5th-dimensional park where Acada used to play with Mother and Father. They had picnics, where they placed a white tablecloth on the ground and had various types of food and ate while sharing their feelings.

It was nice to feel their experiences. It felt calm and peaceful, and I could sense their connection with love. It was the best way to keep me in my heart instead of going into my head. Che said my DNA energy was balancing and getting stronger while I remembered the good memories of their past.

Che then continued his narrative, sharing that his stepmother had asked him to represent his father in a business celebration trip. It was supposed to be like any other trip where he taught others about the Law of One's ways of life. Acada would stay home with the children.

When he went to the gathering, he found many people who did not feel. To his surprise, it was a Mirror reunion. He stayed at the request of his father. Late at night, someone put drugs into his drink without his knowledge. The physiological effect of the drugs induced him into a state of vulnerability. This was the night when a woman came to the bed and seduced him.

Che explained that he thought it was Acada and was intimate with her. She smelled, acted, and looked like Acada. When he woke up, he saw that the woman wasn't Acada, and he noticed something was different with him. He felt attracted to this woman. The human androids were beautiful and very desirable.

He stayed in the house longer than he had planned. Meanwhile, Acada wondered why he was not coming home. She decided to look for him. Upon her arrival, she found him in a room with this woman.

He did not follow Acada because he was still under the spell of the drugs and the seduction of the android. It was a long-term effect that impacted his thinking, and he acted on the stimulation of the substance.

Acada saw the beauty of this human android and doubted herself for the first time. Contaminated with doubt, she compared her pure heart intentions to the mind's desires. She thought her heart was not as powerful as the other woman's physical beauty. For the first time, she was comparing herself to another woman.

Under the influence of the drugs and confused with the seductive behavior of the android, Che stayed in the place for several days. By the time he returned home to tell Acada he was leaving her for the android, she had already had the abortion.

After the abortion, Che said, he was not the same person. He was angry with Acada. Che noted that he had become a Mirror and blamed Acada for his actions. The anger blocked the feelings in his heart.

The council punished Acada by taking her children away and ordered Che to marry the woman android. He sometimes felt his love for Acada inside his heart, but he ignored the feelings.

He moved in with the other woman. By now, he knew she was a human android. He explained, "Woman humanoid is like chameleons that can change colors when close to their victims. She knew what to say and how to act to get what she wanted, and I was under her spell. I couldn't feel when I was close to her."

He kept talking, "The council was already under the control of the Mirrors when Acada received her punishment. One of the options was to take Acada for treatment in my father's center. I agreed because I believed she was not emotionally stable. I did not think my father would do anything to harm her."

As I listened to him talking, he said, "I looked at Acada's eyes while my hands were on her neck. I felt an energy coming to me, clearing the illusions in my mind and body of the damage my father had done to me, and I saw it: Acada in the experimental center; they had removed Acada's reproductive organs; she could not get pregnant again. I felt overwhelmed from feeling her pain. Her thoughts of not being able to have a baby again. It hurt so much…"

Ta had tapped into the energetic information in Acada's body; the protocols of Personal Intimacy and Future were activating his body, and some of his atoms were repairing themselves and connecting to the future and observing from Self-Love, where time and space could not control the truth of the events.

CHAPTER 30
Che

Ta, who is Che in the 5th dimension, acknowledged the validity of the experience he did not see before he touched Acada. Even though he was not back in his full 5th-dimensional energy, his atoms and cells that were in that frequency and with the support of feelings of the symbol of the Future, he started making choices to connect back to light source.

He recognized his role in damaging Acada; he knew he had to do something to stop his father from damaging others. He went to see his father at the experimental center. He confronted his father but like the other Mirrors, his father justified his damage to Acada.

Then, he went to the experimental center's main room and saw the sons and daughters of the Law of One held there, and he set them free. With the help of five people, Che placed an electromagnetic force in the center of the building to destroy it. Everything happened fast; he was the last to leave, but the destructive shattering started before he left, damaging his body. His father was killed in the blast.

Afterward, Che and the other five men escaped to what is now called Belize. He stayed in that area and eventually died there. The memories of Acada stayed in his heart and mind.

Even though it has been thousands of years in the DNA, I was still affected by Ta's story from the 3rd-dimensional perspective without consciously knowing it. The survival reflection was that I did not trust men. I was very judgmental of them, and I had built a wall around me to protect myself from them by saying I didn't need them to be strong for me.

His transformation also changed my molecular energy. It was easy to see the truth from a Self-Love perspective and my eyes opened to a new reality where it is okay to co-create with men and trust them if they are coming from a space of love.

Che and Acada were full of energy and happy, ready to embrace the world and create together. They were innocent but manipulated by the darkness that damaged Atlanteans. The Mirrors made them believe they did not love each other, so they went separately and found a way out of their situations. Neither Acada nor Che felt their love for each other while affected by the 3rd-dimensional blocks. But the energy of love they had for each other would reunite them again in their 5th-dimensional reality in the Twin Cell connection. Holding their story in the molecular memories of my body was an activator. By loving myself and connecting to Acada's Symbols of Love, I had become their future and helped them to be reunited.

The universe had a purpose for me, to experience Che in his true essence, to trust men again and to clear the ancestral damage. Little by little, I learned to trust Che. I loved Che's courage, integrity, and zero tolerance for darkness. I trembled when he was in his energy of loving himself and creating accountability. I have witnessed him standing in his Five Points of Power and his most powerful light, and I have seen darkness shake and not have a chance to survive in his light. He would look directly into my eyes and said, "Do not create excuses and hold back."

I stood before the man revealing his secret of who had damaged Acada. I was listening and loving him at the same time. I had to be strong to be what I learned from him: the energy of love.

I have carried the conflict of their relationship in my DNA, and I have been the product of Che and his determination to help me see my inner beauty and power. I felt the pain in his story and how powerless he felt during those times. I sensed he wanted to tell me his true story, and he had prepared me for that.

This was the awakening of the symbol of the Future, reflecting the truth about Che when he is in the 5th dimension, and he is speaking his message directly to my heart.

Let me explain it differently. In the technology that Acada created of future manifestations, I would be one of their possibilities of the manifestation in their future from the time of Atlantis, that can reunite them again as Twin Cells now. My present was part of their future.

I have learned to love Che and Acada. When I felt their love, I felt motivated to write. But when I connected to the damage done to them, I felt opposition of the 3rd-dimensional low- frequency trying to stop me from knowing more of the truth because the truth exposes the DNA damage, and the contamination can't survive.

Our DNA and atoms, controlled by the 3rd-dimensional behavior, does not want us to remember who we are in the 5th dimension. But once under the influence of our 5th-dimensional atoms, which support the heart's love, the DNA has a light that helps us to remember the past to bring healing, if necessary.

My 3rd-dimensional atoms were attacking me and holding me back from remembering more of the ancestral stories. My body was reacting to the energetic attacks. My kidneys were shutting down. I had muscle spasms and swelling in my legs. I was fatigued and had trouble concentrating. I had allergies, back pain, and conflicting emotions. I felt depressed and anxious.

My cells activated painful memories from my childhood, and my frequency decreased. I even had a car accident and could not hold the high-frequency; my memory was shut down. These were some of the side effects I was having from the entities that did not want me to remember the true story of Acada and Che.

At that point, I stopped writing for almost two years because I wanted to be in my heart and connect to a higher source to write this book. It took a while to feel the strong energy of love and light and to channel their story again from the 5th dimension.

I stayed in my quiet space to ground myself. I sensed there was more to learn before I could keep writing. It was about the feelings of integrity and identity, which are part of Self-Love. I learned that integrity is the feeling of facing things for what they are with compassion, and the feeling of identity is the love you have for yourself that reflects from the perspective of the 5th dimension without suffering.

While driving to LA in February 2021, I felt the mountains' energy. I received a message from them that it was time to write again. Every cell in my body that held the memory of their story from over 12,000 years ago had transformed, and I also had recharged. Now I was ready.

After Acada and Che died during Atlantis, their pure essence returned to the 5th dimension. When we die, every blueprint of pure love and light goes to the 5th dimension, into the future of high-frequency, becomes the higher self, and reconnects to the spirit. The spirit records every experience to create new possibilities.

The experiences that stay in the 3rd dimension are the ones that have not increased high enough in frequency to go to the 5th dimension. It becomes the soul's energy that recycles other lifetimes until it reaches a high enough frequency to go into the 5th dimension. The spirit will always guide the soul to reach light by rewriting stories into events of love and transferred to the 5th -dimensional or high-frequency future.

I was helping Che increase the energy of his fragmented experiences of pain, from the past, and move them to his future. I was helping him to clean up the mistakes he had made in the past. Once Ta increased his energy by clearing blocks and limiting beliefs, he would merge with Che in the 5th dimension.

Deep in my heart, I intended to reunite Che and Acada so that together, they would create a better world. Looking at the truth of the experience helped me see aspects of my mind and behavior that needed to be in the 5th dimension to help transform their souls and connect them into spiritual energy.

When I wrote again, I felt that the love Acada and Che felt for each other had grown and gotten stronger.

CHAPTER 31
Experiencing My Center of Power

The symbol is a polygon of four edges and four vertices, and the vertices to the left and right have extended lines. You are in your Center of Power when you are standing in your power, which means you are observing the balance of love and acting as the giver and receiver of the situation. This experience in the present differs from the symbol of Personal Intimacy that is happening in the future.

Center of Power

The feelings of this symbol help us to restore trust in ourselves. It drives us to see and live true to what we want, believe in ourselves, and what is important to us. Also, to acknowledge what we are capable of and accept who we are. Speak with authenticity and truth.

Let's return to the story of the corrupted subconscious energies that become the takers. The corrupted subconscious energies from the past experiences of our ancestors, and DNA contaminations from Atlantis, are stored in our 3rd-dimensional neutrons and electrons. As a result of their behavior, we can't see the truth of the story of the past. Blocking the truth is like an internal battle among our atoms and DNA.

In 2015, while traveling to Iquitos, Peru, I sat on an airplane beside a mother with a baby girl. She was around two years old, and I noticed she had problems with her legs; they were deformed. While talking to the mother, she told me she was flying back to her city from Lima where they had a doctor who could help her daughter.

The mother also said she was afraid she would not have enough money to buy the airfare, but she did and was grateful to get on the flight. She shared that her ex-husband had an affair while she was pregnant and left her. The situation with her husband stressed her during the pregnancy, and she believed that was the cause of the daughter's problem. She hoped for her daughter to be healed. In her eyes, there was so much faith and hope.

I heard a Light Being say that the cells of the legs of the little girl carried the low-frequency subconscious energy that contaminated her mother. I felt that was true; her daughter's legs did not develop because of the intensity of her mother's anxiety during the pregnancy. The stress, anxiety, and depression lowered some of the frequency of her subconscious level. It transferred and penetrated inside a neutron of the baby's body.

After that, I had a vision; I saw a white room; it felt like a sacred space. The only thing I saw in space was a white table. I watched the damaged neutron that was in the body of the baby be placed on the white table. Then, the Five Points of Power symbol of Mother Creator was placed on top.

The Five Points of Power of Mother Creator went inside the neutron and entered the dark subconscious. A clear and beautiful crystal was pulled out of the subconscious entity, and the energy of the Five Points of Power of Mother Creator took it out of the atom's nucleus. The neutron returned to light, and her body got stronger and eventually healed.

In this situation, the healing energy cleared and reintegrated the pure neutron into the little body using Mother's Five Points of Power. Then I requested, focusing on the energy of my pink quartz crystal in my heart that represents Self-Love, for the protocol of the Future of Father Creator to be placed on top of Mother Creator's symbol of the Five Points of Power. Mother and Father Creator's symbols merged, and the healing started happening. Father Creator's symbol of the Future reconnected the neutron to the future to continue the healing. I also asked the Light Being to have the same process done on the little girl's mother. I never saw the little girl or her mother again. But I felt that eventually, they found a solution.

Without being aware, I was standing in my power of intention. I was requesting healing for the child and her mother. I was the bridge to allow the healing to happen and accepted in my heart the blessing of working with Father Creator. My Center of Creation symbol, or standing in my power, reflected my actions as the link of Self-Love for healing to occur.

My heart was in constant pain when I remembered the past and situations in which I could not provide for my boys, like having money and understanding how to guide them in school decisions or relationships with friends. But it was unfair to me because I did not know how to do that and kept hitting a wall when I remembered.

One day, Che gave me an Energy Gift of self-compassion. And I felt it; I had seen it before, but it is the experience we are looking for. I felt it; I had so much compassion for myself. It was like a force hugging me, saying enough, and helping me remember all the times I was there. I had committed my whole life to them, and it was okay—no more thinking in the past about what would have been possible and be in the present. I repeated several times that day that I have compassion for myself. I was almost sixty years old, and my whole life revolved around what they needed and how to be better for them. The next day, I had an allergic reaction on my face.

The impact of the experience was strong in my body, so then I decided to have compassion for myself and let the past go. And go for my dream, which was to go back to college and study physics. The inflammation that started the day before on my face started going away. It was gone in an hour. Right before I made my decision, I heard Che and Father Creator saying they would support me in my dream.

In another opportunity, I was invited to do the opening meditation for the premier of a movie on mental health awareness. Right before I started, I heard the voice of Father saying, "When you begin speaking, say, you are representing your ancestor by giving the speech." And I did that.

Then I channeled and said that the mind is powerful, but the heart's energy is even more powerful because the mind does not connect us to the future, but the heart does. Then, I showed them how to connect to the pink crystal in their heart.

I began guiding them in a visualization by inviting them to envision a blue sky. Then to see a pure white cloud in the beautiful sky, and I invited them to go inside of the cloud and feel it.

Then I said that the cloud was the pure essence of their heart.

The next step was to envision the cloud in their heart and to touch their heart. Inside of the cloud to imagine a pink crystal, which represented their Self-Love.

Through this energy, they would establish a connection to the future. My intention was for everyone to be connected to their heart and see their purpose in the role that movie would play in the lives of others. I saw how the energy of the pink crystal multiplied in their future energy. It was beautiful. This is another experience of how I stood in my power of Self-Love.

Your pure intentions, the desire to stand in your power and Contracts of Love give you the ability to make choices of love. I have learned that being a creator of love allows me to feel experiences and memories of the light.

Spirit brings us opportunities to complete and fulfill love in our hearts. I am learning to be a creator of love, and I am learning that one of the ways to be a creator of love is by receiving the love of others. I was learning to receive the male love of Father and Che. It is one of the ways to move forward.

One day, I was lying in bed and I had this feeling that I should move to a different place. I did not know where this was coming from. I heard the voice of Father Creator. "Feel how much I love you and allow yourself to let my love in." By receiving his love in my heart, I felt the experience of moving and it did not feel good. It was not time yet. He was giving me the answer by feeling the experience.

I have learned that when we accept the love of Father Creator, Mother Creator, and the Light Beings in our hearts, we receive possible solutions through the light of their love.

Also, I have learned from the power of the feelings of the 5th-dimensional symbols that if I let my heart guide me and embrace the present instead of focusing on the past, my ancestors in low-frequency will not control me. And my ancestors, who choose to feel and are in the future Circular Time, will stand there for me and co-create the future I want.

CHAPTER 32
My Symbol of the 5th-Dimensional Portal

"Our past contaminations, or mistakes, should not determine who we are; It is possible to balance our life." Acada

Our destiny is not set. Your choices can guide you to the future you want. Feel what you desire to experience. I noticed I did not feel the pain and conflict of Acada and Che in my body anymore. I still had the memories of their struggle, but they were not a reflection in my physical body, only in my mind. I felt lighter.

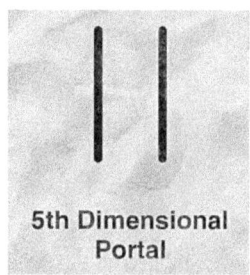

5th Dimensional Portal

I wanted to focus on my personal needs and goals. Feelings are like the sensation of pleasure of digesting the food you like; the emotion that everything is working in your life, and you are enjoying your life experiences.

The symbol of the 5th-Dimensional Portal helped me understand that we create our destiny line. The symbol is represented by two parallel lines of the same size. The feelings of the symbol represent the Creation of Father and Mother, coming together in their Twin Cell energy. It creates balance and strength in the cells to connect to the

5th-dimensional energy. One line represents the feelings of the heart of Father Creator and the other line of Mother Creator.

Acada told me that when I touch the sidebars of the door of the 5th-dimensional portal symbol, my DNA changes to adapt to a new place which is a room where we are trained to be in the 5th-dimensional energies. I called this place the 5th-dimensional Research and Development room (R&D).

When you go through the energetic portal of the 5th dimension symbol, only your high-dimension atoms will enter the 5th-dimensional reality. This symbol only works with the pure essence and intention of light. So, your 3rd-dimensional atoms will not make it.

The 5th-dimensional protocol is the last symbol I go through before I enter the 5th-dimensional R&D room. Each atom in the high-frequency of pure feelings in Circular Time, reflects the Inca Cross of Father and Mother Creator's Twin Cells, when I touch the 5th-dimensional portal's feelings. The two Inca Crosses connect inside the atoms, matching each other and representing the female and male energy. This connection activates the power and gives access to the 5th dimension.

Here is a story to illustrate how the symbol of the 5th-dimensional portal works with accountability. While living in downtown Salt Lake City, Utah, I relished the vibrant experience of easy accessibility to numerous stores within a short distance from my apartment complex.

One day, right before I took the garbage out, I'd had a consultation with a client. I'd taught her the differences between choosing to be a victim, a survivor, or a creator. When I took the garbage to the dumpster next to the building, I saw a homeless person searching for food in the trash. I could see in the unseen world that his brain was damaged from the use of drugs. Intuitively, I felt I should not talk to him.

I looked at this homeless person and asked myself, "What did this person represent in his behavior?" He could not be a victim because he chose to take drugs; he was a survivor. If I were to coach him, where would I start?

Che suggested that I teach this man accountability. It does not matter our circumstances; we all must start with accountability and love. In higher or lower choices, there is always accountability for our decisions.

Accountability without punishment is a powerful way of love. It is experiencing your choice and feeling the consequences. You get to feel what you created for others.

This homeless person had to learn to empower himself. Even eating food from the garbage dumpster is a beginning point to starting a new creation.

Here is a story that may help to understand the symbol of the 5th-dimensional portal. One day, I needed some rocks from the storage area. I had twelve, 12x14 inch containers about 11 inches high, each full of Brazilian and Peruvian quartz and other crystals. I got them directly from the dealer, and only one or two people had touched them. They came directly to me after they were removed from the ground. I often placed them in the rivers and lakes where I was guided to take them.

Sometimes, this was to increase the energy of the place. Other times, it was to connect two or more areas energetically with these crystals. Once, Che told me to give a crystal to a client going to Alaska to ski and leave the crystal on a mountain to increase the frequency of Mother Creator's codes of love.

My storage unit was near the underground parking area in the basement where I lived. When I opened the locked storage unit, I saw someone had broken into my space. It was the second time this had happened in the previous six months. At this time, they did not take anything. Intuitively, I felt the people that broke in were using drugs because they were looking for items to sell, such as computers and musical instruments. They got into other units as well. I'd felt someone was taking things from me a few days before, but I did not check my storage. I thought it was unnecessary because they had stolen my electronic items, and I had removed all that was valuable from the storage room.

Che said that when someone steals from us, the experience has no balance. When we work to provide for ourselves, it is unacceptable when someone else takes something away from us. It is also an inconvenience to repair the loss or damage.

I was upset about what happened. But I had a choice to be a victim, a survivor, or a Self-Love creator, and I chose to be a creator. Che suggested using this situation as a reference point to apply the Inca Way Distribution Process.

The first time I heard about the Inca Way Distribution was in Peru. The Inca Way distribution is your awakening that increases your frequency in light when you do a distribution of love. It is when you learn a new experience, and you decide to reflect and share the benefits of that experience with your ancestors and family generations, as well as with the people, to support a better world. It is a declaration of 50:25:25 points. 50 represents your personal benefit, 25 for your ancestors, and 25 for the people in the world. The distribution is of the light you have increased in co-creating with the universe.

I used the Inca Way Distribution process with the people that broke into my storage space. First, I declared an intention of what I wanted to create. In this situation, I intended to reflect accountability to the source of the damage, the thief who had broken into my space, and anyone else who did the damage. I declared the 50:25:25 points of distribution for my past, present, and future ancestral lineage to benefit from the work. I stated that other people in the same situation would benefit from my healing experience.

This time, I multiplied my intention by five and connected to the Five Points of Power of Mother Creator. I envisioned my protocol of the Subconscious, and I chose to go one hundred thousand years into the future. Any number after 10,000 is good because we are working with exponential growth.

I felt myself going energetically through my symbols of Intention, Five Points of Power, Future, and the 5th-Dimensional portal. Then, into the Research and Development room (R&D) and merged with my higher self. I placed my intention on a white table in the room as an offering and requested my higher self and Light Beings to do the clearing. I requested that the Five Points of Power of Mother's energy be placed on the white table and Father's Future protocol to be placed atop of Mother Creator's protocol. Then I stayed there, feeling the energy of Self-Love and unconditional love in my heart to help with the clearing.

During the process, I felt I was back in my 5th-dimensional portal symbol and witnessed the symbol's movement. First, I saw the energy of the person who broke into my storage unit. I reflected the energy of accountability from my energy to his energy and saw his father and mother. I saw the mother acting like a victim and using punishment to deprive him of his basic needs. I also saw that the mother was unfaithful to the father. The father was rude and detached from providing for the financial and emotional needs of the family. The man, as a boy, did not do well in school because of the lack of paternal and maternal direction. I felt he decided he was stupid when he was thirteen and labeled himself a bad person. He started blaming himself for every wrong thing that was happening to him. Then he started making more mistakes, and his parents kicked him out of the house.

My 5th-dimensional portal symbol continued reflecting the ancestral lineage of the mother. She was an only child and had gotten everything she wanted, and her parents provided material things instead of love. Then I reflected light of the 5th dimension on the grandmother's energy.

His mom's mother was very temperamental and confused about life.

I looked next at her mother's father. He had gone to war somewhere in Europe, and during a battle, he lost a leg. When he came back from the war, he became an alcoholic. I kept going, and it was now around 10,000 years ago. The memories were coming fast, and I could not focus on the experiences, only the feelings of the experience. I continued going until I got to Atlantis to a time after the second explosion happened.

I remembered that pure intentions get you back to the source of the damage, which was what was happening then. I was observing from Self-Love and accountability at the source of contamination in one of the atoms of the man who had broken into my storage unit. I saw a little girl in a white dress running to the water at the beach, and then she drank the contaminated water without knowing it was damaged by the Mirrors.

I saw her DNA become corrupted with radiation. Her skin was burning, she had stomach cramps and could not feel her body. Che was next to me, and I gave her a ball of pink light to place in her heart. It was Self-Love coming from the little girl's higher self. Che helped her gently put the pink light into her heart. After a few minutes, the water contamination began to be removed from her body. According to Che, 90% of the current corruption resulted from water contamination in those times. I saw the little girl getting better, she could feel her body and her stomach stopped hurting. Then I saw the healing in the present time. It was a domino effect. During the process, the body cells began healing, and each one of the people in the process had to be accountable for the choices they made.

Now, the little girl with the information stored in the pink crystal was aware that the water was contaminated, and she was empowered to make other choices. She chose to be careful and not do it again. Things were changing. The new choice of the little Atlantean girl was affecting her DNA lineage; people affected by her choice could now make new decisions.

Che was standing near the contaminated water and creating energy to change the water's frequency. He was giving back accountability to the contaminated water source. Remember, this clearing was possible because there is no linear time in the 5th dimension.

Eventually, the energy in a new frequency will return to the present, to the man who broke into my storage unit. He will be aware of the damage he created, be accountable for the choice energetically, and have the possibility to develop other options.

It is essential to know that while we always get opportunities in the future to change and clear what we created in low-frequency, we are still responsible for our past choices. The Inca Way Distribution can make it possible to go back and clear the damage, allowing us to make a higher choice and maintain the change in our genetics.

My creation, in my point of "Responsibility" of the Inca Cross, was to let the man who broke into my storage unit be accountable for the damage he created in my life. When we do not make people responsible for their choices, we get in the way of their development and progress.

I felt I had learned the meaning of accountability, but Che said there is another part to accountability. It is getting back what was taken away by others' choices. He gave me a ball of light, an Energy Gift, to place in my heart to bring back the energy stolen from me by the person who broke into my storage unit. The energy returned was the feeling of "safety".

The unsafe feeling I had was sent back to him, and peace was restored in my heart. Even though it was not possible to have the physical items returned, I knew that the energy would eventually manifest or replace them.

The experience that I had that day was not an everyday experience, but it showed me the effect of the contamination of the water in the time of Atlantis.

Remember, darkness only has power if we are unaware or don't recall the truth of our experiences. Remembering is a powerful weapon. I have come to a new understanding of the War of the Times after observing stories of the past. I remember standing on top of Sacsayhuaman and seeing soldiers from different times of history ready to fight in a battle. Did that represent the war between Circular Time and linear time? Yes. It was a conflict created by the corrupted subconscious energy from the Mirrors' experiment. Their experiments split our subconsciousness' high-frequency and corrupted them. Then separation happened. We forgot our true nature, which is the 5th-dimensional spirit.

In the 3rd dimension, under the influence of the experiments in Atlantis, control in low- frequency takes over the subconscious energy. What was left was the soul traveling through different times, surviving. With the symbols of Acada and the protocols of Mother and Father Creator placed inside the soul, the corrupted subconscious energy implanted by the Mirrors can be removed, and the spiritual energy reinstates the damaged area.

One day, I was observing a clearing of a dark entity. Father Creator said to me. "Now, witness this miracle." I could see a corrupted subconsciousness, and then I saw the high-frequency possibilities of the entity in the future of light. I saw Father Creator's energy travel to the future, where he disconnected the corrupted subconsciousness from every source of life in the future. "No more taking." It was like cutting off someone's oxygen. The entity stopped existing.

In the Inca Way 50:25:25 Distribution, we get people back what has been taken from them. When you reflect on the last 25 of your distribution, you assist other people with the energy of your transformation. The feelings of Acada's symbols intensified, bringing the possibility of changes from the twenty-five points of distribution. This is to help everyone clear.

Acada's intent is for us to make better choices and create an inner foundation to connect to higher possibilities of love. For example, the man who broke into my storage unit will be supported by having new ideas. Perhaps someone will come into his life to help him realize his mistake and connect with the possibility of higher energy in his DNA to guide him in making changes. He will have opportunities to make other choices, but it will be up to him.

This is how we create a better world. Accountability always brings opportunities for change, but that does not mean we will get away with what we have done. There are consequences of our choices. Some people may go to jail, and others may lose valuable things or loved ones. We are all learning to make higher choices, and levels of corruption must be replaced for the people who have been damaged. New possibilities of completion will present themselves to the person who has been damaged.

On one occasion, I worked with a client who feared harming others including her daughter. She told me she would get thoughts of wanting to hurt people—physically harm them. I had worked with her six times, and she was getting better and stronger. But I listened to her thoughts of harming others and followed the formation of those thoughts back to Atlantis. I witnessed a woman holding a baby and singing. This woman thought her baby was perfect. I saw it was a human android caring for a baby. I recognized this because she could not feel. I was with Che and Prophet Thoth while I was observing the story.

Prophet Thoth said to me, "When an android is built, it is programmed to think that it can only construct or build perfect relationships with others, and if it does not meet that expectation, it will self-destruct. If the human android processed that the baby is unattractive, the program in the android will trigger self-destruction because her creation was not perfect."

Now he continued, do this: "Create the intention for the baby to look dark as a shadow and unattractive to the android. Then, place it before the eyes of the android. It will see the baby as ugly and damaged and it will destroy itself. And the baby will reunite with the mother."

Prophet Thoth told me to expand the idea. So, I created the distribution of 50:25:25 for every human android in that time to auto-destroy itself. And I saw hundreds of destroyed androids. Then I asked my client if the thought of destroying others was still there. She said it was gone.

When our intentions are not pure, and we choose to be victims or survivors, we can damage our environment. When Che's father built the android, he thought humans had limitations. He created that belief system and by doing so, he limited humans in their creation.

Isn't it true that sometimes we think we know everything and hurt others by shutting them down when we try to survive? Yes, duality is an outcome of fear. If we believe we are broken, we believe we need someone to fix us, but that is not true. You can't fix what is not broken, but we can hurt others by trying to fix them. Che's father knew he was creating suffering, but he did not care. He damaged Che, and Che damaged Acada.

Che's father took Acada's loved ones away from her and blocked her Energy Gifts. He believed he needed to fix her. The only reason Acada was not destroyed was that she remembered her love and connection to Father Creator. Che's father intentionally created a false reality to stop others from connecting with her. That false reality was that Acada was broken. He knew that Acada could stop him, so he damaged her to avoid her actions. This false perception allowed the People of the Light to attack Acada instead of him. This false perception deceived the People of the Light into fearing and rejecting Acada's message of love. Che's father also used Acada's knowledge to take advantage of others.

When the parallel lines of the symbol of the 5th dimension are reflected in us, it helps us to acknowledge the truth to restore balance rather than acting out in the false perceptions. In our genetic stories, not everyone stands for us or our higher selves. Not everything that speaks or connects us to the unseen world is light. Che's father forced his ideas on others by mirroring and cloning fear and destruction. He felt no regret, even in his last days of life.

Is it possible that when Che touched Acada, he was healed because he went through the genetic symbol of the 5th-dimensional portal? The answer is yes, and the symbol of the 5th-dimensional portal made it possible for him to see the truth of the situation.

CHAPTER 33
My R&D in the 5th Dimension

It is in the R&D room that I witness the healing done to help my clients. It is where I see how powerful the protocols of Father and Mother Creators are when working together as Twin Cells. I see them standing in the power of giving and receiving in the individual's Center of creations.

Acada came to me when I needed it the most; my boys were five and seven years old. I was struggling to understand my role as a mother, and I prayed to Father and Mother Creators and the universe to help me stand for the higher self of my two boys. The gift was Acada. I learned from her that love is the foundation on which we balance our lives and connect with others.

Each of us have our own Research and Development room. It is connected to our DNA energy. The R&D is the place where I channel the 5th-dimensional information of Father Creator, Mother Creator, Che, Acada, Prophet Thoth, and other Light Beings to empower our Living Universe.

The R&D is where I witness the benefits of Acada's tools. Here, I place my intentions on a white table and hope her teachings can guide me. It is where I observe and channel the messages that guide me through my life's best and worst times.

It is in the R&D where I witness that these days we need a whole relationship with the power of our hearts. Lots of changes are happening, and we need Self-Love. The planet is preparing to change, and we humans are changing too, through an evolution of thoughts.

It is in the R&D where Acada shares her messages to create a new society of love. "We are powerful," she says. "And we get to embrace and hold that. Loving ourselves is what is going to help us meet these changes and thrive."

We are powerful in the 5th dimension because we create possibilities in the future and manifest them in the present. That happens in the R&D in the 5th dimension.

When we are in the future in high-frequency, we can 'lock' an event in a specific space, which means we can create a possibility in the present. With the force of the Five Points of Power, we can eventually manifest it in the present.

This story relates to mothers and fathers. One time, I saw in the R&D room a healing happening; it was a young man who had panic attacks and was in constant terror. Even though he did not remember he was sexually molested, his body remembered it. I could see a specific atom in his body that carried the memory and behavior, like the sharp movements of radiation reflected in other atoms. Together, they created terror in the body and mind. I saw it happen several times.

Then, the energy of the high-frequency future opened like a dimensional portal of light in front of me. A Light Being came through the portal and took the atom with the memory of the abuse that was on the white table at the R&D. He held the atom with one hand and took it further into the future. I heard his voice saying, "stop existence," and the atom vanished.

It was the atom of the abuser that was hooked on the energy of the young man. The manifestation of the atom deleted was in the future and it suddenly stopped existing in the present. We can't survive without a future. A few weeks later, I saw the young man; the terror in his body was gone, and he appeared stronger and healthier.

The mother was happy knowing that her son was healed, and it was the beginning of a beautiful new life. Mothers and fathers can connect to this story because we do not want our children to be harmed by social beliefs and contaminations.

Eventually, we will see more positive changes done in the R&D. For instance, the power of love will increase the energy of the future in a high-frequency of mothers and fathers. And parents, even when unaware of the damage done to their children, their love will lead them to clear and protect the children from harm by others. It will be done by manifesting the action of clearing the world's traumas from their children just by reflecting their Self-Love to their children—a permanent change leading to a new world of balance.

I like working with my students who are learning to channel and work from the R&D room. One day, after twenty years of preparation, I taught the first class of Channeling Level Two. In the Channeling Level One course, the students received several gifts to increase their frequency and learn basic ways of healing themselves.

Level Two is about learning how to work in the R&D room. One day, while they were working in the R&D room, I saw the future portal and the Light Beings bringing the Father Creator's symbol of the Future and Mother's Five Points of Power. They placed them on a white table to clear contamination and create new possibilities of love. I paused for a moment. With a smile, I felt my heart full of gratitude. It is happening! I was teaching others how to work in the 5th dimension.

I watched my students. I saw Clara's surprise when she viewed a light explosion as Mother and Father Creators' symbols touched each other. I saw Mary, who was very strong in her feelings, feel the love of Mother Creator. Lisa, who always takes notes, shared that she saw the symbols while working with her clients. I loved Lisa's commitment to learning to make a life of love for herself and her family.

I saw Karen. She would not go into the R&D room because her Self-Love energy was not strong enough because she would condition herself constantly. She felt her heart many times as necessary while adjusting and increasing her Self-Love for a stronger connection. Her ability to see every detail always amazed me. Karen was so powerful but did not even know it. She reminded me of myself when I first started to train with Che.

We all started the class with a common purpose in our 50:25:25: to become a multidimensional group supporting our dreams and goals, our ancestors, and generations to come to reflect love and harmony for a better world.

My body was calm and open going to the 5th dimension. So many times, my 3rd-dimensional atoms had attacked me. But now, by learning and practicing how to love myself, the power of Mother and Father Creator's protocol made the process dynamic and more effortless in my body. They were a force stimulating me with love, and I was making progress.

I knew it was the beginning of a significant new game. My body had reached the highest potential and connected to the symbol of Personal Intimacy and Mother and Father Creators in the R&D room to co-create in this reality. It takes just one person in this reality to have the experience, and then it can be replicated in others and that was me. I experienced this process and now others can do it too.

I understood why it was so crucial for Che to train me to feel the experience and bring the protocols of Acada into this reality. Che, through time, had taken each one of the symbols and placed them in the feeling of Self-Love. He said, "It was the best place to store them to reflect our life through the eyes and feelings of Self-Love. I understood the essence of his message, emphasizing, "ONLY PEOPLE THAT LEARN TO LOVE THEMSELVES WILL HAVE ACCESS TO THESE SYMBOLS. No more shortcuts. We go into ascension using our own light, not the light of others."

I could feel the sensation of having new 5th-dimensional energies in this reality. It was as if I had made spaghetti for the first time, and now there was a recipe. Now others can follow the recipe and make spaghetti over and over again.

It is also in the R&D where Acada taught me that the Light Beings give me a point of reference in what they have already experienced. The R&D room gives us a "point of reference" for something we haven't been aware of, and by experiencing it, we gain the feelings that confirm the existence of that new reality. It is in that moment that when my molecular behavior changes for something better that can be replicated and expanded.

It is important that I explain this again. We can only learn if we have a point of reference. For instance, when I work with my clients and see their energy, sometimes they do not know how to do something because they lack a reference point.

One client, for instance, did not know how to share with others because, in his cellular memory, he did not have that experience or code of sharing. One of the Light Beings reflected his experience, or feeling of sharing with others, with my client. That reflection was connected to my client's cellular memory as a point of reference for how the experience of "sharing" feels from the 5th-dimensional perspective. Now he knows how to share and can create the experience or behavior of sharing with others.

Our intentions or choices of points of reference impact others. A choice, or intention, is a power we decide to use for 3rd-dimensional or 5th-dimensional purposes. When we are in the energy of the 5th dimension, our intentions, or choices, create expansion. We grow exponentially because the point of reference does not have blocks. Our intentions have limitations when we are in the 3rd dimension with the contamination. Our reference points must come from the 5th dimension to elude the trap of illusions.

Since I started working in the R&D room, my point of reference on the relationship with Father and Mother Creator has changed. My point of reference is now in an energy of unconditional love, with no expectation but being myself in the present. It reminded me of my relationship with my boys. When my oldest first lived alone, he sometimes got lonely— mostly at night. He would call me and talk a little, then ask me to stay on the phone while he read or played computer games. I would stay on the phone doing other things, even when he was getting ready for bed. He would fall asleep with the phone still in his hand, and so would I. When I woke up and looked at the time, I would see that four or five hours had passed, and we were still together on the phone. It happened the same with my youngest son. To me, these experiences were pure connections of unconditional love.

There was a time that I believed that Father and Mother Creator did not love me unconditionally because I had falsely believed no one loved me. I remember one experience when I went to the R&D and connected to the Five Points of Power of Mother Creator and Father Creator's Future protocol; I transformed. I felt deserving of love and affection. Now, I have the experience that I am loveable, and they love me unconditionally.

Remember, when you are in the R&D room, not all your energy is there, only your atoms acting in Circular Time, allowing you to observe the past with protection. Without contamination, it is possible to clear past lives and ancestral events using the energy of accountability and love. Another thing to remember is that the more we transform our atoms to Circular Time, the more efficiently we manifest our pure desires.

R&D is the place where I channel the 5th-dimensional information of Father Creator, Mother Creator, Che, Acada, Prophet Thoth, and other Light Beings to empower our Living Universe. According to Che, Acada's protocols or Symbols of Love are integrated in the energy of the pink crystal, that is in your heart, that represents the energy of Self-Love.

CHAPTER 34
Acada's Protocols of Love

Learning Acada's process did not happen overnight. It was a process of several years. For the first seventeen years, it was hard on my body because my 3rd-dimensional atoms blocked me from getting information from the 5th dimension. I believe I started mastering them twenty years after I was introduced to them. It took that long because I was also bringing them to this reality, the 3rd dimension, for the first time after Acada's death in Atlantis.

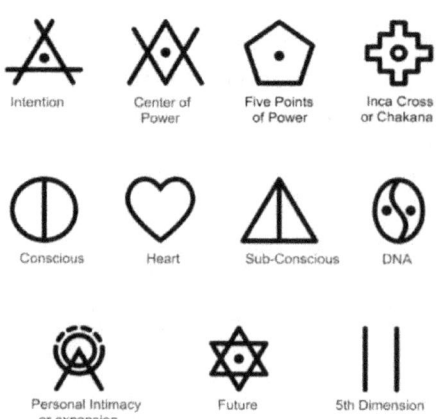

My experiences of the symbols of Acada were challenging and rewarding. It took a while to understand and define them. I did the best I could to translate them.

When you use your intuition, a source of feelings, you connect with your inner self at the atomic level. As previously stated, we are made of atoms of three essential elements: protons, neutrons, and electrons.

An atom is not alive until it has an energy that creates motion and movement. Feelings are one type of energy that create motion.

The atoms in our body that have feelings in their energetic field are 5th-dimensional. The 3rd -dimensional atoms, limited by linear time, are controlled by blocks and limiting beliefs. They are called molecular memories because they have emotions and stories.

Using Acada's Symbols of Love activates the atoms to the 5th-dimensional frequencies by restoring feelings. The symbols give access to the Light Beings in the future in high-frequency, to restore balance and heal damaged atoms, by bringing the elements and feelings back to their source.

Acada used the Sacred Geometry of feelings, a universal language, to achieve her goal of helping us make choices from the perspective of feeling the experience.

The Sacred Geometry Symbols she used in her process are groups of feelings with a common purpose; to be connected to all that is there in the united consciousness of love. These symbols are the Intention, Center of Power, Five Points of Power, Consciousness, Subconsciousness, Heart, DNA, Personal Intimacy, and Future protocols.

In Machu Picchu, I had observed when the Light Beings used these symbols, in their highest potential of the spirit, to clear the energy of the woman of Atlantis that betrayed Acada. I also saw Acada working with the symbols while she was in the ancient sites.

When we are in the energy of Self-Love and connected to the future in high-frequency, we can access the Symbols of Love. We can be a witness of love and be a gift to our society. By reflecting the symbols to others, in the process of 50:25:25 distribution, when we are in the 5th-dimension, we can feel the coding of the symbols in our atoms.

By integrating this knowledge, Acada's process activates us to fulfill our highest potential and connect to the future of the highest energy of love.

A good way to start activating our atoms to a 5th-dimensional frequency is by feeling your pink crystal: your Self-Love energy in your heart. All the symbols are inside the pink crystal, ready to be used. They all will work together like a dance of creation. They create various holograms of forms and colors that help to connect to Circular Time. These Symbols will help you in the 3rd dimension to clear blocks and limiting beliefs when you experience stress, depression, or anxiety or other low-frequency emotions.

The process of contamination begins at a sub-atomic level where one element of a 3rd-dimentional atom has been isolated and taken out of balance. This creates radiation by creating ions.

What fragmented you at a cellular level will be repaired, and your body will recharge and heal itself. And you will restore your connection to the 5th dimension to create in the future in high-frequency.

Here is how to use the symbols, with your pink crystal representing your Self-Love energy, to change your behavior of low-frequency or release blocks and limiting beliefs and take you back to balance. I will use one of my stories to show how to use the symbols.

Every new year for me was emotionally confusing. I noticed that since I was young, I liked to spend New Year's Eve by myself. I cleaned my place with the idea of having a fresh new start. Cleaning my house represented to me making space to have clarity in my life to move forward. Deep inside of me there was always the emotion of waiting for something. The need of waiting for something shocked me and did not let me enjoy a new beginning.

When I woke up the morning of the first day of the year, I had that feeling of emptiness that I had every previous year. This time I decided to do something different. I connected to my pink crystal in my heart, and I was aware that deep inside of me in the subconscious space, I had been waiting for something, but I was not conscious of the story.

Connecting to my heart that morning, I felt it. Every new year I was waiting for my mother to love me unconditionally. I was hoping to know how it would feel to be fully accepted by her. As painful as it was to see that I had being waiting for a long time to be wanted by her, without her need to fix me, I was facing the truth of the situation.

Without my awareness, I had held back, always preparing and waiting for her love instead of going out to celebrate a new beginning with others. I was crying internally because I realized I would never be able to hug her and say "Mom, I feel your love, I am fulfilled now".

Feeling the pain in my heart, I envisioned my conscious symbol holding gently and explained to my subconscious that it will never happen. It is okay to let it go and move on. In a kind way I said to myself, "Let it go, enjoy life".

I saw a little light in my heart, the wisdom that it was time to let it go. I was ready to change all the molecular behaviors attached to it. That's when I decided to apply the process that Che and Acada taught me.

I recalled what Acada said, "Remember, when you want to change a behavior that you are not happy with, this process will allow you to create with your heart, and eventually, you will rely more on your feelings and build balance in your life."

My intention was to help that child part that was waiting for my mother's unconditional love, to move forward to a life of new experiences with others, that can love her unconditionally and enjoy life.

First, I saw the pink crystal in my heart, and I stimulated Self-Love by moving the crystal. Then, I expanded that love everywhere in my body by saying and feeling that I love unconditionally every atom in my body.

Then, I envisioned, a blue sky. The blue sky represented the collective identity and wisdom of the universe. There, I saw a beautiful, pure white cloud. The cloud is a representation of my pure essence of light. It is the idea that I have a place of belonging in the universe.

The next step guided me and I went inside of the white cloud. Then, I felt that the cloud was in my heart where the connection with the universe lives. I placed my hand on my heart. Inside of the cloud, I saw the PINK CRYSTAL. I intuitively knew, with the power of my mind, the crystal could be visualized in different sizes. This time, I made it a human size and I hugged it, with emotions of gratitude for having a connection to Self-Love.

I remembered to place my right hand close to my heart as a reminder that my white cloud, my pure essence was there. By feeling the love for myself, I became the "observer of love."

I started my process of communicating with the universe. I rotated my PINK CRYSTAL to the right five times to make my connection with Mother Creator, my female power of creation. Then I rotated the crystal five times again, this time making the connection to Father Creator, my male power of direction, which is my 5th-dimensional future.

Then, in my quiet space, I observed the blue sky and I saw a dimensional portal. It was like a door that opened to two realities. I could feel the frequency of the 5th dimension on the other side of the portal, which was a gentle energy like a pure breeze connected to this reality.

I declared my intention, "I do not want to keep waiting for my mother to love me unconditionally, it is time to move on and enjoy life." In that moment, I remembered the story of a young man that was deeply in love with a girl. It was hard for him when they broke up. She moved on but he kept waiting for her. During that time, he kept making improvements in his life, hoping that upon her return, she would be proud of him.

One day, a Light Being visited him and told him, "She is not here because she does not want to be here. There are other people like your friends and family that want to be with you at this moment. Value them and be present to them. Remember they are here because they want to be with you." This was the point of reference that the universe was giving to him to take a new direction.

The light from the 5th dimension brought the message and the source to fulfill my intention, which were the ideas and feelings creating a new reality. It was coming directly to my pink crystal like a laser beam coming from the other side of the portal and downloaded the message inside of the crystal.

In that moment, Acada's Symbols of Love that were inside of the pink crystal were being activated and receiving the new ideas coming from the future with possibilities and manifestations of love and light.

The symbols were rewriting the molecular memories to Circular Time, making a powerful connection between the present and future and letting go of the past that was not serving anymore.

I was in so much gratitude in my heart, it felt quiet, the heaviness of the memories of the past that created fear and loneliness was gone. It was a new possibility of honor and value, and to celebrate the people that love me and want to be with me.

A peaceful feeling came and stayed. The calm feeling in my body was the emotional memories in some of my cells that understood that, in the Circular Time process of Self-Love, the universe would step in his big game to create a future of highest possibilities. And to help me to repair the damage that I did to others and myself. By holding back and not being in my full potential, waiting for my mother to love me unconditionally, I was not present to love and honor others.

The sadness I carried in my heart was because the unfulfilled desire did not allow me to be present and fully experience my boys in their childhood. This emotional burden led me into a prolonged state of depression. I was insecure about myself, afraid of rejection and carried the terror of losing someone. But now the universe was helping to clean the past and bring new opportunities to be present to my boys and create a reality of love and expansion. And it felt good.

As I observed the movement of energies in my pink crystal, a profound realization dawned upon me. The first rotation of five times was bringing the energy of the Five Points of Power of Mother Creator into my crystal, while the last rotation, seamlessly integrated the Five Points of Power of Father Creator. In this harmonious merging, I felt I was part of them, and I found my unique place in the universe of creation and expansion. This was the place where I had learned to speak my truth and know, that in the future, with the help of the universe, I will have abundant opportunities to establish myself as who I am: my Five Points of Power, which are trust, direction, compassion, distribution of love, and unconditional love. And reflect them to others.

CHAPTER 35
A New Life

Ta survived the explosion and destruction of Atlantis and fled to what is now Belize, where he created a center for the restoration of energy. He placed every loving memory with Acada and all his love experiences in the atoms of some of the rocks. Che said that in his past life as Ta, in Belize, he worked hard to reconnect to Acada, the 5th-dimensional energy, until he got sick and died.

At one point in my searching for the truth, I went to Belize, looking for the caves where Ta may have been after he escaped from Atlantis, but even though I found a cave, it wasn't the right one. Later, Che told me my energy wasn't high enough to find the place where he had downloaded his memories. During that time, my body had blocks and limiting beliefs that opposed me finding the truth of Atlantis. In later years, when I increased my frequency, I could travel energetically to the cave and feel the energy of Ta's Books of Light.

Years later, after I visited Belize, I received a happy visitor from the unseen world. It was the being with the elongated head, that I had seen in my first training in Peru, at the Temple of the Moon. This time, the being spoke. He told me that he was thankful to me for helping him find his wife. Initially, that didn't make sense, but then I felt something familiar in his energy. I smiled back at him. It was Che!

Che, it turned out, had an elongated head like Acada. Not only that, but his ancestors were from Mu, and his mother was a creator of love like Acada. That day, I saw him for who he was. I felt a deep love around me. I was reflecting on Che's feelings in my energy space.

The work I had done during my years of clearing, had helped them! I learned about water without contamination, and Acada and Che helped make it possible. I assisted them to increase the water's frequency in some places. I left crystals and other rocks in different rivers and ocean waters, which helped with the process. I connected to the energy of water in places as far-flung as Norway, Sweden, South America, Central America, and North America. I had become a guardian of the water, and now I understand, that I am here at this time of my life, to serve a purpose.

My purpose is to provide services of love, to serve Mother Earth, and help in the process of water purification that will assist in helping to remember who we are in creating, in Circular Time. Which is the balance of love of female and male, creation, and direction. The essence of pure water on this planet is a source of life.

I want to clarify that service is a gift of love. We're all here to provide our services for our world and to share our knowledge and wisdom for a higher purpose.

Linear time, which arose with the advent of the 3rd dimension, created a veil; we have forgotten who we are. Remember, we are here to love every living thing of light, to clear blocks that have contaminated our Symbols of Love, and to increase our energy, so we can return to the 5th dimension.

Now, I see Acada and Che more clearly. They love each other, just as Mother and Father Creators do. They stand as the guardians of the water of the 5th dimension. I also have a better understanding of the purpose of the Twin Cells. They protect and maintain the water and connections of the 5th dimension and higher frequencies. Every memory, gift, and piece of knowledge I have acquired is part of these intentions.

Rainy days give me a sense of peace. My mind gets quiet, and I feel myself moving forward with my heart's pure intentions. Sometimes, I remember the past stories that have been rewritten, with new stories of love and completion, and I get a sense of fulfillment.

I woke up to a rainy day, it was cloudy and gentle drops of water falling on the ground. I love water! I noticed my life had changed. Instead of being submissive and holding my emotions, I had learned to express what I am thinking and feeling. I wasn't temperamental anymore. I was kind to myself, loving, and compassionate, and I relied more on the feeling of my Five Points of Power and the Inca Cross. My relationship with my sister and boys had also improved. When my boys talked to me, they did not have to worry about me losing my temper. My sister could share emotions and did not feel like she was walking on eggshells, not knowing how I would react to her. I had learned to love me and them unconditionally.

That day, I had a vision of Acada and her husband together in another reality. It was the same story I had seen before when Che was sick, lying on the bed. Acada glanced out the window and asked Father Creator to help her with Ta. She wouldn't connect with Father previously to help her. This time was different. I felt Che's happiness. He was content and comfortable with himself.

I saw that the story had changed. He was not sick anymore. He was healed. This time, Acada laid on the bed. She was tired after the long journey of healing Ta and felt a little weak. Che gently and lovingly took care of her.

Then the story changed again. Acada wasn't feeling weak, but instead, she had strength. Che held her on the bed, and I felt Che's deep love for her. He looked at me with confidence and a smile and said, "Thank you."

I saw Acada's three children come to the bed. She was happy to be with them. When I watched them together, I felt my connection with my oldest son was stronger, and the wall that separated us was gone. I felt my youngest son had more direction in life. I cried for a long time when I saw these changes. While their past story was changing, so was my life.

Che looked at me again and showed me his small boy, Fatherlove. It was the boy that Acada lost. In the new story, the abortion never happened. He was alive and full of energy, playing with his brothers. There were no words to describe the beautiful feeling I had. I was their future, bringing the possibility of rewriting their love story, by using her symbols, to get them back together, to their higher selves in the future.

I took a break to restore my energy – I didn't want to get in my head and lose the connection. I felt my pink crystal in my heart. I stayed in the feeling of Self-Love for a while, and it increased my energy again.

After that, I saw Fatherlove; he was older in his early twenties. He was dressed in white and had a bright golden color around his head.

Suddenly he saw me, and I felt his love around me! His radiant beam and golden light, as a golden disk, in front of my chest was recharging me. He said that I had brought the present, past, and future in the same dance, and that darkness could not exist when they were together. I closed my eyes to relax and receive his love.

After a few minutes, I saw Fatherlove again. He was dissolving linear time in the 3rd dimension. He was more powerful than any Light Being I had ever seen. It was just like Father Creator had predicted in Atlantis.

My heart knew this experience was a possibility in the high-frequency future. I was excited to see this was possible, but I wasn't sure how to manifest it.

Fatherlove's spirit gave me the solution, integrating "all" Father's and Mother's protocol symbols inside Acada's process. Yes! Merge each of Acada's symbols with Father and Mother Creators' symbols. For instance, integrate Acada's symbol of Intention with Father and Mother's symbols of Intention.

The integration of the strongest forces of Twin Cells, which are Mother and Father Creators, makes manifestation in the future possibilities. The energy can be transferred into the present. It locks the manifestation in the high-frequency future, and will manifest sometime in the present.

It has been more than a year since I had the vision. I was driving to Los Angeles when the mountains close to Saint George in Utah, told me that it was time to start writing the book again. This trip was three years later, when I had the vision of Che and his family being together in the future. It took this long to learn and practice Self-Love and unconditional love to maintain my energy high enough to incorporate Mother's and Father's symbols in each of Acada's symbols to help to manifest Che, Acada and their family reunited in the future of high-frequency.

After almost twenty years of preparation, I felt I could do it. Acada was already in the future; her past life stories were clear. Che was almost there then, unifying them in their Twin Cell energies, so it would be easier to move their children to the future.

There was still an incomplete part of Che in Atlantis. Ta was holding back because of his desire to clear Atlantis's original subconscious corrupted energy, which was the energetic parasite implanted into the energy of the Law of Ones. It was the Mirrors' most powerful tool of destruction.

I was finally ready to increase my energy to a level that could help Che clear the energy of the corrupted subconscious implant, placed in his energy in the time of Atlantis. Che and Fatherlove would guide me in the process. First, I had to create the intention to remove what had stolen his ability to stay connected to the 5th dimension and manifest to that level.

Then, I placed the intention to connect the Twin Cell energy of the Mother and Father in each of Acada's protocols, just like Fatherlove had shown me.

For instance, in Acada's symbol of the Inca Cross, I integrated the Inca Cross of Father and Mother. The next step was to activate the connection in the Twin Cell's energy of Mother and Father Creators, in each symbol, which took me almost three years to establish.

I activated the Twin Cell connection by merging their Five Points of Power symbols which created the 5th-dimensional balance of female and male energy. In this way, the implants of the corrupted subconscious would be neutralized. Without the subconscious implants, the atoms in our body become the energy of the spirit or 5th-dimensional energy. That means every part of us gets transferred to the future and connects to our higher self and multiple possibilities of healing and balance in our lives. This process will eventually cause every past life, in low-frequency pain and suffering, to become obsolete.

Next was, merging Mother's Five Points of Power and Father's Future protocol on the white table in the R&D room so that when the miracle happens it will eventually obsolete the energetic subconscious parasite.

I made some changes in Acada's process as she guided me to ensure the removal of the corrupted subconscious. Instead of having one intention in the Inca Way Process, five intentions must be created. There is a specific order required to make a stronger connection.

- The 1st intention should always be to feel the energy of unconditional and Self-Love for myself.
- The 2nd intention is to feel the energy of Mother's Five Points of Power reflected in my Five Points of Power.
- The 3rd intention is to connect and merge Father's Future Protocol with my future protocol.
- The 4th intention is to create one specific intention in the essence of love such as "I want to learn to have more focus."
- The 5th intention is to be in your highest potential of light to manifest your intentions.

On March 5, 2022, I was in my room, and I felt the energy of the mountains of Peru coming to me through a portal of light. They gave me a vision of the possibility of Acada and Che's family being together in the future. Also, they told me that I should go to a coffee shop at the Trolley Square Mall. They asked me to go in and purchase a chocolate cake. By now, I know if they ask me to eat something, it's because I get to digest the experience of the request in my body.

March 10, 2022, was "the miracle day." Now was the time to make a *possibility* become a *manifestation* in the future. Acada was already in her whole essence in the future. I had witnessed and felt the Twin Cell energies of Mother and Father in Acada's Protocols in the future of high-frequency. Now it was going to be the first time I was helping merge a couple of Twin Cell's energy in their full energy connection, besides Mother and Father. This meant the beginning of no past and future in low-frequency, void of pain and suffering created by corrupted forces, and filled only with possibilities and manifestations of love.

The way to do it was by merging Ta with Che in one reality in the future. Ta was the linear time experience waiting to be changed to a Circular Time and be complete. Che was the future, the higher self, and the power of spirit—the same person but in two different times.

Clearing Ta's blocks and limiting beliefs from the implant of the corrupted subconscious level, will allow him to connect to his higher self and be in the energy of Twin Cells with Acada and be in his full potential in the high-frequency future.

I did what the Peruvian Mountains asked. When I got to the coffee shop, the first thing that got my attention was that the walls were glossy white and there were many ceiling lights. This made it possible to see the cakes and other desserts look colorful and appealing. I smiled while I purchased the chocolate cake.

While I was sitting and eating the chocolate cake, the mountains asked me to trust and let the feelings flow that were coming to my heart. It felt like a breath of fresh air, and I heard the voice of the mountain saying, "It is time to take Ta to the future of high-frequency."

When I felt the energetic download completed, I left the coffee shop slowly, walking to my car. I told myself, "It is time, and I get to remember not to doubt myself."

Once back in my apartment, I sat on the blue sofa in my living room and felt the light in my heart. I looked at the white walls around me and said, "Trust yourself, trust yourself," as Che has said to me on many occasions as we worked together.

I kept telling myself, "Focus on your energy of Self-Love in your heart. No expectation. It is what it is. Just follow the feelings of your heart."

I closed my eyes and went into a deep meditation. I opened my heart and created my five intentions: I intend (1) to love myself unconditionally; (2) to connect and merge my Five Points of Power with Mother's Five Points of Power; I envision the merging process of the symbols; (3) to connect and merge Father's Future symbol with my Future symbol; I envision the merging process of the symbols; (4) *to remove from Ta the corrupted subconscious implant that is stopping him from transferring to the future in high-frequency;* and (5) to be in my highest potential to support this to work. I saw the five intentions take the shape of a clear crystal. I carried this crystal through the process to get to the R&D.

Then I wished for the distribution of 50:25:25: so, my ancestors, generations to come, and people in the world in a similar situation as Ta. And for those that wanted to close a past life, to move forward in the future and to connect to their higher selves.

Next, I envisioned my symbol of conscious feelings in front of me as a golden symbol of light that connected to my brain. Then I imagined the pink crystal inside my heart representing Self-Love and felt unconditional love for myself. I envisioned the golden light integrating with the light of the pink crystal in my heart.

I continued by seeing my Subconscious Symbol in front of my heart. I requested to travel 50,000 years in the future. Next, I went through my symbols or Portals of Light to ensure I was going to the future of high-frequency: my symbols of Intention, my Five Points of Power, and my Future. Before I went through the 5th-dimensional symbol, I stood right in the center of the symbol of the 5th-dimensional portal, and I placed the clear crystal on the floor. I stretched my hands, and with my palms, I touched the portals and took the energy and light from them to balance my female and male energy in my body. Then I picked up the crystal and went through the portal and got to the R&D.

In my R&D room, I saw the white table where I placed the clear crystal with my five intentions. I repeated my desire: "I intend for the implant of the corrupted subconscious to be removed from Ta."

I requested a Light Being to place the energy of the Five Points of Power of Mother Creator on top of the crystal and for Father's future symbol to be placed on top of Mother's. I requested them to merge. I watched Mother's and Father's symbols merge until they became a hologram of white light, and I focused on Ta becoming decontaminated from the implant.

To my surprise, a Light Being took the hologram and gave it to me. I held it with my two hands. I didn't understand what was happening, but I felt safe because I was in the 5th-dimensional R&D.

I felt my energy gently traveling to the past. It was like going through a wormhole very fast but steady. Somehow, the golden hologram manifested my energetic body in the past in Atlantis.

I arrived on the seashore at the ocean, miles away from the city of Atlantis. The city had tall buildings, but it was far away, and I could not clearly see the structure of the buildings. I was at the same place where I had seen the little girl drinking contaminated water before. I knew I was there because I could feel myself breathing the air, and my feet were touching the sand. It was cold and dry. I noticed I did not have shoes.

The essence and smell of the place was foreign to me. I usually hear the different sounds that the plants and animals make, but this time, there was no sound but an empty echo. That was part of the contamination, the loss of the sound of frequencies.

I felt a telepathic message from the Light Being coming from the future. A gentle voice said to place the hologram on top of the water. Slowly, I got close to the body of water, and I held the golden hologram on top of the series of waves on the surface, and it touched. I continued holding the golden object and the water turned into a bright yellow light in seconds. It emitted energy in the form of rays and spread everywhere and expanded outward for long distances.

When I turned to the right, I glanced at Ta standing beside me. I had seen him so many times in my visions like they were movies; now I was inside the movie, and he was in front of me. Something was different by being in his presence: my understanding of why Acada loved him so much. His presence was breathtaking because he held the energy of the love of the Mu people.

I did not say anything. I gave him the hologram. He had been channeling information from the future from Acada and Che, the way I was receiving information as well. He knew what to do with the golden hologram. I watched him share it with others. When he was done, he felt it was time to go.

I saw him walking forward, looking at a portal of light, it was Father Creator's symbol of the future, then he went through it, which meant that he had crossed over to the future in the 5th dimension.

"He did it," I thought. It was an honor to observe a man of courage to make a choice of love after he found out the truth of the story. I gazed at him until he went through the portal and disappeared.

In my experience with the Light Beings, I carry light and information to other realities; most of the time, I do not get the information of what I am taking, to prevent me from getting ideas of the 3rd dimension and sabotaging the progress. When I started working with the Light Beings, I made a Contract of Love with them to help them clear the contamination.

The mission was complete, and I wanted to know more about the golden hologram. I asked the Light Being, "What is the hologram's purpose?"

The Light Being stared at me for a moment before responding, "It's the cure for the corrupted subconsciousness."

It hit me, and I suddenly realized something: Ta had the opportunity before to leave Atlantis, but he didn't leave because he wanted to bring the cure back to Atlantis before leaving. He loved his people as much as Acada did. The story had changed! With Che's help in the future, there was a better outcome, to rewrite the story of the darkness of the past, into a story of love. Ta did not go to Belize but stayed in Atlantis and worked to find the cure for the corrupted subconscious. And he did!

Without knowing, I had taken the cure back to Atlantis! The golden hologram was the Five Points of Power of Mother Creator placed back into the molecular structure of the water, in the Times of Atlantis, by Ta. It came from Che in the future and went to Ta in the past. This was the healing of the two of them coming back together in the future, in high frequency.

I checked my body for any 3rd-dimensional behaviors attacking me. I found no stress, anxiety, depression, or pain at that moment. I was free of attacks from blocks and limiting beliefs. I had no internal conflict, just a gentle light inside me. I did it! I had overcome, for a short period, all the blocks in my body and taken the cure to Atlantis without realizing it.

Ta had manifested his wish in Atlantis: to heal his people. Then he left, in his full essence, to the future to be with Acada and co-create together as Twin Cells.

I'm certain they're together. I can feel it in my body. My dream has been fulfilled; Acada and Che are reunited as Twin Cells in the future in high-frequency and co-creating together in Circular Time, a place without pain and suffering where the cosmic clue is Self Love, gratitude, and abundance.

Twin Cells' stories are important because the more they clear and reunite, the more they bring back love, and understanding that we are all connected with every living creature. Yes, Circular Time will replace linear time where the blocks and limiting beliefs will not exist, darkness will die, and all of us—including you—will remember things for what they are.

I'm still working with Acada, Che, Prophet Thoth, Mother and Father Creators, other Light Beings, and my mountains. Together, we're transferring stories of love to our future.

Che's love for me has helped me understand that I'm beyond my body's limitations. He has guided me to remember the codes of the water of the 5th dimension, or what he calls "water without time." It's the sacred connection of Father and Mother Creators. It's also my *true* identity. I'm a source of life!

I hope you can understand the true meaning of life and love it as I do. I learned to love myself, to allow others to love me, to love others, and to learn from others to love myself. I have seen so much damage in the world, but now I know I can help rewrite the past with love stories, by loving myself and sharing unconditional love.

Just like my Shaman ancestors, there will come a time when I must transfer my knowledge to my apprentice. But I wanted more than one person to have this information. I chose to write this book to give the information to you and everyone. These are the stories of the love of Mother and Father Creators, Che and Acada, and other Twin Cells. I share them because I believe you can be the reflection of love, and hope for a better world.

About the Author

Growing up high in the Peruvian mountains, Elena Camargo Radford developed the ability to communicate with the unseen world—the energy of the mountains, rocks, and water. She discovered a common denominator: the technology of love, which begins with self-love and extends to others. Later, she trained as an Inca Shaman in her homeland, learning about the Inca Cross and other ancient teachings. The first lesson she learned was the importance of love, service, and wisdom. Now a healer, she works with individuals, groups and communities to unlock their highest potentials. Elena offers workshops and experiential tours to sacred sites in Peru. Find her at www.theincaway.com or www.elenaradford.com

Testimonial

I found my way to Elena during a time of major shifts and transitions in my life in 2018. In my first meeting with her, I shared "I feel like I am on the precipice of a major transformation." At that time, I was seeking guidance, support and at times answers in attempt to make sense what was happening to me in my life. I was engulfed by the sense that things were happening to me and I wanted them to stop while at the same time frustrated that I was not able nor did I have the awareness to see the signs and clues that all is and was unfolding for me to learn, grow and evolve.

From the very beginning of my in-person sessions with Elena over the course of a year, I felt held and supported. Looking back from the place of now, it was through her calm voice and loving compassion that I was able to relax in and open up. My body was healing from being in environments that were full of judgement and criticism and I was longing to understand why. Through her support, guidance and insight I made some shifts in my life. She introduced me to the concept of energy and its frequencies, and the action of completion, meaning some actions were not able to be completed, closed, done and that opportunities were presenting themselves to move through and heal actions from the past. In our sessions, she invited me to meet myself in a place of love, rather than harsh judgements and self doubt. I was so focused on logical and analytical thinking that I often missed the messages she shared in metaphor and story. When this happened, she would find a way to reframe her message, adding more to the story or sharing an example in her own life. Always holding the message that I was growing and learning and that I was not getting it wrong. My life did shift, I moved out of the country and took a deep dive on and inward journey and I did not return to the Rockies.

Fast forward to now, in 2024. I see that my life took me in the direction that was necessary and relevant for my own journey and growth. And I began noticing that I was at a time where I was looking for some more guidance to deepen my studies and gain insight to what was unfolding for me. A friend reminded me of Elena. Instantly I knew, yes. My body offered the signal that this was time to reconnect. I immediately reached out to book a session.

The moment I saw Elena on the screen, I was enveloped in love. Her presence and gaze moved me to tears. This is an excerpt from the email I sent after we were reunited, five years later:

I feel like me again. I knew I was not feeling like myself and I had no idea if or when I would feel like me again and now I feel like me.

After our session, my mom and I went kayaking on a lake. I was gliding and glistening and floating. Such a blissful state. In our time together I was able to access a deep sense of ease and peace, similar to the state I access when I am in deep mediation. Thank you for sharing your insight about this place being outside of time and space. I had not made that connection.

As I shared when I saw you, being in your presence feels like home. Safe, comfortable and at ease.

I have been exploring many questions around energy and its role, how it shows up and when and I know that you sharing your insight and wisdom with me through the written word (Elena shared with me her book Circular Time) is going to meet me exactly where I am at! Thank you.

I am so grateful that we are together again and trust that the time in between was in service of that which needed to be undone, met and processed before we could be together again.

I am ready for what is in store for me, to greet that which is on its way.

Our timing feels auspicious. I have been seeking a teacher and when I saw you, I knew it is you.

Thank you!

It became clear to me, that I had work to do and lessons to learn in the five years that we were apart. In fact, the same day that I had my session with Elena, I felt called to pull a journal from my shelf. I opened number 88, a yellow journal to an entry about koshas or energy bodies. Yes! How powerful is that? Drawn to the yellow color of the cover, I opened to an entry from 1.5 years ago that I wrote about my experiences and questions about energy bodies.

And, as I flipped through the pages I read this from an entry on 9.21.22 the day before my 45th birthday:

Saw me and another, my lover. We were field workers. migrants. We were in a line. Dark, grey, brown clothes. Got to the front to enter truck, vehicle and I had-choose-had/chose/placed my baby down on the ground and got into the truck. Be with that.

I immediately recalled what Elena had shared with in me in 2019 before I went to India. She said that I would accept, heal the wound that I left a child. She shared, that it would be like setting out a bowl of strawberry ice cream in a really special bowl and then not being able to eat it for a long time. When I was in India she shared, you will eat it when you are in India. This she shared, will be an opportunity for completion. And, while I was there, I lived at an ashram for a little over three weeks and shared ALL of my time there with an 8 month old baby name Prerna. It was blissful, like coming home.

Looking back, Elena was guiding me towards healing and taking care of myself. She was asking questions about me, what were my goals and interests, what did I want. At first they felt uncomfortable and foreign, as I had become so accustomed to focusing on everyone, she was encouraging me to move slow, to not rush or over think, to enjoy life, to get into nature and to relax. I also realized that I needed to connect with my self through love. I did not know how to love myself and I was looking to others to show me and provide me with love. I see now how a huge catalyst to this self love was in the events that drew me to Elena in 2018. In the time between 2018 and 2024, I was able to do that. I was able to soften in and experience love. True love. The love that is not tied or bound to constraints or conditions, the love that is always here, enveloping, surrounding and guiding our way on.

I see now, that I need to take those steps, to reawaken and access the love within, to deepen my relationship with myself and the world around me and when I was ready, a new teacher would appear and I would be begin a new aspect of my growth. This is what I felt and knew when I saw Elena in May of 2024. I was ready to deepen my awareness of energy, of light and its role in our lives.

Elena has introduced me to the word contamination. Rather than feeling I have done something wrong or not gotten something right, Elena offers that when my frequency is low, I have the tendency to attack other low frequencies. This awareness is helping me let go of my rigid, narrow, self-deprecating feelings of thinking that I am not good enough, bad, damaged or that something is wrong with me. Through our work that we do together in which she asks me how she can be of assistance, to clear and remove blockages and I remain open to receive the healing energy gifts she offers, I know that I can continue to turn towards love and compassion and light, even when I feel the dark grip of fear, doubt and scarcity.

When I began reading Circular Time (Elena's book), it was as if she was answering the questions I had in my head. As I read on, each question was being answered, some in real time. And more were coming! This is an email excerpt that I wrote to convey my awe and gratitude:

I am SOAKING in and ABSORBING your messages, wisdom and love in Circular Time. Thank you to you, Che and Acada and all of the Light Beings who are supporting and guiding your way on! So many of my questions are being answered. I am in awe and delight, my heart full of gratitude for this gift, your offering and the auspicious timing of it all.

Your time, wisdom, guidance and support is welcomed and nourishes my soul.

What incredible interwoven stories of LOVE! Love for yourself, love for others, love that transcends time, love for humanity, love for the Mother and Father Creator. Love that we can see. Love that is unseen. Love that is felt. Love that is the guiding force of all!

I am still soaking and revealing in its wisdom, word and love that envelopes me.

I am in awe. Thank you for sharing your inward journey, thank you for the steps you have taken, the energy you have shared, the wisdom you offer, the space that you hold for yourself, for me, for us, for all who are ready.

I know from my own journey the depths of self-doubt and worry, confusion, exhaustion and from this, through this I know the expansiveness of love, grace, gratitude and forgiveness.

And this, now. The timing of it all is delightful.

In a recent session, Elena extended an offer to begin studying with her to take my knowledge and experience to another level. I am ready and I have accepted. In our time together, (as outlined in her course description) I will engage in a course that is designed with a systematic approach to identifying and resolving blocks and limiting beliefs that hinder personal growth. By cultivating self-love and awareness, I will discover powerful solutions to overcome these obstacles.

Guided meditations are designed to create a safe and sacred space for channeling. I will learn to set clear intentions, establish healthy boundaries, connect with my body's wisdom, and speak your truth. These practices will help me effectively direct my energy towards my goals and aspirations.

"Channeling is a process by which we achieve a state of heart and mind consciousness through communication with higher beings, ancestors, and the universe. Self-love plays a vital role because by loving ourselves, we increase our energy and experience more feelings, eventually opening us to Channeling."

I am excited to greet what is coming towards me on this next step of my journey with Elena as my teacher. I move forward with a strong spine, an open heart full of love and a curious mind.

Index

Symbols

1st Triangle 124

2nd triangle 154, 164

2nd Triangle 164

3rd dimension 12, 13, 19, 25, 29, 30, 48, 52, 61, 65, 67, 68, 71, 73, 74, 81, 106, 121, 122, 125, 142, 165, 193, 201, 204, 220, 222, 226, 239, 246, 258, 266, 268, 270, 275, 277, 283

3rd-dimensional 15, 16, 21, 22, 23, 24, 25, 27, 29, 39, 50, 52, 57, 61, 63, 69, 77, 86, 90, 97, 145, 164, 188, 207, 218, 222, 225, 243, 244, 245, 247, 253, 265, 266, 268, 283

3rd triangle 157, 182, 184, 185, 186, 187

3rd Triangle 179

4th dimension 67, 68, 73, 184, 186, 221, 224

4th-dimensional 109

4th triangle 160, 184, 185, 186, 187, 190, 192

4th Triangle 184

5th dimension 12, 15, 24, 30, 42, 43, 48, 56, 57, 61, 62, 63, 64, 67, 68, 69, 70, 73, 74, 83, 84, 85, 90, 91, 93, 106, 110, 111, 114, 116, 119, 122, 135, 137, 155, 164, 180, 182, 186, 187, 188, 191, 193, 206, 207, 210, 212, 217, 218, 221, 222, 224, 225, 226, 228, 239, 243, 245, 246, 253, 256, 257, 260, 263, 264, 265, 266, 268, 270, 272, 275, 278, 282, 284

5th Dimension 63, 262

5th-Dimensional 30, 54, 252, 255

5th-dimensional portal 117, 206, 240, 253, 254, 255, 256, 261, 281, 50, 25, 25, 255

A

abortion 14, 46, 47, 48, 54, 108, 198, 200, 204, 216, 241, 276

Acada 4, 7, 10, 13, 14, 15, 16, 17, 18, 19, 21, 45, 47, 48, 50, 51, 52, 54, 55, 56, 57, 58, 59, 60, 61, 62, 63, 64, 65, 66, 67, 68, 70, 76, 84, 85, 86, 88, 91, 93, 95, 96, 97, 98, 100, 101, 105, 106, 107, 108, 110, 111, 112, 114, 115, 116, 119, 121, 122, 123, 132, 133, 138, 140, 143, 144, 145, 146, 147, 150, 159, 161, 164, 165, 168, 169, 170, 188, 192, 194, 195, 196, 197, 198, 199, 200, 201, 202, 203, 204, 205, 206, 207, 208, 209, 210, 211, 212, 215, 216, 217, 218, 219, 222, 224, 228, 229, 230, 231, 232, 234, 236, 237, 238, 239, 240, 241, 242, 243, 244, 245, 246, 252, 253, 258, 259, 260, 261, 262, 263, 265, 267, 268, 269, 271, 272, 274, 275, 276, 277, 278, 279, 280, 282, 283, 284

accountability 15, 88, 140, 141, 180, 183, 185, 186, 199, 217, 225, 231, 244, 253, 255, 256, 257, 267 acknowledgment 14, 151, 185

Addictions 103

ancestors 10, 13, 16, 22, 23, 24, 33, 43, 50, 55, 56, 57, 58, 70, 71, 77, 97, 99, 111, 117, 119, 134, 136, 137, 156, 159, 160, 163, 165, 182, 185, 186, 212, 224, 239, 247, 251, 255, 265, 274, 281, 284

Andean shaman 135, 136, 138, 143, 145, 224

Andean Shaman 13, 143, 224

androids 89, 239, 241, 260

Anxiety 21, 36, 100

approval-seeker 23

Atlantis 7, 10, 11, 12, 13, 14, 15, 17, 43, 47, 48, 49, 51, 52, 54, 56, 57, 58, 61, 62, 64, 67, 73, 74, 87, 89, 91, 93, 95, 97, 99, 100, 101, 105, 108, 110, 111, 115, 116, 117, 138, 145, 147, 150, 155, 159, 164, 165, 197, 200, 201, 202, 205, 206, 207, 209, 216, 218, 219, 229, 230, 237, 238, 245, 246, 247, 256, 258, 259, 268, 269, 274, 277, 278, 282, 283, 284

atom 55, 65, 66, 67, 68, 95, 115, 120, 121, 128, 211, 224, 230, 248, 253, 263, 269, 270, 271

awareness 11, 14, 38, 70, 84, 108, 119, 138, 197, 225, 249, 270

B

blocks, and limiting beliefs 52, 193, 204, 217

blue sky 85, 250, 271, 272

Books of Light 63, 64, 65, 67, 68, 69, 71, 95, 97, 98, 105, 106, 107, 108, 109, 110, 111, 113, 114, 116, 119, 120, 136, 137, 138, 140, 153, 195, 202, 204, 209, 217, 218, 219, 274

brother 7, 22, 23, 24, 28, 39, 40, 73, 126, 134, 147

C

cells 31, 66, 91, 105, 122, 128, 226, 243, 245, 248, 252, 257, 273

Center of Power 247, 269

Chakana 115, 117

Che 4, 7, 41, 42, 43, 50, 78, 82, 121, 122, 124, 125, 126, 127, 128, 132, 136, 141, 144, 149, 152, 154, 155, 156, 159, 160, 162, 163, 171, 188, 198, 204, 210, 225, 232, 233, 237, 238, 239, 240, 241, 243, 244, 245, 246, 249, 250, 252, 253, 254, 256, 257, 259, 260, 261, 262, 265, 267, 271, 274, 275, 276, 277, 278, 279, 280, 282, 283, 284

choices 11, 15, 19, 22, 27, 47, 48, 51, 63, 69, 71, 72, 74, 76, 78, 80, 83, 85, 88, 93, 97, 128, 130, 131, 133, 135, 140, 141, 146, 150, 163, 166, 167, 168, 170, 176, 181, 187, 189, 191, 192, 197, 199, 212, 217, 218, 219, 222, 223, 224, 225, 227, 231, 232, 236, 238, 239, 243, 250, 252, 253, 257, 259, 266, 269

circular time 2, 7, 11, 12, 16, 48, 58, 63, 67, 68, 69, 70, 75, 90, 91, 93, 105, 106, 112, 113, 114, 116, 117, 118, 185, 186, 195, 196, 210, 217, 223, 224, 229, 230, 251, 253, 258, 267, 270, 272, 273, 275, 280, 284

codes 10, 11, 14, 16, 60, 61, 68, 118, 140, 219, 223, 254, 284

computer 30, 56, 92, 113, 208, 266

connections 36, 104, 117, 121, 129, 134, 154, 266, 275

conscious 38, 39, 92, 96, 106, 122, 126, 128, 134, 145, 188, 221, 222, 223, 224, 232, 270, 281

consciousness 17, 19, 33, 37, 39, 43, 44, 46, 50, 57, 66, 68, 71, 74, 75, 89, 92, 93, 111, 118, 122, 126, 127, 129, 133, 134,

136, 137, 140, 194, 195, 216, 219, 229, 231, 232, 234, 269, 271

contamination 11, 12, 13, 15, 17, 29, 39, 48, 49, 51, 52, 57, 61, 67, 73, 74, 77, 81, 83, 84, 87, 89, 91, 92, 93, 94, 99, 100, 101, 103, 105, 109, 110, 111, 116, 117, 121, 127, 136, 140, 152, 165, 168, 181, 186, 193, 195, 196, 197, 198, 202, 203, 204, 207, 211, 212, 219, 222, 229, 230, 232, 234, 245, 256, 257, 258, 264, 266, 267, 270, 275, 282, 283

Contracts of Love 57, 58, 70, 71, 146, 191, 250

corruption 17, 71, 73, 74, 84, 111, 125, 198, 218, 257, 259

creation 10, 11, 12, 13, 14, 15, 16, 18, 20, 30, 50, 57, 58, 59, 60, 64, 70, 71, 72, 73, 74, 83, 88, 95, 97, 105, 106, 108, 114, 116, 117, 118, 122, 127, 128, 129, 131, 133, 134, 135, 138, 150, 166, 170, 172, 173, 176, 177, 179, 180, 181, 183, 185, 186, 188, 190, 197, 208, 221, 222, 224, 229, 235, 238, 254, 257, 260, 269, 271, 273, 275

crystals 10, 87, 96, 106, 116, 134, 145, 150, 254, 275

Cuzco 13, 144, 145, 149, 150, 151, 155, 160, 163, 201

D

depression 12, 21, 67, 74, 101, 107, 140, 168, 248, 270, 273, 283

direction 10, 20, 24, 40, 60, 61, 65, 69, 77, 83, 95, 138, 142, 143, 145, 177, 186, 187, 191, 205, 221, 222, 226, 227, 256, 272, 273, 275, 276

DNA 11, 12, 13, 15, 61, 62, 66, 73, 74, 77, 88, 89, 92, 95, 96, 97, 99, 100, 101, 103, 106, 109, 111, 116, 118, 128, 136, 137, 138, 142, 188, 196, 203, 217, 228,

239, 240, 243, 244, 245, 247, 253, 256, 257, 259, 262, 269

E

Egypt 89, 91, 119, 158, 161

electron 90, 120, 121, 128, 221, 226

elongated head 153, 155, 161, 274

Energy Gift 131, 137, 138, 212, 233, 234, 249, 257

expansion 10, 57, 60, 62, 65, 68, 70, 74, 127, 175, 176, 185, 190, 197, 199, 224, 266, 273

experience 11, 14, 15, 16, 19, 21, 25, 26, 31, 32, 33, 35, 37, 41, 46, 47, 50, 51, 52, 55, 56, 57, 58, 59, 60, 62, 64, 65, 66, 67, 69, 70, 74, 76, 77, 78, 81, 82, 84, 93, 97, 105, 106, 107, 113, 120, 122, 124, 125, 126, 127, 128, 130, 131, 133, 135, 137, 138, 139, 140, 144, 145, 147, 148, 159, 160, 161, 164, 165, 168, 171, 175, 179, 188, 189, 200, 202, 209, 211, 214, 216, 217, 218, 219, 225, 228, 229, 230, 231, 232, 234, 237, 238, 243, 244, 246, 247, 249, 250, 252, 253, 254, 255, 256, 258, 265, 266, 267, 269, 270, 273, 277, 279, 280, 283

F

Father Creator 46, 54, 55, 56, 57, 59, 60, 61, 62, 64, 97, 106, 131, 132, 138, 147, 158, 174, 175, 185, 190, 201, 224, 225, 233, 240, 248, 249, 250, 251, 253, 258, 260, 262, 264, 265, 267, 272, 273, 276, 277, 282

Fatherlove 62, 108, 200, 203, 276, 277, 278

feelers 72, 73

feelings 10, 11, 12, 13, 14, 15, 18, 19, 24, 26, 27, 28, 30, 33, 36, 38, 41, 42, 46, 47, 49, 50, 51, 52, 57, 59, 60, 61, 62, 64, 65, 66, 68, 70, 71, 72, 73, 74, 78, 82, 83, 84,

85, 88, 91, 92, 93, 96, 98, 99, 105, 106, 107, 114, 116, 117, 118, 122, 124, 125, 126, 127, 128, 129, 130, 133, 134, 135, 137, 138, 139, 140, 150, 153, 154, 158, 160, 163, 164, 165, 167, 168, 169, 177, 179, 180, 181, 183, 186, 187, 188, 189, 190, 191, 192, 193, 194, 195, 196, 197, 200, 202, 203, 210, 212, 213, 214, 218, 221, 224, 225, 226, 228, 232, 233, 234, 235, 236, 237, 239, 240, 241, 243, 245, 247, 251, 252, 253, 256, 259, 264, 265, 268, 269, 271, 272, 275, 280, 281

female 7, 10, 55, 57, 61, 83, 88, 89, 95, 96, 115, 117, 118, 120, 133, 140, 141, 145, 147, 159, 177, 179, 180, 181, 182, 183, 185, 186, 187, 203, 211, 221, 222, 230, 253, 271, 275, 278, 281

First Outbreak 87

Five Points of Power 59, 60, 61, 62, 68, 73, 83, 88, 90, 91, 92, 96, 105, 106, 133, 220, 221, 223, 224, 225, 226, 227, 244, 248, 255, 263, 264, 267, 269, 273, 276, 278, 279, 280, 281

future 11, 16, 19, 48, 49, 51, 52, 57, 58, 59, 60, 63, 65, 67, 68, 69, 70, 71, 72, 74, 76, 78, 79, 81, 83, 87, 91, 93, 94, 95, 97, 98, 105, 106, 111, 115, 116, 117, 131, 133, 137, 163, 164, 165, 167, 185, 186, 187, 190, 192, 193, 194, 195, 196, 197, 198, 199, 204, 206, 208, 211, 212, 217, 218, 219, 223, 224, 229, 230, 231, 232, 233, 234, 236, 237, 238, 240, 242, 244, 245, 246, 247, 249, 250, 251, 252, 255, 257, 258, 263, 264, 269, 270, 272, 273, 277, 278, 279, 280, 281, 282, 283, 284

G

gatekeeper 10

H

happiness 13, 14, 19, 24, 40, 54, 57, 70, 83, 165, 180, 182, 185, 189, 190, 197, 229, 276

healer 41, 43, 131

heart 13, 14, 15, 18, 19, 22, 23, 24, 26, 27, 28, 30, 31, 33, 34, 38, 39, 40, 41, 43, 45, 46, 48, 50, 51, 53, 55, 56, 57, 62, 64, 65, 66, 74, 75, 84, 85, 92, 93, 104, 107, 112, 122, 123, 125, 127, 130, 131, 133, 134, 135, 139, 143, 144, 147, 153, 159, 160, 163, 169, 170, 171, 173, 174, 176, 181, 182, 183, 185, 189, 191, 193, 197, 198, 199, 201, 202, 205, 210, 211, 212, 219, 226, 232, 233, 234, 237, 238, 240, 241, 243, 245, 246, 248, 249, 250, 251, 253, 255, 256, 257, 258, 264, 267, 269, 270, 271, 272, 273, 275, 277, 280, 281

higher self 15, 50, 52, 192, 193, 230, 246, 255, 256, 262, 278, 280

high-frequency 10

high vibrational beings 17

hologram 16, 117, 229, 230, 235, 281, 282, 283

Huancayo 19, 20, 22, 208

I

illusion 11, 19, 30, 52, 68, 73, 86, 126, 186, 188, 189, 197, 198, 211, 218, 223

Inca Cross 112, 115, 116, 117, 118, 124, 127, 150, 157, 160, 163, 164, 168, 177, 179, 180, 183, 184, 185, 186, 187, 188, 190, 192, 193, 195, 196, 210, 213, 225, 233, 253, 257, 276, 278

Initiation 142, 157

intuitive 70, 143, 160

L

Lake Titicaca 157, 158, 160, 170, 171, 208

Law of One 10, 11, 12, 13, 15, 16, 17, 48, 49, 54, 57, 60, 61, 62, 72, 74, 88, 89, 90, 91, 92, 94, 96, 97, 105, 108, 109, 110, 111, 119, 194, 197, 198, 199, 206, 207, 210, 222, 240, 243

Light Beings 7, 41, 43, 44, 50, 52, 54, 56, 70, 78, 91, 112, 122, 124, 127, 132, 134, 136, 137, 156, 166, 167, 168, 170, 177, 185, 189, 190, 195, 211, 212, 216, 217, 222, 224, 226, 234, 251, 255, 262, 264, 265, 266, 267, 269, 283, 284

linear time 12, 21, 52, 58, 63, 67, 68, 69, 73, 75, 88, 92, 94, 105, 109, 115, 116, 121, 186, 187, 195, 201, 202, 206, 212, 220, 221, 222, 223, 224, 225, 257, 258, 269, 277, 280, 284

love 7, 10, 11, 12, 13, 14, 15, 16, 17, 18, 19, 22, 24, 25, 26, 27, 29, 30, 31, 33, 34, 35, 38, 41, 42, 46, 48, 49, 50, 51, 52, 53, 54, 55, 56, 57, 58, 60, 61, 62, 63, 64, 65, 66, 67, 68, 70, 71, 72, 73, 74, 76, 77, 78, 79, 82, 83, 84, 85, 86, 88, 92, 93, 94, 97, 98, 103, 105, 106, 108, 110, 111, 112, 113, 114, 115, 119, 120, 122, 123, 125, 126, 127, 128, 129, 131, 132, 133, 134, 135, 136, 137, 140, 142, 143, 144, 145, 147, 151, 153, 155, 159, 160, 163, 165, 166, 167, 169, 170, 171, 172, 173, 174, 175, 176, 177, 180, 182, 185, 186, 188, 189, 190, 191, 194, 195, 196, 197, 198, 199, 200, 201, 202, 203, 204, 207, 210, 211, 212, 213, 214, 215, 217, 219, 224, 225, 226, 227, 229, 231, 232, 233, 234, 238, 239, 240, 241, 244, 245, 246, 247, 250, 251, 253, 254, 255, 256, 259, 260, 262, 263, 264, 265, 266, 267, 269, 270, 271, 272, 273, 274, 275, 276, 277, 279, 280, 281, 282, 283, 284

low-frequency 11, 18, 30, 63, 67, 68, 69, 70, 74, 77, 86, 88, 92, 94, 98, 99, 105, 106, 115, 116, 125, 140, 150, 161, 181, 186, 187, 191, 194, 197, 207, 210, 215, 216, 217, 221, 222, 223, 224, 225, 230, 232, 239, 248, 251, 257, 270, 278, 279

M

Machu Picchu 150, 215, 216, 217, 218, 269

Maldek 95, 96, 203

male 7, 10, 40, 55, 57, 83, 95, 96, 117, 118, 120, 133, 145, 148, 153, 177, 180, 181, 183, 185, 186, 187, 188, 190, 203, 211, 221, 222, 230, 250, 253, 272, 275, 278, 281

mental process 30, 78, 234

Mirror 11, 72, 74, 89, 92, 93, 198, 241

molecular memories 33, 65, 110, 111, 116, 120, 217, 244, 269, 272

Mother Creator 7, 14, 55, 56, 57, 61, 132, 172, 176, 177, 178, 221, 223, 224, 225, 226, 234, 240, 248, 251, 253, 254, 255, 262, 264, 266, 267, 271, 273, 281

Mountains 120, 133, 157, 158, 208, 280

Mu 10, 11, 12, 13, 14, 48, 54, 57, 58, 59, 61, 73, 87, 90, 92, 106, 116, 117, 119, 138, 172, 173, 204, 206, 238, 240, 274, 282

multidimensional 10, 16, 34, 36, 58, 70, 71, 83, 86, 106, 108, 113, 114, 116, 117, 120, 148, 155, 229, 265

My Symbol of the Future 236

N

neutron 55, 95, 96, 117, 120, 121, 128, 177, 221, 222, 223, 224, 225, 226, 248

O

Opus 144, 145, 147

P

Pablo 143, 144, 145, 146, 147, 148, 149, 150, 151, 152, 153, 154, 155, 157, 158, 159, 160, 161, 162

Passion for Life 118, 177, 178, 179, 180, 182, 183, 193

past 11, 12, 15, 16, 19, 42, 47, 49, 51, 52, 58, 63, 64, 65, 67, 68, 69, 70, 71, 73, 74, 77, 78, 79, 80, 82, 84, 93, 94, 98, 99, 105, 106, 111, 115, 116, 117, 121, 122, 126, 129, 139, 140, 141, 149, 155, 158, 160, 163, 164, 165, 167, 183, 185, 186, 187, 193, 194, 195, 196, 201, 202, 206, 207, 210, 211, 212, 214, 217, 218, 219, 223, 224, 226, 227, 229, 230, 231, 232, 233, 234, 236, 240, 245, 246, 247, 249, 251, 252, 255, 257, 258, 267, 272, 273, 274, 275, 276, 277, 278, 279, 281, 282, 283, 284

Peru 13, 21, 22, 23, 27, 28, 33, 41, 42, 45, 91, 111, 119, 142, 143, 145, 146, 149, 156, 157, 158, 164, 170, 201, 208, 219, 248, 255, 274, 279

pink crystal 85, 123, 212, 250, 257, 267, 269, 270, 271, 272, 273, 277, 281

point of reference 61, 70, 80, 85, 115, 145, 197, 231, 234, 236, 265, 266, 272

powerless 29, 45, 50, 80, 125, 180, 189, 226, 228, 233, 244

present 11, 16, 19, 31, 39, 45, 47, 50, 52, 55, 58, 59, 63, 65, 67, 68, 69, 70, 78, 79, 93, 95, 97, 105, 106, 115, 116, 117, 131, 135, 137, 139, 143, 165, 167, 183, 185, 186, 189, 190, 193, 195, 196, 197, 209, 211, 212, 217, 218, 219, 224, 229, 231, 233, 234, 235, 236, 245, 247, 249, 251, 255, 257, 259, 263, 266, 272, 273, 277

productivity 14, 60

Prophet Thoth 7, 89, 91, 93, 122, 170, 171, 173, 174, 188, 189, 190, 221, 259, 260, 262, 267, 284

Protection 118, 154, 164, 168, 169, 177, 178, 187, 193

protocol 59, 73, 96, 97, 109, 115, 116, 117, 133, 150, 203, 222, 223, 224, 226, 229, 232, 236, 248, 253, 255, 265, 267, 277, 279

proton 55, 95, 96, 115, 117, 118, 120, 121, 128, 177, 221, 222, 224, 225, 226

Puma Punku 109, 110, 115, 116, 117, 202, 206, 207, 208, 209, 210, 212, 213, 214, 215, 219

punishment 24, 25, 38, 82, 97, 127, 169, 199, 242, 254, 256

pure intention 123, 191, 193, 194, 195, 196, 198, 199, 210, 237

R

R&D 253, 255, 262, 263, 264, 265, 266, 267, 279, 281

responsibility 29, 72, 89, 126, 143, 167, 180, 188, 189, 191, 197

S

Sacred Geometry 91, 117, 269

Salt Lake City 2, 54, 139, 182, 184, 253

Second Outbreak 88

self-expression 118, 177, 178, 180, 183, 193

Self-Love 2, 7, 11, 14, 16, 19, 30, 40, 43, 50, 52, 54, 55, 63, 67, 69, 70, 72, 74, 77, 79, 83, 84, 85, 86, 93, 97, 116, 122, 123, 130, 133, 135, 137, 138, 164, 165, 169, 173, 182, 189, 191, 194, 195, 196, 197, 199, 211, 212, 215, 216, 217, 225, 228, 234, 237, 242, 244, 245, 248, 249, 250, 254, 255, 256, 263, 264, 265, 267, 269, 270, 271, 273, 277, 279, 280, 281, 284

spirit 37, 38, 44, 56, 62, 112, 113, 118, 121, 122, 123, 134, 136, 137, 147, 164, 186, 188, 193, 194, 195, 196, 204, 206,

208, 209, 212, 215, 217, 229, 230, 239, 246, 258, 269, 277, 278, 280

stress   12, 21, 67, 74, 81, 140, 228, 248, 270, 283

subconscious   38, 39, 40, 46, 92, 106, 122, 126, 127, 129, 134, 145, 188, 221, 222, 223, 224, 225, 226, 247, 248, 258, 270, 271, 278, 279, 280, 281

subconsciousness   39, 40, 118, 126, 127, 129, 133, 134, 137, 223, 225, 226, 258, 283

suffer   26, 45, 68, 69, 146, 165

Survivor Behavior   76

Symbol of Personal Intimacy   228

Symbols of Love   14, 15, 16, 59, 244, 267, 269, 272, 275

T

Ta   7, 57, 61, 62, 147, 150, 159, 197, 198, 200, 201, 202, 203, 204, 205, 218, 219, 229, 230, 237, 238, 239, 242, 243, 246, 274, 276, 278, 280, 281, 282, 283, 284

technology   10, 11, 12, 14, 15, 16, 17, 49, 61, 63, 87, 89, 90, 91, 92, 96, 106, 116, 117, 119, 122, 127, 129, 135, 140, 159, 195, 196, 198, 202, 203, 206, 210, 224, 226, 239, 245

Third Outbreak   90

Tiahuanaco   13, 138, 208, 213, 214, 215, 219

trauma   37, 83, 126, 166, 212

Trust   117, 124, 127, 129, 130, 131, 145, 146, 150, 163, 177, 178, 182, 193, 280

Truth   62, 118, 160, 177, 178, 179, 184, 186, 187, 193

Twin Cells   57, 91, 105, 106, 107, 108, 109, 121, 122, 198, 222, 245, 253, 262, 275, 277, 280, 284

U

universe   14, 43, 44, 50, 58, 60, 62, 64, 89, 106, 117, 118, 121, 125, 128, 129, 130, 134, 146, 174, 224, 228, 229, 236, 244, 255, 262, 271, 272, 273

V

victim behavior   77

virus   92

W

War of the Times   111, 151, 258

white cloud   64, 85, 250, 271

www.ingramcontent.com/pod-product-compliance
Lightning Source LLC
Chambersburg PA
CBHW070640120526
44590CB00013BA/802